An American Saga

An American Saga

Some East Tennessee Taylors

W. Eugene Cox and Joyce Cox

iUniverse, Inc.
Bloomington

An American Saga
Some East Tennessee Taylors

iUniverse books may be ordered through booksellers or by contacting:

iUniverse
1663 Liberty Drive
Bloomington, IN 47403
www.iuniverse.com
1-800-Authors (1-800-288-4677)

ISBN: 978-1-4620-4343-9 (sc)
ISBN: 978-1-4620-4344-6 (ebk)

Printed in the United States of America

iUniverse rev. date: 04/12/2012

Contents

Foreword

All of us are born into a family and the first thing that family gives us is a name. For better or worse we carry that name, certainly in the case of men, until we die. We have no choice. Strictly speaking, we do not have a say-so in our first or Christian name either. We may, as we get older, ask that we be called by our middle name, or by initials, or even by a nickname. Regardless, Shakespeare be damned, we are not a rose and our name does matter.

I am a Taylor. That is who I was on the day I was born because that was my daddy's name, and I shall be a Taylor when I die. I am proud of it, but only because it is mine, and we all should be proud of who we are and where we came from.

Who are the Taylors? Good question, but it is several questions really. If you mean where did we come from, I can say Carter County, Tennessee, or more precisely the Milligan Community of Carter County. (More precisely still, "east of Gap Creek," that body of water being a clear cut marker between various clans and communities hereabouts.) We are thought to be from Scotland and Ireland by lineage, migrating here with thousands of our fellow countrymen. Daddy said there are sixteen different families named Taylor in East Tennessee that are not related. I do not know where he got his information, but even if he is off by a few, the point is that we took God's edict to Adam and Eve to heart and did our best to populate these parts.

You can answer "who are the Taylors?" by defining what we do for a living. I am told that in Old Britain families took their names from their professions so perhaps we sewed and weaved and mended other peoples' clothes. Maybe, but it does not explain daddy's proclamation that the Taylors were the kings' executioners. I believe daddy made this up because swinging an axe with a hood over your head is more compelling than darning socks. This leads to another way to define "who are the Taylors?" What do we do now or at least what did we do during the term of the saga written by Gene and Joyce Cox?

Judging by the embellishment my daddy gave to our "original" occupation, you would be correct in saying many of us became lawyers. If this sounds like criticism, it is not, for what is good trial lawyering if not the art of delivering a particular narrative in a persuasive manner. But, like all families, we were not one thing.

We were soldiers, politicians, preachers, teachers, writers, publishers, and hardware salesmen. We were not mathematicians or scientists and only rarely engineers. For some reason human contact and discourse was where we were most at home, whether it was persuading a voter that we had the answer to their problem if only elected to office or that tenpenny nails were more suitable to their job than flathead ones.

But maybe this, too, misses the mark. All of us train to become something and then do it, either for love or money or both. But what do we care about and what would we sacrifice for?

Again, Taylors are like many others. We love and would die for God, our family, our country. I know this to be true because it has happened. My daddy's tombstone does not say he was president of the Tennessee Bar or a former circuit court judge (though it could). No, it says simply "Sergeant U.S. Army." We are simple, straightforward people who are humbled by all God has given us as a people and as a family. We would fight more quickly over principle than money; love children; elevate dogs above all other pets; respect women; believe baseball is the king of all sports; abhor self promotion and flashiness; and prefer beer over scotch, bourbon over beer, and moonshine over them all.

And above all else is the story, the original tale passed down at the dinner table through the generations, until some believe it worthy of being written down. Gene and Joyce Cox have written a most worthy tale of the Taylors. They are fair in their presentation, unflinching in their criticism, balanced in their praise, and comprehensive in scope. Occasionally they write of unpleasant things. (My great uncle really did make moonshine in the Governor's Mansion as a teenager and he did leave the cooking fire unattended, great damage to public property resulting from the ensuing explosion. And, alas, he did go thereafter to military school, and the prisoners, sent over to tend the grounds who provided the recipe, were returned, unceremoniously, to more mundane pursuits.) No matter. My family is like yours in that success or failure, famous or infamous, they are all there, and the story is not nearly as rich or authentic if they are missing. So too the Taylors. Enjoy. I did.

John S. Taylor
Great-grandson of former Governor Alf A. Taylor

Preface

On Monday morning, September 21, 2009, Harrison and Ramona Taylor approached us about writing a manuscript documenting the story of their branch of the Taylor family and their place in history. For ten years Harrison, working with Ramona, had been accumulating information about his genealogical line of Taylors. They subsequently commissioned us to record the rich and compelling family history that is intertwined with emigration, the founding of our nation, and the birth of Tennessee. The Taylor family participated in the creation of Carter County, soldiered in the American Revolution, the War of 1812, endured the suffering of the Civil War, and aided in the Civil War relief efforts of East Tennessee. They served as U.S. congressmen, and treated with Native Americans on the national scene. Two brothers, Alf and Bob, reached the governor's office, and Bob later became a U.S. Senator. Theirs is a story of public service and prominence in Carter County, the state of Tennessee, and the nation, covering almost three centuries. If there is a centerpiece of this narrative it might be Nathaniel Greene Taylor, who is book-ended with his direct line ancestors and descendants. Harrison and Ramona turned over their research to us, and we used this research material to write the manuscript, supplementing as we could. We were honored to be selected by them, pleased to get to know them better during the project, and trust the result meets all their expectations.

Gene, having worked for the National Park Service (NPS) which is an agency of the U.S. Department of the Interior as is the Bureau of Indian Affairs, was amazed at how the Taylor's were connected to so many NPS sites. These national treasures are included in the endnotes, helping readers realize just how far the influence of the Tennessee Taylors reached during this time in history. And, for those who are interested, these sites provide more background into their lives and the nation's history.

Many individuals and institutions assisted in the preparation of this narrative. In researching the early Taylors, Jennifer Bauer, superintendent, Sycamore Shoals State Historic Area, Elizabethton, Tennessee, made available H.T. Spoden & Associates,

Sycamore Shoals State Park and Colonel John Carter House report. We appreciate her time and assistance. Dona Lewis, retired librarian, and Cheryl Grizzle, her replacement, Jonesborough-Washington County Library, Jonesborough, Tennessee, were of immense value in responding to our many interlibrary loan requests which helped document the lives of the Taylors. Mr. Ronald Lee, Tennessee State Library and Archives, Nashville, was very helpful in our early research and was always quick to respond to our needs and questions for which we are grateful.

Good friend and retired professor of history, Louis Athey, Ph.D., Franklin and Marshal College, Lancaster, Pennsylvania, provided an in depth review of chapter two about Nathaniel Taylor, improving it considerably. We are grateful for his help in providing research and other assistance. Tom Kanon, Ph.D., archivist at the Tennessee State Library and Archives was equally helpful in our research. A War of 1812 scholar, he also reviewed our chapter on Brigadier General Nathaniel Taylor.

Robert M. Utley, author of many western histories and a former chief historian of the National Park Service, graciously reviewed the facts on western history in chapter four about Nathaniel Greene Taylor. Bob Moore, historian, Jefferson National Expansion Memorial, St. Louis, Missouri, took the time to make an incredibly helpful in depth review of chapter four which we appreciate. George Elmore, Fort Larned National Historic Site, Larned, Kansas, was also gracious enough to provide a review of chapter four. Jim Pahris of Jonesborough helped us immeasurably with railroad schedules, names of railroads, and other arcane railroad history that only someone with his talents and interests could uncover. Thanks Jim.

History professor, Tom Lee, East Tennessee State University, reviewed chapter five, and his straightforward comments improved organization significantly. His suggestions about Alfred Alexander Taylor and Robert L. Taylor, helped us find balance in the social and political lives of these two great Tennesseans.

Don K. Ferguson, executive director, The Historical Society of the United States District Court for the Eastern District of Tennessee, Inc., who also covered the trial following the Clinton High School desegregation of 1956, helped clarify major points and also provided documentation about federal Judge Robert Love Taylor in chapter six on Benjamin Harrison Taylor.

Robert L. Taylor Jr., Ph.D., son of federal Judge Robert Love Taylor, grandson of Governor Alfred A. Taylor, and retired history professor, Middle Tennessee State University, Murfreesboro, Tennessee, reviewed the entire manuscript. He provided an insight ordinarily not achieved in a manuscript with family history, and we appreciate his input on Reconstruction during Andrew Johnson's presidency. Michael Toomey, Ph.D., adjunct history professor, Lincoln Memorial University, Harrogate,

Tennessee, former editor (1999-2009) of *The Journal of East Tennessee History*, and friend, graciously agreed to review yet another of our works. His thorough review included editorial suggestions, organizational restructuring, and input about Tennessee history that added considerably to the text. We are grateful to all those who took such an avid interest in this project and so enthusiastically supported us.

W. Eugene Cox
Joyce Cox

Introduction

Mystification best describes my memories. My father died in 1930 when I was five years old. I have few memories of him. I do remember that, when he died, his body was "laid out" in the living room of our home at 181 East Highland Road, Johnson City, Tennessee. A lot of people crowded into our house.

I was mystified. Who are all these people? What are they doing here? Where is my daddy?

Some man heard me whispering these questions and picked me up to show me my daddy lying in what they called a coffin. I was mystified by it all. I went into the dining room and tried to cry. That was the thing to do, I thought.

As I grew I began gathering facts about myself, my family, and the world. Such facts do not come complete, chronological, or self-evident. They are all jumbled-up. Historians are needed with records, books, and time lines. So in a mystified state I wandered through—back and forth, up and down, in and out. This led to school-grammar, high school, college, seminary, graduate school. They teach what you can know, never know-but want to know, to put the pieces together. Still mystified.

This volume is an attempt to put some loose ends, gaps, and errors in proper perspective. After several years of searching, traveling, and reading, I called on Ed Speer to help with some research and then Gene and Joyce Cox-historians! This is not intended to be a complete history of Tennessee or Taylors. There are too many of those. Only the Taylors who were more directly in my own line-not extensive or in depth-but those who brought me into and along this limited life span, are included.

So here are some more pieces to the puzzle that has guided, shaped, and directed my life. I am grateful and still mystified, but moving on, humming the ballad "Where do you come from? Where do you go?"

The Rev. Dr. Benjamin Harrison Taylor
Son of Ben H. Taylor (1888-1930) and grandson of Alf Taylor (1848-1931).

East Tennessee Taylors Genealogical Chart of the Andrew Taylor Line

Andrew Taylor born in 1730 married Elizabeth Wilson in about 1763. When she died he married her sister Ann in probably 1769. In 1778 he migrated from Virginia to the Watauga settlement, North Carolina. Andrew settled on a small flat at the confluence of Powder Branch and Buffalo Creek, a tributary of the Watauga River. This would later become known as Happy Valley, Carter County, Tennessee. Andrew died in 1787.

Andrew and Ann's first son, Nathaniel Taylor, was born February 4, 1771, in Virginia. He married Mary Patton on November 15, 1791, in Virginia. Nathaniel served in the House, Tennessee Eighth General Assembly, representing Carter County from 1809 to 1811. During the War of 1812, his East Tennessee Militia command served in the defense of Mobile, Mississippi Territory, now Alabama, in 1814. Nathaniel died at his residence on February 20, 1816.

James Patton Taylor was born November 5, 1792, in the Territory of the United States, South of the River Ohio, and married Mary Cocke on August 22, 1816. The eldest son of Nathaniel and Mary, he was Attorney General of the First Judicial District and met an untimely death on January 12, 1833.

Nathaniel Greene Taylor born on December 29, 1819, in Carter County, Tennessee, was the oldest child of James Patton and Mary Taylor He married Emeline Haynes on January 30, 1844. Nathaniel, a lawyer and Methodist minister, served in the U.S. Congress from March 1854 to March 1855 and for a full term from 1865 to 1867. He was the founder of the East Tennessee Relief Association in 1864 and went north to help raise a quarter of a million dollars for the association. President Andrew Johnson appointed him Commissioner of Indian Affairs, and he served from 1867 to 1869. He died on April 1, 1887.

Alfred Alexander Taylor, the second son of Nathaniel Greene and Emeline Taylor, was born on August 6, 1848, in Carter County. In 1874 he served in the Tennessee General Assembly. On June 22, 1881, he married Florence Jane J. Anderson. From

March 4, 1889, to March 3, 1895, he served as a Republican in the Fifty-first, Fifty-second, and Fifty-third U.S. Congresses. He was governor of Tennessee from 1921 to1923. Women voted for the first time in his election. Alf, as he was known, died on November 2, 1931.

His brother, Robert Love Taylor born on March 31, 1850, was married to Sarah Baird, Mamie St. John, and Alice Hill. He served as a Democratic congressman from the First District (1879-1881). Robert or "Our Bob," as he was better known, served three terms as governor of Tennessee, from 1887 to 1891 and 1897 to 1899. He was serving as a U.S. Senator when he died unexpectedly on March 31, 1912.

Benjamin Harrison Taylor, better known as Ben H. Taylor, was born on August 4, 1888, and on September 28, 1920, married Lela Amanda Ramsey. His premature death occurred on March 26, 1930, in Johnson City, Tennessee. His son, Benjamin Harrison Taylor, Johnson City, Tennessee, conceived the idea for this narrative.

Chapter 1

Andrew Taylor
1730-1787

Six Generations of Taylors

The saga of the East Tennessee Taylor family from 1730 to 1956 presents a portrait of Americana with its hopes, dreams, successes, and failures. As we search our past we have a tendency to spotlight certain facts about our ancestors and often neglect to place them in their time and to remember that they were men and women as we are. In this narrative we wanted to place the Taylors in the larger context of state and national history. Like many of us, they were preoccupied with finances for they enjoyed living well. They were family oriented, strong on education, had high moral values, and embraced politics.

The Taylors might be viewed as a mirror unto ourselves as we delve into their lives. Their ambition, desires, and finances were perhaps no different from others of their day except for the scale on which they were carried out. They were farmers, slave owners, Indian fighters, Unionists, businessmen, lawyers, and large land owners. Their ranks included a militia officer, Tennessee senator and assemblyman, an attorney-general, postmaster, newspaperman, an Indian commissioner, and professor, but unlike most of us they also held the highest office in Tennessee and the U.S. Congress. Although they represented ordinary people, they were not ordinary themselves. What is true is that the warp and woof of Taylor history is tied to the fabric of Tennessee and America's history, and that is the main thesis of this publication.

The saga begins before statehood in Tennessee with Andrew and Ann Taylor's arrival in 1778. They were among those brave and adventuresome first European families to settle East Tennessee. Their two sons were in the militia, beginning a Taylor tradition that remains to the present. Andrew assessed taxable property in the state's first county, thus beginning another Taylor tradition of public service that they would be best remembered for. Andrew Taylor settled on the Watauga River where a representative government was formed four years before our Declaration of Independence was written. Textbooks of the American Revolution often do not focus on the back country, but Andrew was there at the gathering of the frontiersmen at Sycamore Shoals which led to the subsequent victory of the mountain men over the British at Kings Mountain. His family was there when Europeans were struggling with the Cherokee for control of the land in order to establish a permanent settlement in northeast Tennessee.

Nathaniel Taylor, Andrew's son, was a slave owner, militia officer, Indian fighter, surveyor, state legislator, businessman, and iron works manufacturer. No ordinary frontiersman, his first public office was held in 1793. His prominent role in early Carter County and Tennessee shows him to be one of the builders that lay the foundation of statehood for Tennessee. The militia, in which he served as an officer for his entire life, provided a sense of security in the fledgling state and was put to the test in the War of 1812. Nathaniel had a field command in the war, helping protect the territory around Mobile, Alabama. This war, little known or understood will soon celebrate its 200th anniversary making his story timely. After Nathaniel's death, his wife, Mary built Sabine Hill prior to 1821. The house is now owned by the State of Tennessee. Once in operation, Sabine Hill will help tell the story of East Tennessee's early frontier and Mary and Nathaniel's life in such a pivotal time.

The Taylors were memorialized when the county seat of Johnson County was named Taylorsville for James Patton Taylor, the son of Nathaniel and father of Nathaniel Greene Taylor. Few people are aware of the role Nathaniel Greene Taylor played in East Tennessee. His was a life that events impacted and one that should be remembered for the impact he had on East Tennessee and the nation. Although a slave owner, he was a Unionist who helped keep our nation intact at great risk to his life, during the Civil War. By 1863 shortages of food and labor and the internecine warfare in East Tennessee had made the region destitute. Nathaniel's heroic efforts at that time are shared, not only in recognition of him, but to give a glimpse into what people suffered. His fundraising efforts were significant to the welfare of East Tennesseans.

Tennessee's political history as seen through the eyes of Nathaniel and his once political enemy and later friend, President Andrew Johnson who selected him to be his Commissioner of Indian Affairs in 1867, is explored. Those fascinated with the American west will find that the commissioner's office played a major role in the lives of Native Americans. This narrative fills a void in East Tennessee history in describing Nathaniel's life in Tennessee politics and his reformist movement as Indian commissioner which affected national policy. Actions of this East Tennessean left a clear imprint on the direction of Indian policy for several decades.

With the Civil War and Reconstruction behind them, Tennesseans saw the decade of the 1870s as an opportunity to improve the state's economic system. These were difficult times financially for the Taylors and placed many hardships on the family while Nathaniel was serving East Tennessee as a fundraiser, a congressman, and the nation as Indian commissioner.

Alf Taylor, Nathaniel's son, entered the Tennessee General Assembly in 1875 and introduced legislation that created one of Tennessee's counties. Years later the Republicans nominated thirty-eight year old Alfred A. Taylor for the governor's race. Robert E. Corlew, in his book, *Tennessee A Short History*, calls the 1886-1896 decade a troubled one with factional politics continuing unabated in the Democratic Party. This lack of harmony within the Democratic Party encouraged the members to seek a candidate who could unite them. That candidate, Robert Love Taylor (Bob), Alf's brother, was nominated because of his strong unifying leadership in the Democratic Party.

Thirty-six year old Bob Taylor of Carter County is woven into his brother Alf's chapter, making him the sixth Taylor to be written about. Running against each other for governor, their colorful campaign became known as the "War of the Roses" capturing the imagination of Tennesseans as well as the nation. In earlier Tennessee campaigns Civil War and Reconstruction prejudices were part of the rhetoric. The Taylors, in the War of the Roses, changed that and helped Tennesseans shift from the past to the present and to become more forward looking, although they may not have been entirely aware of doing so.

After his term as governor, Bob became a lecturer in 1892, on the profitable Chautauqua tour. When Alf left Congress, his main occupation was giving lectures on the Chautauqua circuit for about twenty-six years. The brothers helped put Tennessee on the map with their lectures. These tours were grueling and kept both men away from home for long periods of time but made them financially able to have a comfortable life. During this period, Bob served as a third term governor from 1897 to 1899. He was elected U.S. Senator in 1907 and served until his death in 1912.

Alf ran for governor in 1920 and was aided in his successful election bid by "Old Limber," a foxhound. The brothers from East Tennessee knew just about every president from Abraham Lincoln to Herbert Hoover, and they rubbed shoulders with a great many leaders of Tennessee and the nation. They had far ranging contacts, and it was perhaps the social contact in political life they craved as much as the competiveness of seeking political office and supporting their party.

In the last chapter we write about Benjamin Harrison Taylor, Alf's son, who was a prominent East Tennessee attorney and a Democrat. His peers said he would have been the next governor of Tennessee had his life not been cut short. The eighth Taylor featured in the narrative is federal Judge Robert L. Taylor, included because of the role he had in the Clinton desegregation crisis of 1956, a part of East Tennessee and national history. His decision as judge was felt nationally and in 1957 enabled one African American student at Clinton High School to become the first black graduate from any integrated public high school in the South.

The Beginning of Present Tennessee

The events that foreshadowed Andrew Taylor's move to the Watauga settlement began over a century before his arrival. In 1684 the British, as it was in their self interest to maintain good relations with the Cherokee, consummated the first Cherokee treaty with the "representatives from the Lower Towns of 'Toxawa and Keowa.'" The deerskin trade was developing quickly, and by the 1700s, was a full-blown enterprise with more than fifty thousand hides being exported from Charleston annually. "In exchange for deerskins, the Cherokee received firearms, ammunition, metal knives, pots, axes, and garden implements, as well as an assortment of beads, baubles, vermillion for paint, clothing, and quantities of rum."[1] For a society that had none, the durable metal objects radically changed the lives of the Cherokee who were eager to trade for these products.

In the 1760s this desire for animal pelts as trade items brought the European long hunters into the market and to what is now northeast Tennessee. The ancestral Cherokee had lived here for centuries, but in the 1760s the area around the Watauga Settlement was only sparsely inhabited by them. The Cherokee claimed a hunting territory that encompassed 40,000 square miles and was located in portions of eight future states.[2] Future Carter County, Tennessee, where Andrew Taylor settled, was in this vast Cherokee empire.

In the late 1760s and early 1770s, news about the lands along the Clinch, Holston, Nolichucky, Powell, and Watauga Rivers, attracted people like bears to honey. The settlement that blossomed on the Watauga River around Sycamore Shoals is significant not only in Tennessee history but also in the history of the nation. When King George III issued his Proclamation of 1763, he prohibited colonists from living or establishing settlements west of the designated proclamation line which ran through the Appalachian Mountains and the Indians owned the lands on the western boundary.

Sometime around 1766 Julius C. Dugger located his home on the north side of the Watauga River. William Bean arrived on nearby Boones Creek in 1769, and in 1770 James Robertson built a cabin about where the present town of Elizabethton is located. Also in 1770, Jacob Brown arrived from South Carolina and started a settlement on the Nolichucky River, about seventeen miles away from the Watauga Settlement. In 1770 or 1771 John Carter (1737-1781) came from Virginia to the west side of the Holston River (now Hawkins County) with his family, but in 1772, because of Indian robberies, he moved to the Watauga settlement. Another Virginian, Valentine Sevier Sr., arrived in 1772 just upstream from Sycamore Shoals where most of the early colonists settled. In December 1773 Valentine Sevier's son, John, came with his family to Sycamore Shoals.

The Watauga Association

In 1772 the Watauga Association based on the laws of Virginia was organized and five magistrates were elected. It is not known who these magistrates were nor has a copy of their famous agreement been found. The association was not an attempt at a separate government but was a temporary democratic form of self government, within limits, initiated by the Wataugans themselves, and only meant to serve as a government until the area was accepted by either Virginia or North Carolina.[3] Also in 1772, the colonists on the Watauga thwarted the Proclamation of 1763 by signing a ten year lease with the Cherokee which allowed them to live there.

As a result of the Watauga Association being formed, Lord John Murray Dunmore, Governor of Virginia, wrote in 1774 that "[The Wataugans] have appointed magistrates, and framed laws, for their present occasions, and to all intents and purposes, erected themselves into, though an inconsiderable, yet a separate State. . . . It at least sets a dangerous example to the people of America, of forming governments distinct from and independent of his majesty's authority."[4]

Richard Henderson, a North Carolina judge, was successful in his quest, to purchase land from the Cherokee, and, on March 17, 1775, the chiefs of the Cherokee Nation conveyed to Richard Henderson and Company for a reported ten thousand pounds some twenty million acres of land in Kentucky and Tennessee.[5] Known as the Transylvania Purchase, it was, to that time, the largest private purchase of land in America.[6] The Cherokee gave permission for a "Path Deed," signed on March 17,

1775, at Sycamore Shoals, which allowed the Wataugans to construct a road from the Watauga settlement through the Cumberland Gap into Kentucky.[7]

A treaty, signed at Sycamore Shoals on March 19, 1775, and known as the "Wataugah Land Purchases" included land on the Watauga, Holston, and New Rivers, which Watauga residents purchased from the Cherokee. On the banks of Sycamore Shoals on the Watauga River, Henry Lyle owned a 640 acre tract of land. It was upstream, or northeast, and adjacent to the tract on which the 1776 Fort Watauga stood. Lyle had purchased the land on October 19, 1775, and before 1778 had built a house on the property. Thirty some years later John Scoggins, a later owner, would sell 361 acres to Nathaniel Taylor for $3,000. This land became known in the Taylor family as the "Sycamore Shoals Plantation" and was the same site on which the overmountain men had gathered thirty years before for the march to Kings Mountain.[8]

The inhabitants of Watauga were afraid of Indian attacks, and sometime in the first half of 1776 they began to build Fort Watauga, or Caswell, as it was originally named on the south side of the Watauga River west of Elizabethton where the Sycamore Shoals Monument is now located.[9] The Wataugans, still laboring under the self government which they had formed, knew they needed the organizational structure of colonial government. Uppermost in their minds was the desire to establish legal title to their land, obtain funding to protect themselves, and if need be wage war. In 1776 they addressed their position and grievances by having clerk William Tatham write to the Provincial Council of North Carolina. Tatham wrote that because they were on the edge of the frontier they feared people would settle there, take out credit, and abruptly leave, defrauding their creditors without them having legal means to prosecute. In this petition they requested to be annexed to North Carolina. Counting the committee members, 260 freemen signed the petition.[10]

On Thursday, August 22, 1776, the petition from the Watauga and Holstein settlements, identifying themselves as the Washington District, was received at the Provincial Council of North Carolina. Upon receipt the council recommended that the "freemen" [those who owned property] hold an election on October 15 to elect five delegates to represent the Washington District, at the Provincial Council meeting in Halifax, North Carolina, convening on Sunday, November 10.[11] On Tuesday the petition was accepted and Charles Robertson, John Carter, and John Haile from Washington District were allowed to take their seats. On December 3 John Sevier took his seat in Congress as a delegate from the Watauga Settlement and Washington District. On Monday, December 23 the House issued commissions for the District of Washington to John Carter as Colonel, John Sevier, Lieutenant

Colonel, Charles Robertson, 1st Major, and Jacob Womack, 2nd Major, enabling them to organize, prepare for defense, and be supported financially by the state.[12] This was the beginning of Tennessee's military history and was a forerunner to the Forty-fifth General Assembly in 1887 which created the Tennessee National Guard.[13]

So many colonists were arriving, that British Superintendent John Stuart wrote on August 26, 1776, saying "many hundreds of families" are on the Holston and Watauga Rivers. As a result of the 1776 petition sent to North Carolina, the petitioners were advised to hold an election on March 10, 1777, to choose a senator and two members for the House of Commons. John Carter was elected to the North Carolina Senate, and John Sevier was elected to the House of Commons where he proposed that Washington District become a county. In 1777 Washington County, with its western boundary reaching to the Mississippi River, became the first county in what would later be the state of Tennessee. On February 23, 1778, the first court for Washington County, North Carolina, convened.[14]

Andrew Taylor Arrives in Washington County, North Carolina

As of 2011 the descendants of Andrew Taylor could trace their origins back 281 years to 1730, the approximate year Andrew Taylor Sr. was born.[15] In 1755 or 1756, Andrew Taylor Sr. married Elizabeth Wilson, the daughter of John Wilson. Andrew and Elizabeth lived on Mill Creek in Rockbridge County, Virginia, with their four children, Isaac, Elizabeth, Andrew Jr., and Matthew. Elizabeth died around 1768, and Andrew married Ann Wilson, Elizabeth's sister, probably in 1769. They had three children, Nathaniel, Rhoda, and Rebecca.

In the agricultural society of the 1700s, not all farmers knew how to fertilize and refurbish their land for growing crops. When the land was no longer fertile, they often moved on. Historically, they would leave after the harvest and relocate before the next planting season. Whether this was Andrew's reason for moving or not, he left Virginia in the spring of 1778 after obtaining a land grant in North Carolina.[16] Court records support his arrival in North Carolina by showing Andrew as a property owner, and eligible to serve as a grand juror. On August 27, 1778, he was selected for the upcoming court, confirming that he was on the Watauga earlier that year.[17]

It is not clear how Andrew obtained the land grant. He may have purchased the warrant, as was a common practice. Andrew moved onto the land before he had the warrant which was not entered until April 4, 1779, indicating some arrangements had previously been made. He took the warrant to the North Carolina entry taker, John

Carter, who happened to be his neighbor. Carter entered the warrant and requested that the 450 acres of land located on both sides of Buffalo Creek, be surveyed. This was approved and signed by Governor Alexander Martin.[18]

Andrew settled on a small flat at the confluence of Powder Branch and Buffalo Creek, a tributary of the Watauga River, where he probably built a small cabin to hold his large household. Family lore tells us that he built what was referred to as a "lean to." Another thought is that the two-story log house, thought to be his, was probably built years later by Alfred W. Taylor. Large log homes were being built at this early date. For example, sometime between 1776 and 1778, Christopher Taylor (no known relation) built a two-story log home that still stands, although it has been moved from its original location to Jonesborough. Also, in 1797 John Casebolt had a two-story log house built in Elizabethton.[19]

Sometime around August 1779 the Washington County court began to assess taxable property for the first time. Andrew Taylor, Mathew Talbot Sr., and Clevis Barksvill (Barksdale) were assigned this task. They assessed the property "below the Iron Mountains including the waters on the north side of Brush Creek and Watauga and also all the taxable property on the north side of Watauga and [made a] return to Thomas Houghton." People were also living on Stony Creek below, or west of, Iron Mountain. The assessors probably went down both sides of Stony Creek, then continued their work on the north side of the Watauga. Andrew Taylor received another land grant, surveyed on November 24, 1779, for thirty-one acres "joining the land [where] Taylor now lives."[20]

The constant threat of attack by the Cherokee hovered over the Taylors and their neighbors, but the militia was beginning to carry the campaign to the Indians. In 1778 John Sevier, Lieutenant Colonel of the militia, was living at his home, Mount Pleasant, on the south side of the Nolichucky River. In 1779 during the campaign against the Chickamauga Indians, he and his men served under Col. Evan Shelby. Andrew Taylor Jr., son of Andrew Sr., served under Capt. David McNabb, Andrew Jr.'s brother-in-law. These Cherokee Indians were dissatisfied with the Watauga treaties, and under Dragging Canoe's leadership they had broken away in 1776 and were known as the Chickamauga Cherokee. In February and March of 1780 Andrew and Isaac Taylor served in the militia under Capt. Robert Sevier and Col. John Sevier. Andrew Jr., in his claim for a pension, stated that he was drafted (as a fourteen year old) "from Buffalo Creek [where his father lived] as a militiaman in the fall of 1780 [*sic* 1779] for a three-month tour serving under Captain McNabb and Colonel John Sevier." They "marched to the Overhill Town, and burned their town, cut up the corn, destroyed their stock, and killed many Indians." Afterwards, they marched home and were discharged in the neighborhood of his residence by Colonel Sevier. It is odd that there is no mention of service by Andrew at Kings Mountain, which, though brief, was such an important event.[21]

The British also posed a threat that the backcountry people had to be aware of. In the summer of 1780, Captain McNabb raised a company of militia and marched south, joining Gen. Joseph McDowell in North Carolina for a three month tour of duty. Isaac Taylor, Andrew Jr.'s brother, was with McNabb. Under McDowell, they arrived after the battle at Ramsour's Mill, South Carolina, and then ranged along the New River. The company was commanded by Colonel Robertson, and after joining McDowell, they captured ninety-two British at the Twenty-Two Mile House in South Carolina.[22]

The American Revolution, now five years old, was headed for the mountains with all its fury. On May 12, 1780, Gen. Benjamin Lincoln surrendered the garrison at Charleston, South Carolina, with its attendant loss of men and arms, to British Gen. Charles Cornwallis. The British hoped to follow this victory by marching into the Carolinas and Georgia. To encourage the Loyalists and punish the rebels, Maj. Patrick Ferguson swept into the backcountry in September where vicious guerilla warfare continued for some time. Meanwhile, Cornwallis had moved to Charlotte, North Carolina, and ordered Ferguson to gather all the Loyalists he could from the back country to protect his left flank. With this accomplished, he hoped to capture the Chiswell's lead mine on the New River near Wytheville, Virginia, invade that state, and encourage the Indians to attack the backwoodsmen. Ferguson, from Gilbertown on the edge of the mountains, sent a message by a prisoner to men on the Watauga, Nolichucky, and Holston Rivers, saying that, "if they did not desist from their opposition to British arms, he would march his army over the mountains, hang their leaders, and lay their country waste with fire and sword."[23]

This threat by Ferguson and its ramifications infuriated the militia leaders. To them, their homes and families were now under attack. Col. Isaac Shelby of Sullivan County received the message and rode to Col. John Sevier's home below Jonesborough to inform him of the threat. They began to devise a plan to collect as large a force as possible and launch a surprise attack on Ferguson. Col. Charles McDowell and Col. Andrew Hampton, with about 160 men and refugees, were encamped at John Carter's on the Watauga River, having fled from Ferguson at Cane Creek and the Upper Catawba in August. Col. William Campbell, in nearby Virginia, was notified that a rendezvous would be held on September 25 on Carter's land, sometimes referred to as Sycamore Flats on the Watauga.[24]

The Gathering, Religion, and the State of Franklin

Men began arriving at Sycamore Shoals and Fort Watauga, about a mile below present day Elizabethton before the appointed day of September 25, 1780. The arriving "overmountain" men, as they were later called, were several hundred strong with as many horses plus cattle which they planned to drive for food. Andrew Taylor Sr.'s cabin was located approximately two and a half miles south, on a hill from which the smoke and blazing fires of the encampment were plainly visible. It was a gathering not to be easily discounted or forgotten.

The Reverend Samuel Doak, licensed to preach on October 31, 1777, by the Hanover Presbytery, became a great spiritual leader in Virginia and Tennessee. He gave the inspirational prayer for the men before they departed Sycamore Shoals for the Battle of Kings Mountain in 1780.

The Reverend Samuel Doak traveled twenty-five miles from Salem, Tennessee, to invoke God's blessing on the frontiersmen destined to march to the battle of Kings Mountain. On September 26, before their departure, he ended his prayer with a quote from Judges 7:20, saying that when Gideon surrounded the Midianites they cried out "The Sword of the Lord, and of Gideon." The frontiersmen echoed this war cry in the stillness along the Watauga.[25] The Taylors were Presbyterians like Doak and no doubt were in attendance. They, as Doak wanted, were interested in establishing their church on the frontier. The minutes of the Hanover Presbytery, September 14, 1784, state, "a verbal request, [indicating there was a congregation and perhaps a church] for supplies [ministers] from French Broad, from the fork at Nola-Chucky [*sic*] and Watauga" was made. This "Watauga Church" was the forerunner of the future First Presbyterian Church in Elizabethton, where members of the Taylor family worshipped.[26]

When the impressive encampment broke up on September 26, the militia rode out, going down Gap Creek to the east of Andrew Taylor's property. Andrew Taylor and his family among others were there to bid them farewell. It was a long march to Kings Mountain where the frontiersmen, as planned, caught Major Ferguson by surprise. They camped that last night at the Cowpens, and from their increased number some 900 of the best equipped were chosen to make the attack. On October 7 this number surrounded Ferguson's camp of some 1,100 men and in a vicious one hour fight killed Ferguson and reaped a decisive victory. The news spread quickly and while the patriots' spirits soared, those of the loyalists dropped, along with their desire to enlist with the British forces.[27]

In 1781 the May Term of the Washington County Pleas and Quarter Session appointed justices and assessors for the year. Appointed for the Second District were Thomas Houghton, William Cocke, James Henry, Andrew Taylor Sr., and Isaac Taylor, his son.[28] Andrew Taylor Sr. and his family were caught up in another frontier event, the State of Franklin, which was an attempt to separate the northeast counties of Tennessee from North Carolina and form a separate state. Nationally, different groups attempted to create separate states throughout the country while the government was trying to "unite" the thirteen states already in existence. Among those to almost accomplish this were the State of Franklin adherents who met at Jonesborough in August and December of 1784. A committee report from one of the conventions, date unknown, stated "that the counties of Washington, Sullivan, and Greene . . . form themselves into an Association . . . [toward] laying off a new state." The committee members included Christopher Taylor (no known relation to the subject Taylor line), who lived near Jonesborough. No other Taylor was listed. A vote was called for, and a Taylor (no first name but most likely Christopher) and an A. Taylor who was not listed among the members present, voted for secession. We do not know whether or not A. Taylor is Andrew Taylor Sr. In March 1785 the members elected John Sevier as the first and only governor of the State of Franklin.[29] There was much opposition to this movement for separation, including the state of North Carolina, and we do not know for sure which side the Taylors were on. When George Washington became president on April 30, 1789, the Constitution went into effect. This nullified any attempt to create a new state.[30]

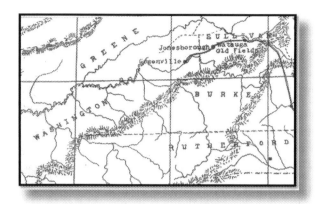

In 1783 only one road entered present Tennessee from North Carolina. From Morgantown, North Carolina, in Burke County, it crossed Roan Mountain, went through the Watauga Old Fields to Jonesborough and ended at Greeneville. The Tennessee counties represented are Greene, Sullivan, and Washington. Adapted from E.W. Myers, *The State Records of North Carolina*, vol. 18.

In Andrew Taylor Senior's will, dated May 22, 1787, in Washington County, North Carolina, he gave to Ann, his wife, the dwelling house and a grist mill. After her death, his son Nathaniel received the property. Nathaniel was to provide for Ann's "maintenance and support and [that of Andrew's] two daughters." Nathaniel and his wife, Mary, lived with his mother until they purchased the "Sycamore Shoals Plantation," another property, in 1810.[31]

Andrew's house, as described to Franklin D. Love by William and Maj. George Taylor grandsons of Gen. Nathaniel Taylor, was as follows: "The house was constructed of logs, with an open passage way between the north and south ends. It was two stories, and had six rooms, rear and front, and a porch in front and in the rear. It had a shed kitchen." According to Andrew Taylor Sr.'s will he owned three slaves at the time of his death in the fall of 1787.[32]

Andrew is buried on an eminence east of the old Taylor homestead. The burial ground, known in the family as "the oldest Taylor Graveyard," is located on a hill just before entering Elizabethton. It is about 600 yards east of the original Andrew Taylor homestead (mouth of Powder Branch). Either Andrew Taylor or his daughter Elizabeth was probably the first one to be buried there. It is perhaps the oldest graveyard in the Watauga Settlement.[33]

Chapter 2

Nathaniel Taylor
1771-1816

Nathaniel, son of Andrew and his second wife Ann, was born in Rockbridge County, Virginia, on February 4, 1771. At age seven, almost two years after the American colonists declared their independence from Great Britain, he moved with his parents to Washington County, North Carolina, settling not too far from where Buffalo Creek flows into the Watauga River. When the Taylors moved, they were aware that the Cherokee were a threat to those living on the Watauga River. Nathaniel's brothers, Andrew and Isaac, were defenders of the frontier and fought under John Sevier, a man that Nathaniel was acquainted with the rest of his life.

The steady growth and importance of Sycamore Shoals on the Watauga during the 1780s appears evident from its emerging road network. On Monday, February 5, 1787, the Washington County court ordered that "a wagon road be cleared from the Dividing Ridge between Gap Creek and Doe River to the center of the Watauga River near Jacob Smith's." This road continued from the Watauga River up Roan Creek toward North Carolina. On Tuesday, February 6, the court ordered Nathaniel's stepbrothers, Isaac and Andrew Taylor Jr., to help "lay off" a road from James Stuarts to Sycamore Shoals. This route continued on to the Nolichucky River in Tennessee. In May the court ordered a wagon road cleared from the Sycamore Shoals toward Indian Creek, running along the north side of the Watauga River. As a teenager Nathaniel may have traveled one of these new roads with his father to Jonesborough, the county seat of Washington County. Had he been there on May 12, 1788, he might have noticed the tall lanky young man from North Carolina who had presented his credentials to practice law in Washington County. The lawyer was Andrew Jackson, the future hero of New Orleans who Nathaniel as a militia officer later served under.

In 1789 when Nathaniel was eighteen years old, events which would influence the future of the Taylors, the county, the state, and the nation occurred. First was the demise of the State of Franklin, and second was the creation of the newly formed Constitution of the United States. A third event, equally important, was the creation by Congress, on May 26, 1790, of the Territory of the United States, South of the River Ohio, routinely referred to as the Southwest Territory. President George Washington appointed William Blount as governor of the Southwest Territory, and Blount established the first territorial capital at William Cobb's home, known as Rocky Mount, between the forks of the Holston and Watauga Rivers. Cobb had arrived in 1770 and built a "nine-room, two story house of white oak logs" about six miles from where Nathaniel's family settled. On October 3, 1790, Governor Blount formed the District of Washington from the counties of Washington, Sullivan, Greene, and Hawkins. The Taylors found themselves incorporated into the Washington District. On October 11, Governor Blount arrived at his new residence, the William Cobb place in Washington County, and on October 20 he wrote that he felt "very well accommodated with a room with glass windows, fireplace, and so forth." The capital remained there until March 1792 when Governor Blount moved it to Knoxville.

According to family lore, in 1791 after the crops were in, Nathaniel "exchanged" sixty-five acres of land on Buffalo Creek for a black pony that he took to Virginia to carry home his new bride. Another family story, with some credence, is that Nathaniel, when about sixteen, was sent to Rockbridge County, Virginia, for schooling. There he met Mary Patton. She was the daughter of James Patton, one of the early colonists in Virginia who had reportedly emigrated from Ireland with the Taylors. Upon arrival in Virginia, Nathaniel began a courtship with Mary, and on November 15, 1791, twenty-two year old Nathaniel was married to Mary on her nineteenth birthday by a Presbyterian minister named Brown. "James Patton gave a substantial dowry to his daughter and son-in-law, a horse, bridle, and saddle each, a yoke of steers, a wagon, house hold goods and garden seeds, and a Negro man." The young couple returned to the Watauga country and the home place of Andrew Taylor Sr. located on Powder Branch off Buffalo Creek where they resided with Nathaniel's mother, Ann.

In manhood Nathaniel Taylor was described as six feet tall with deep set dark eyes, brown hair, and possessed of a military bearing. Mary was described as strong willed and capable. She was five feet, six inches tall, blonde with blue eyes, a florid complexion and a well rounded face. She was said to be rather stout in middle life. Nathaniel Taylor quickly acquired a number of slaves and thousands of acres of land. He was politically involved in the militia and had many business ventures, including the manufacture of bar iron, flour, and gunpowder. Due to his remarkable business ability, he was one of the wealthiest men in Carter County.

The Militia, Creation of Tennessee, and Carter County

The earliest Tennessee Militia was organized under the militia laws of North Carolina, with each county having a regiment named for its respective county and divided into captain's companies. The county tax collection procedure required captains of the militia have the responsibility of compiling an annual "list of taxable property" for each landowner which they submitted to the county court. The county was divided into taxable districts, and from the captain's list taxes would be assigned and collected. This practice was not dropped until 1834 when Tennessee's new constitution was approved, and the districts were called "Civil Districts." Nathaniel was captain of a company in the Carter County Regiment of Militia, and the earliest he assessed taxes for his taxable district was in 1790.

President George Washington commissioned John Sevier as brigadier general for the Watauga District on November 21, 1789. The newly created War Department was assigned responsibility for the Indian tribes. Washington made the territorial governors Superintendents of Indian Affairs. In 1790 he established the precedence for providing annuity payments for land ceded to the United States. In 1793 appropriated funds were made available for negotiating treaties and for supporting them. The relationship that the fledging United States established with Native Americans at the beginning of George Washington's administration was far reaching and had a bearing on one of the Taylors in the 1860s.

Nathaniel ranged the Nolichucky River fighting against the Indians. One encounter occurred on Indian Creek when the Indians killed members of the Lewis family, burning their house and taking a daughter captive. Captain Taylor and his company pursued the Indians who headed south where they crossed the French Broad River, losing their pursuers. The daughter was later traded for a gun and then reunited with her remaining family. Another encounter involving Nathaniel was the Etowah Campaign which occurred in 1793 as a result of Capt. John Beard and about forty militiamen killing a number of Cherokee, resulted in the Indians attacking Samuel Henry's station. John Sevier and his militia responded to the raid, reinforced by Col. John Blair and Capt. Nathaniel Taylor with additional troops, which increased Sevier force to about 600 or 700 men. This large force gave chase to the Cherokee, Sevier and his men burning one abandoned Indian village before crossing the Etowah River to the Indian town of Etowah, near Rome, Georgia. Sevier's troops routed the Cherokee and burned the town. The militia returned to their homes, ending the campaign.

Nathaniel Taylor gained his first public office on November 21, 1793, when he was appointed Justice of the Peace for Washington County, Southwest Territory, by Governor William Blount. Less than three years later, on March 28, 1796, the first Tennessee General Assembly met at Knoxville, former territorial capital and the capital of the newly formed State of Tennessee from 1796 until 1816, authorizing the creation of Carter County. The legislation stated that Washington County, from which Carter County was being established, covered such a large area that travel time to court, general-musters, elections and other public duties was onerous. Joseph Brown and Nathaniel Taylor were appointed as commissioners. They were paid two dollars a day to survey the dividing lines for the county which was named for Landon Carter (1760-1800), the son of John and Elizabeth Carter. Carter was a member of the North Carolina General Assembly in 1784 and 1789.

This home built by Landon and Elizabeth Carter before he died in 1800 is one of the most architecturally significant houses in early Tennessee. It has six rooms, a cellar, and garret. Known as the Carter Mansion and located in Elizabethton, Tennessee, it is today part of Sycamore Shoals State Historic Area. W. Eugene Cox.

Tennessee became the sixteenth state of the Union on June 1, 1796. An immediate task of the Carter County Pleas and Quarter Session court, which first met on July 4, 1796, at the home of Samuel Tipton, was to select various officials. The nine justices of the peace the court selected for the new county included Nathaniel Taylor. Although the minutes for the first years of the court are not available, Goodspeeds'

History of Tennessee does list the magistrates, perhaps from the original documents that were available at the time of its publication in 1887. Nathaniel Taylor was commissioned First Major for the Carter County Regiment of Militia, on October 4, 1796, making him one of the county's first military officers. Taylor was also selected by the court as the first sheriff of Carter County and served from 1796 until 1799.

The legislature appointed Landon Carter, Reuben Thornton, Andrew Greer Sr., Zachariah Campbell, and David McNabb to locate a site for a courthouse, a site which later in 1797 became the county seat. A fifty acre tract "at the foot of Lynn Mountain, east of Doe River, about a mile above where the river empties into the larger Watauga" belonging to Samuel Tipton was chosen. In 1799 the prominent Landon Carter family further placed their stamp on the county by having the county seat named Elizabethton after Landon's wife, Elizabeth. Goodspeed's history states that Nathaniel Taylor and Nathaniel Folsom were paid fifty dollars by the court to survey Elizabethton. Another example of Nathaniel's surveying skills occurred on March 5, 1795, when as deputy surveyor he surveyed a tract of land for John Bean "agreeable to the Entry Taker."

The population of four year old Carter County was 4,813 in 1800 and included 208 slaves. Tennessee's population in December 1801 was 105,602. Nathaniel was listed as head of household in the 1800 census, and he and Mary had five children, owned five taxable slaves, and 1,500 acres of land. Taylor's public life was closely allied with Carter County, and as the county prospered financially, so did he. His appointment as a magistrate indicates he was highly respected by his neighbors. In addition to state legislation and early deeds, part of the record of Nathaniel's public life may be found in the Pleas and Quarter Session records of the county court. On June 5, 1800, Nathaniel was called with others to "lay out a road from the road that leads from Gap Creek into the road that leads from the Sycamore Shoals to the Greasy Cove beginning at Nathaniel Taylor's." At the time, he was living on the property his father Andrew had acquired.

In 1792 Landon Carter built the first iron works of future Carter County at Elizabethton. The mountain ranges in the county contained the iron ore, limestone, timber, and water power required to manufacture iron. As transportation was limited and difficult, there was a great need for locally manufactured iron products. Iron was considered so valuable that it was often used as a medium of exchange. Nathaniel's business acumen was evident when he purchased an iron works from Godfrey Carriger Jr. in 1803. It was located in a section of Carter County that would later become part of Johnson County. Known as the Roan Creek Iron Works, it was the first iron industry in the area that would later become Johnson County. From time to time, Nathaniel rented out the operation, and while he was away during the War of 1812, his son, James P.

Taylor, acting as his agent, rented it to James Patterson. Nathaniel owned the property until his death in 1816, at which time it was willed to the family.

Nathaniel was popular enough to win the votes to serve in the Tennessee Fifth General Assembly as a senator, representing Carter and Washington Counties from 1803 to 1805. By 1803 Nathaniel had advanced to the rank of colonel in the militia. Whether due to personal popularity or leadership ability, he continued to rise in the militia. In 1804 Taylor ran against Col. John Tipton for the elective post of brigadier general. The regimental officers who did the voting selected Nathaniel, and he was placed in command of the First Brigade, composed of five regiments from upper East Tennessee.

Education was important to early Tennesseans in general and to the Taylor family in particular. On July 28, 1806, the Tennessee General Assembly authorized the formation of Duffield Academy founded by attorney George Duffield at Elizabethton. In 1806 Nathaniel was one of the first trustees of the academy. That same year he was on the cusp of a huge financial purchase when he signed an article of agreement with Andrew Greer Sr. and George Williams to share in the profits of a 32,000 acre purchase. Greer was to purchase the property for them, but the outcome of this agreement is unknown.

In 1805 the county court brought charges against Nathaniel Taylor and Julius Conner for a supposed debt of seventy-seven dollars plus damages owed to Godfrey Carriger. The writ, issued on June 24, was served on Nathaniel on June 26 by Sheriff Abraham Byler. The sheriff could not find Julius Connor, but it was not unusual for an individual to skip on a debt. The outcome of this suit is not known. There were often lawsuits for debts against Nathaniel in the early part of the nineteenth century. In November 1807 Fuller Gresham, Elijah Crouch, and Nathaniel Taylor were called to the February 1808 court. Godfrey Carriger Sr. had filed a suit against them for $500 that they supposedly owed him. Sheriff Abraham Williams issued the writ on Nathaniel and Gresham. The debt was paid, although Elijah had absconded. The Watauga Petition of 1776 referenced debtors who fled from the Watauga country to places where they could not be legally prosecuted. Evidently it was still a fairly common practice in 1808. From 1809 to 1811 Nathaniel, representing Carter County, served a second term in the House of the Eighth Tennessee General Assembly.

The War of 1812 and the Southern Campaign

Although they were actually an ill equipped and poorly prepared militia, the image and myth of the romantic minuteman of Concord and Lexington who defeated a larger force was very real to nineteenth century citizens. The militia was utilized throughout the country and became very important in the separate states. An 1812 publication showed the military organization of Tennessee's state militia. It stated there was universal conscription by an Act of 1803, and all freemen and indentured servants from age eighteen to forty-five were part of the state militia. A later militia act required that recruits must be able-bodied men between the ages of eighteen and fifty who would receive 160 acres of land upon enlistment. On the Watauga River, militia first protected the citizens from Indians. It grew into an organization that drilled and helped celebrate Independence Day with marches and the discharging of weapons. Leadership was based on cronyism, with the more prominent citizens becoming officers. Training and learning the art and strategy of war was not high on the militias list of important skills. Nathaniel Taylor was a militia officer who had fought the Cherokee twenty years earlier and had, perhaps stayed in the militia for political as well as for patriotic reasons. As an officer he had the loyalty of his men and was assured of some of their votes in his political endeavors. The militia kept him connected to other officers, not only regionally but at the state level. As a businessman with a variety of interests, these relationships could be significant. Further, the United States had not fought a war of any size between the end of the American Revolution in 1783 and the War of 1812. Its militia and regular standing army was complacent.

In 1812 an infantry officer's uniform was described as having a blue coat faced with red; buttonholes and pockets worked with gold cord; a white vest and breeches with black knee bands; white stockings; black gaiters made of velvet; stock of black leather or velvet; ruffle shirt; head powdered; and a cocked hat with a feather in it.

Donald J. Long's painting, "Generals and Field Officers, North Carolina Militia, 1813" illustrates the uniform that is similar to the one the Tennesseans wore. Shown from left to right are a colonel of the infantry, major of artillery, major of cavalry, major general with white ruffled shirt such as Nathaniel Taylor would have worn, and an aide-de-camp. Used by artist's permission and the Company of Military Historians, Plate 602.

In 1811 the Tennessee militia was divided into a First and Second Division. Maj. Gen. John Cocke commanded the First Division from East Tennessee, and Maj. Gen. Andrew Jackson commanded the Second Division from West, now Middle Tennessee. Under the First Division of East Tennessee there were three brigades with four brigadiers in command. They were Nathaniel Taylor, George Doherty, James White, and Thomas Coulter. We are not sure why four generals are listed for three brigades. General Coulter commanded East Tennessee troops based in Georgia in 1814, and this may account for the odd number. In 1811 Brig. Gen. Nathaniel Taylor was listed in command of the First Brigade which had five regiments. The Second Brigade consisted of the Sixth Regiment through the Ninth, and the Third Brigade had the Tenth through the Fourteenth Regiment.

One especially irritating grievance against Britain stemmed from a long standing practice by the British Navy of impressing able bodied men and boys into naval service. This was carried out in seaports and on the high seas where vessels were boarded and crew members impressed. The Embargo Act of 1806, passed by the U.S. Congress, brought a heavy decline in trade and was meant to retaliate against the men being impressed at sea or in port. As tension mounted, many politicians began to favor war as an answer, and among the most vocal were a congressional group called the War Hawks. They were part of the Twelfth United States Congress that convened on November 4, 1811. Robin Reilly argues in his well written book that the most likely cause of the war was nationalism and the contempt with which the British treated the Americans as colonials. So great was the enthusiasm for war that legislators seemed not to notice that they were unprepared. Repercussion from these grievances would eventually reach Carter County.

In 1812 President James Madison recommended that Congress declare war on Great Britain over the impressing of seamen and the inciting of Indians against the United States. Tennessee Governor, Willie Blount, on June 30, 1812, notified Maj. Gen. John Cocke of Rutledge, Grainger County, that war had been declared against Great Britain on June 18. The British strategy was for a "quick, decisive, and advantageous settlement. Essentially, it was designed to foster disunion, disillusionment, and political turmoil in the United States." Their hope was that the American government would "sue for a hasty peace."

The Creek War

In Frank Owsley's excellent and aptly named book, *Struggle for the Borderlands*, the largely untold story of the south in the War of 1812 is discussed. He divides the story into two parts, the Creek War which culminated at the battle of Horseshoe Bend and the British Gulf coast offensive ending with the Battle of New Orleans. The campaign for the Gulf Coast "attracted the British because it was sparsely populated and lightly defended. They believed there were many potential allies there, including Indians, particularly the Seminoles and Creeks, and black people, both slave and free." There were also about 1,000 pirates who lived on the coast which the British hoped to entice to their cause, but they would not be able to garner the support of any of these groups.

The Mississippi Territory in 1810. Historically the Creek had lived in towns, and according to trader James Adair were, in 1775, one of the most powerful of the tribes. The Creek War of 1813-1814 began as a civil war in present Alabama. One of the causes was the faction known as Red Sticks who pitted themselves against those Creek who allowed white settlements on their lands. This escalated and was swept up in Maj. Gen. Andrew Jackson's campaign of the same time frame. Frank Lawrence Owsley Jr., *Struggle for the Gulf Borderlands.* Reprinted with permission of the University Press of Florida.

In July 1813 a party of Red Sticks, so called because of their clubs which were painted red to signify war, as was the Creek custom, visited Pensacola, Florida, to trade for European goods and to obtain arms promised to them by the Spanish officials. On July 27 the Mississippi militia attacked them in what became known as the Battle of Burnt Corn. Thus began the Creek War "which transformed a civil war in the Creek Confederation into a larger war with the United States." On August 30, 1813, "the creeks retaliated . . . by attacking Fort Mims, a stockade forty miles north of Mobile, surprising the 300 occupants where some 250 Americans were killed including 120 militia."

Secretary of War John Armstrong placed Maj. Gen. Thomas Pinckney of South Carolina in overall command of the Creek campaign. Under Pinckney's command was Andrew Jackson who had been appointed by Tennessee Governor Willie Blount as Major General of the United States Volunteers. In the southern campaign, Jackson had many issues facing him; subordinates questioned him as to who was in command, recruitment and militia enlistments were especially tiring with their short terms, communication was poor, there were not enough arms, and there were constant food shortages for both men and animals. As Jackson prepared for the Creek campaign, he had to deal with these and other command issues.

Despite these issues Jackson was successful in the Battle of Horseshoe Bend on March 27, 1814, which was a cataclysmic event for the Creek Indians. It was the last battle of the Creek War, and as a result, they lost much of their homeland. Gen. Andrew Jackson, with East and West Tennesseans and ironically 600 Cherokee and lower Creek allies totaling 3,300 men, attacked 1,000 Upper Creek warriors. The Americans and their Indian allies killed 800 Creek, the largest loss of American Indians in a single battle. After the battle, the remaining hostile Creek were subdued. On April 18 General Jackson started his men clearing the ground for the erection of Fort Jackson on the site of the old French Fort Toulouse. The site was located at the junction of the Coosa and Tallapoosa Rivers near present day Montgomery, Alabama.

Taylor and the Tennessee Militia

One of Maj. Gen. Andrew Jackson's command issues involved Brig. Gen. Nathaniel Taylor of Carter County. On January 20, 1814, Jackson and Maj. Gen. John Cocke, commander of the Eastern Division of Tennessee, were discussing whether Taylor or George Doherty of Jefferson County should have command of the First Brigade.

We do not know why or when this became a problem. It may have been a personal rivalry between Taylor and Doherty. There was one extra Brigadier General in the East Tennessee roster, and this may or may not have had some bearing on the issue. On January 31, 1814, this threat of losing command of the First Brigade resulted in Taylor sending a letter to Andrew Jackson asking who was in command of the brigade. In response, on February 2 Jackson wrote Nathaniel and copying Cocke, told Taylor he was instructing Cocke to settle the command issue. Both Taylor and Brig. Gen. George Doherty received their officer commissions on the same day, and therefore neither outranked the other, preventing a decision based on rank. In February Jackson wrote Doherty that the command issue has been resolved in his favor. Taylor was not happy with this decision and on March 8 complained again to Jackson. However, Jackson was satisfied and congratulated Doherty for restoring order in the brigade. After the engagement at Horseshoe Bend on March 27, Jackson may have been even more pleased with the selection of Doherty as his men played a critical role in that battle.

Brigadier General Nathaniel Taylor's wartime papers are few and give us only glimpses into the details of his service. That he commanded the First Brigade, as is often stated, is correct until February 1814. After that date we are not sure what title his command carried. Bryon and Sistler's book lists a brigade quartermaster serving under him which further confuses the command issue. Official records indicate that General Taylor was ordered into federal service on August 4, 1814, and his staff was "called into service of the United States from Tennessee under the laws of 28 February 1795 and 18 April 1814." In Taylor's command of the East Tennessee militia and later parts of the West Tennessee militia, his aide-de-camp was his friend, attorney George Duffield of Elizabethton. Generals were allowed two civilian servants or waiters, as they were listed on the muster roll, and Taylor took P. Martin, an African American from his family farm.

An organizational chart for Brigadier General Taylor's command, except for some of his staff, could not be found, and it is doubtful if one exists. A partial listing of field regiments follows, and, like the companies, brigades may have changed by 1814. Our listing is developed by the Tennessee State Library and Archives (TSLA) and draws heavily from Bryon and Samuel Sistler's book, *Tennesseans in the War of 1812*. Spelling of names varies from source to source, as well as within sources, and we chose the one most often used in modern day spelling.

In 1804 Nathaniel Taylor of Carter County was promoted to brigadier general. After mustering his command at Knoxville, Tennessee, on September 20, 1814, his troops, although ill equipped and armed, departed on October 14 for the Mississippi Territory, there to protect Mobile and environs. The date of this portrait is unknown and could have been painted anytime between 1804 and 1814. Nat T. Winston.

Taylor's field command included Col. Nicholas T. Perkins, Franklin, Tennessee, 1st Regiment West Tennessee Mounted Volunteers, and Col. Alexander Lowery, 2nd Regiment, West Tennessee Militia, from counties located mostly around Nashville. Colonel Lowery submitted his resignation on November 7, 1814, and was replaced that same month by Lt. Col. Leroy Hammonds. Hammonds' 2nd Regiment "was scattered throughout the Creek Territory . . . [and manned] various forts in the region, including Forts Jackson, Montgomery, Claiborne, and Pierce. Some of the companies participated in the taking of Pensacola (November 7, 1814) from Spanish authorities." Col. William Johnson, Knoxville, 3rd Regiment, East Tennessee Drafted Militia, died on October 27, 1814, and his replacement is unknown.

If recruitment did not fill the quota of troops, the remainder was picked by lot and the term "drafted militia" used. These "drafted militia [were] mustered in at Knoxville and marched to the vicinity of Mobile via Camp Ross, Fort Jackson, Fort Claiborne, and Fort Montgomery, [Mississippi Territory, now the state of Alabama]. Along the way the men were used as road builders and wagon guards. In February 1814 many of them were stationed at Camp Mandeville [near Mobile] where there was much disease."

In Sistler's book, Taylor's staff and field officers are listed, but they could not be placed in the command structure. These officers were Col. James Raulston, 3rd Regiment Tennessee Militia Infantry, 2nd Maj. James C. McGee, 3rd Regiment East Tennessee Drafted Militia, Lt. Col. John Anderson, drafted militia from Knoxville, Cornelius F. Spoor, Judge Advocate, Robert W. Hart, Assistant Adjutant General from West Tennessee, and Brigade Major John Russell. Some of these may have been at the battalion level.

Pensacola, West Florida, and the British Offensive

Less than a year after the action of Fort Mims by the Creek, "Andrew Jackson was offered the rank of brigadier general of the line and the brevet rank of major general in the United States Army. On May 28, 1814, the date of this rank, Maj. Gen. Andrew Jackson was placed in command of the Seventh Military District, replacing Major General Flournoy. The Seventh District included most of the Creek Nation, and Jackson, as a representative of the land-hungry westerners, wanted to be rid of the Creek once and for all."

The Treaty of Fort Jackson was held on August 9, 1814, and "the Creek were required to cede some twenty million acres of land" to the United States. This would eventually result in the removal of the eastern Indians to the West. "Critics have attacked the policy of Indian removal and assimilation, but certainly into the nineteenth century this was an alternative to extermination." On September 18, 1803, Thomas Jefferson wrote that the Louisiana Purchase would "open as asylum" for the Indians.

The Red Stick leader of the Creek Indians, William Weatherford (c. 1781-1824), surrendering to Maj. Gen. Andrew Jackson at the end of the Creek War of 1813-1814.

Weatherford was one of the leaders that led the successful Creek attack against Fort Mims. Alabama Department of Archives and History, Montgomery, Alabama.

On August 14, 1814, British Maj. Edward Nicholls occupied the Spanish port city of Pensacola with its "access to the interior." On August 27, 1814, General Jackson arrived in Mobile "placing him in a much better position to watch the activities of the British and to be prepared to meet any attack." Spies had provided intelligence that an attack was forthcoming on Mobile Point. If the bay was captured, the British could penetrate the Indian Country and, as Jackson, said "excite the Indians to war, the Negroes to insurrection, and then proceed to the Mississippi [River] and cut off communication between the upper and lower part of the country." Brig. Gen. Nathaniel Taylor and his field command were part of this defense system.

While General Jackson was in Mobile the British were planning to attack Fort Bowyer on the Gulf of Mexico. Nathaniel Taylor in the meantime was gathering his East Tennessee militia. The term of service for his men began on September 20 at Knoxville, Tennessee, their place of rendezvous. At Knoxville, Taylor had difficulty obtaining arms from John Williams, a local attorney. Previously, Williams had marched his Mounted Volunteers of Tennessee Militia to fight in Georgia, in early 1813. Williams skillfully led his regiment at the Battle of Horseshoe Bend and was praised by Gen. Andrew Jackson. Largely as a result of this expedition, he was commissioned a colonel in the 39th U.S. Infantry. He returned home to Knoxville to recruit and obtain clothing and arms for the regiment. When Taylor arrived in September 1814, Williams had collected 1,000 stands of arms.

There was a question among the U.S. Army regulars as to whether militia officers in higher grades outranked them. This was put to the test on Monday, September 26, when General Taylor wrote a very explicit letter outlining his needs. In the letter, he advised "Colonel Williams that small arms and accoutrements were not available for the men under his command; General Jackson had ordered him to march without delay and to be equipped for service." Taylor pointed out to Williams that without weapons he could not adequately protect his command nor carry out the military mission that might be assigned by Jackson. He asked Williams for five hundred stands of arms, and Williams replied, "it is not in my power to furnish the militia under your command with arms." Taylor quickly responded stating that he needed the arms to carry out his duties, and using his rank he made a "peremptory demand" on behalf of the United States for them. Williams stated that "you have been already informed that it is not in my power to part from the arms in my possession. I am under the necessity of refusing positively a compliance with your order. I deem it unnecessary at this time to investigate your authority to give me an order."

General Taylor complained to General Jackson who wrote to Colonel Williams saying that he had received, by express rider, copies of his correspondence with General Taylor. He did not know why it was forwarded as no charges accompanied the communication, but added, it "may be intended by the general as a foundation for your arrest." Jackson said that he regretted the arms were not furnished as Taylor had a right to command any officer of lower grade. He also stated the obvious, that there was no possibility of Taylor arming his men after leaving Knoxville. Williams' slow recruiting indicated that only half of the arms he had gathered were necessary for the recruits, and there would have been enough for Taylor's militia. Jackson said, "this is not a time to investigate nice military questions of rank. It is the duty of all officers even to recede a little from their own rights where a public benefit would ensue." Williams did not take well to this rebuke and sent a letter on November 1 to Jackson stating his defense. Taylor, however, had to leave for the Mississippi Territory without the arms. Charles McClung, a prominent citizen and a former militia officer of Knoxville, supported his brother-in-law, Colonel Williams, by writing to Jackson about "the unfitness of Nathaniel Taylor."

On September 28, 1814, Brigadier General Taylor reported to Jackson that his "1,000 poorly armed militiamen [had] left Knoxville" to join his army. In early October Taylor received a letter from Adj. Gen. Andrew Hynes who was on Governor Blount's staff. The letter discussed Taylor's supply problems and inquired as to when he was departing to join the army. Taylor had left before this letter arrived. Unaware of the September attack on Fort Bowyer, and with the threat of an attack at Mobile, Taylor was directed, on October 11, to march "with the least possible delay" for Fort Claiborne. Fort Claiborne was located on the left bank of the Alabama River in present Monroe County, Alabama, and was seventy miles northeast of Mobile.

Major General Jackson was "convinced that Pensacola was the key to British operations" on the Gulf Coast, but in Washington the government officials feared an attack on Pensacola would start a war with Spain. Word was sent to Jackson not to attack, but it arrived too late. On November 7, 1814, Jackson attacked Pensacola with a force of 4,100 regulars, militia, and Indians meeting little resistance. As they left, the British blew up the forts, neutralizing Pensacola, and Jackson marched back to Mobile.

Jackson divided his district for strategic purposes and called on a friend from Nashville to command the Eastern Section of the Seventh Military District. On November 6, 1814, this friend, Brig. Gen. James Winchester who had been freed by the British after the battle at Raisin River in 1813, departed Nashville for Mobile. Brig. Gen. Nathaniel Taylor with approximately 1,000 Tennesseans was placed under Winchester's command. Brig, Gen. James Winchester agreed to take command with the understanding that he would do so only until his relief, Maj. Gen. John McIntosh, arrived with his Georgia militia. The force designated for the Eastern Section, commanded by McIntosh, was to total 8,000 effectives to protect and to provide Jackson reinforcements as needed. This, in reality, was only a paper force.

Capt. James Craig, a company commander in the 2nd Regiment West Tennessee Militia, left a personal account of his military service from 1814 to 1815. His account helps us to understand and gain perspective about the difficulties encountered by a company commander in the War of 1812. Since he was part of Taylor's field command, it also gives us a heretofore unavailable look into how Taylor's militia performed, although it is unclear how Taylor came to be in command of West Tennesseans. On September 14, 1814, Captain Craig of Reynoldsburg was ordered to muster in at Fayetteville, Tennessee. He arrived on the evening of September 20 with his company from Dickson, Hickman, and part of Stewart County. Their service date began on September 20, the same as for Taylor's brigade. The company officers reporting to Craig were 1st Lt. Edmond W. Gee, 2nd Lt. Truston B. Thomas, 3rd Lt. Thomas Nesbit, and Ensign Jonathan King. Samuel Young was the First Sergeant. In addition the company included four more sergeants, six corporals, and ninety-three enlisted men for a company total of 109 men. Captain Craig's record keeping shows how a company commander had to maintain accountability and keep receipts for arms, assignment of rations, accounts for forage or lack thereof, required inventory of personal effects of the deceased, and sundry other information. A captain's pay for six months was $246.33 while a private made about twenty-seven cents daily for six months service totaling $49.33.

On September 25, 1814, the 2nd Regiment West Tennessee Militia was ordered to march from Fayetteville to Fort Deposit, Mississippi Territory. They arrived on the 30th and camped there for four days. On October 4 they departed, arriving at Fort Strother on October 10. Leaving the next day they continued roughly 130 miles to Fort Jackson, arriving on the 18th. On October 17 Robert W. Hart, Assistant Adjutant General from West Tennessee, who was on General Taylor's staff, sent a letter to General Jackson stating that 1,000 West Tennessee Militia from Fayetteville, Tennessee, had departed Fort Jackson. They departed on the nineteenth, arriving on October 26 at Fort Claiborne. On this date H. Haynes, Inspector General, on orders from Major General Jackson, ordered Captain Craig to take command of Fort

Claiborne and "defend it to the last possible Extremity." Fort Claiborne was seventy miles northeast of Mobile.

On September 30, 1814, Capt. Joseph Kirk, 3rd Regiment, East Tennessee Militia, was at Kingston near Knoxville and General Taylor's command was nearby. After leaving Tennessee, Taylor's force marched through the thinly populated Mississippi Territory (present Alabama and Mississippi). Prior to 1800 Alabama had only 1,250 residents, and in 1814 no food or forage could be expected from such a small population. It was impossible for Taylor's army to carry everything they needed. During the campaign, they were constantly plagued with inadequate provisions and arms. In the War of 1812 civilian military contractors provided supplies and food to the army, but even when functioning properly this was not an entirely satisfactory arrangement.

On Wednesday, October 12, Taylor ordered his men to begin their march on the thirteenth from Camp Duffield and Camp Ross. Their orders were to march to Camp Jackson on the Coosa and Tallapoosa Rivers, 240 miles away. Major C.F. Spoor had just returned from Fort Strother, Mississippi Territory, located on the upper Coosa River in present northeast Alabama, and informed the officers that provisions were not available. They were reluctant to leave the camp without knowing that provisions could be provided on the march. Since the field command had only nine days of supplies, the officers did not think it advisable to depart. Plus, they were short on wagons and requested that they stay in place until sufficient quantities of rations were supplied. Accordingly, the officers and their men did not depart, but wrote to Taylor, explaining their reasons for not obeying his order.

On October 14 they were still in place at Camp Ross, located at the mouth of Chattanooga Creek on the south side of the Moccasin Bend of the Tennessee River, present Chattanooga. Captains Tunnell, Powell, Stewart, Lawson, Milikan, and Scott of the, 3rd Regiment, East Tennessee Militia, wrote General Taylor that the contractor, John McKee, wanted them to sign off for their rations without McKee listing the value, which they refused to do. General Taylor expressed his concern to General Winchester on October 15.

It is unknown when or if the supply problem was solved, but General Taylor was at Camp Misery and began his march on October 14. General Taylor wrote to the civilian contractor's agent at Fort Claiborne, telling him to forward "fifteen hundred complete rations and three barrels of whiskey for the hospital department [to] meet the Tennessee troops on their line of march." On October 31 John Russell of Knoxville, listed as a brigade major in Taylor's command, wrote Jackson saying "General Taylor is the most anxious man I ever saw to press on and accelerate our march, but sickness

[is] delaying them, measles, pleurisy, and flux that has affected about one-third of our men." This was a high number, and without proper roads, food, forage, and medical supplies in a largely unpopulated region, it was a daunting task to keep the men alive. On October 22 Russell reported that Lt. Col. John Anderson Jr. (1778-1814) of the East Tennessee Drafted Militia, much loved by the men, died at Fort Strother. Russell also complained about the poor quality of food that the contractor was supplying.

To illustrate how few supplies there were at Fort Claiborne on November 1, Captain Craig wrote the commanding officer of Fort Montgomery stating he was in need of stationery and if he could receive a sufficient supply he would be obliged. Even more importantly, there was an urgent need for forage, and on November 2 Craig wrote Capt. John T. Wirt, Assistant Quarter Master General, that he needed forage for the "Daily Express" rider for Brigadier General Taylor and other officers. On the same day, Captain Craig issued orders that a public boat must always be ready for use on the Alabama River, and all officers, soldiers, and civilians, must not interrupt this traffic by taking the boat. Eleven days later he wrote requesting that the drovers and guards that plied between Fort Jackson and Fort Claiborne be provided powder and cartridges.

Brigadier General Taylor seemed to think he was being rushed too much on his march without any consideration for his difficulties. On Saturday, November 5, he wrote to Major General Jackson and shared with him the "difficulties in moving and equipping" his East Tennessee troops. Taylor followed this up on November 12, informing Jackson of his "supply problems and his march southward."

In November Brigadier General Winchester wrote Major General Jackson that he was at Fort Stephens, about sixty-five miles north of Mobile. Jackson, learning that New Orleans was to be assaulted, could not wait for him, and left Mobile. On November 20 Major General Jackson, from his headquarters in Mobile, wrote to Secretary of War James Monroe that it was with regret that he was leaving for New Orleans before the arrival of Brigadier General Winchester. He wrote that Brigadier General Taylor had delayed his militia on their march, was constantly complaining, and rumors indicated he was "subject to intoxication," but as the eldest officer he would assume command. By special order, Jackson "confined [Taylor's] command to the militia" and left Lt. Col. Mathew Arbuckle, 3rd Infantry, a career officer from Virginia, in command of Fort Charlotte, Fort Bowyer, and the 3rd Regiment, U.S. Infantry. Arbuckle was ordered to cooperate with Taylor until Winchester arrived. Jackson shared with Monroe that he felt the security of the Eastern Division depended on Winchester's timely arrival. Major General Jackson left on November 22, traveling overland to reach New Orleans on December 1, 1814.

By the end of the November Winchester was in Mobile, Mississippi Territory, where he entered the small village that had a population of about 500 people living in about 150 wooden houses. Fort Bowyer on the Gulf of Mexico guarded Mobile Bay and was thirty miles away from Mobile. Winchester's command, the Eastern Section of the Seventh Military District, encompassed a huge area whose southern border ran from Pascagoula, Mississippi, along the Gulf Coast, eastward to the Perdido River (present Florida state line). It technically extended northward to the Tennessee River, but his forces were mostly focused on the region around Mobile Bay.

Eventually Taylor was given command of all the interior forts, which Winchester soon began inspecting. At Fort Montgomery he found Taylor negligent, as "the public stores [were] in very bad condition and ordered store houses to be built within the fort and all valuable hospital and quartermaster stores moved into them. Huts for hospitals and sheds for artificers [were] to be built outside the fort."

The mobility of the British amphibious force was of great concern. If Jackson moved all or most of his force to Mobile, he left New Orleans vulnerable. If he did the reverse and strengthened New Orleans then Mobile could be taken. Further, the American naval forces were weak, but fortunately Jackson had disrupted British plans by taking Pensacola. In November the intelligence indicated that the British were going to attack New Orleans which forced Jackson to move more troops to that location. New Orleans sat close to the Gulf of Mexico making it a prime target.

While the larger plans were being contemplated at higher command, Captain Craig, at the company level, was coping with his losses. To give an example of the plight of the soldiers, between November 26, 1814, and March 28, 1815, he lost fourteen men to sickness. An inventory of property for Cpl. James Jackson who died on November 26, 1814, shows how few possessions the soldiers had. He owned one pair of shoes, socks, two pairs of pantaloons (trousers), one hat, one wescoat (waistcoat, a vest) and shirt, a knapsack, one pair of mittens, one tomahawk, a butcher knife, one pint bottle (canteen), and one twist of tobacco. He had $1.06 in cash. All his belongings were auctioned off for $5.44, which, with the $1.06, would have been sent to his family.

In early December the British cut the supply line between New Orleans and Mobile. In anticipation of this occurrence, civilian military contractors, Pope and Brahnam, were supposed to stockpile reserve supplies for Brigadier General Winchester's use at Forts Jackson, Strother, and Williams, but this was not carried out. In another development, Winchester was warned by Jackson that over 100 British vessels were along the Gulf coast. In response Winchester moved Brig. Gen. Nathaniel Taylor's Tennessee brigade of militia from Fort Montgomery to Mobile.

The signing of the Treaty of Ghent, Belgium, on Christmas Eve, 1814, ended the War of 1812 but not the hostilities. Before news of the signing could reach the United States the decisive battle of New Orleans ended this unpopular war. The American commissioners were John Quincy Adams, James A. Baynard, Henry Clay, Albert Gallatin, and Jonathan Russell. Sir Amèdé Forestier. Smithsonian American Art Museum.

Brig. Gen. John Coffee's Tennessee Mounted Infantrymen had departed on a forced march to New Orleans. There was still no word of McIntosh, Hawkins, or Coulter. On December 27, 1814, Col. William Johnston, commanding the 3rd Regiment East Tennessee Drafted Militia, wrote to Captain Craig at Fort Claiborne on behalf of Brigadier General Taylor. Taylor ordered Craig to take his and Captain Delaney's companies and depart on a forced march to the port of Mobile. They were to take the quickest route to Brig. Gen. James Winchester. Craig and the two companies arrived at Mobile on January 9, 1815, and were ordered to Camp Mandeville to join their regiment. In mid-January Winchester, at Choctaw Point, moved "most of his combat-ready troops to Camp Mandeville" located south of Mobile on the bay around Garrows Bend. From February 4 to March 13, 1815, Brigadier General Taylor's headquarters were at Camp Mandeville.

On January 8, 1815, Jackson's troops, an estimated 3,500 to 4,500 strong, in entrenched positions against the exposed British, won a decisive victory at the Battle of New Orleans. "Of the approximately 5,300 British soldiers in the attacking columns and reserve, 2,037 became casualties: dead, wounded, or missing. Jackson lost seven killed, six wounded." The victory also became a nationalistic symbol for a growing, vibrant country.

While Jackson was winning the Battle of New Orleans, Winchester, ensconced in Mobile, continued to confront the problem of inadequate supplies. Capt. William Woodfolk, commander of Fort Jackson, had to place his men on half rations. Brig. Gen. Nathaniel Taylor wrote complaining from Fort Jackson that his men were poorly clothed and inadequately fed, and even feed for his horses was in short supply. The civilian contractors who were supposed to supply the army were once again not fulfilling their obligations.

On January 20, 1815, General Orders issued by Jackson stated that Col. Nicholas T. Perkins, 1st Regiment West Tennessee Mounted Volunteers, had assumed command of the troops stationed at Camp Mandeville. The army was having problems with desertion, resulting in stricter rules and regulations that were stringently enforced. At a court martial held in December 1814 at Mobile six Tennessee militiamen were sentenced to death for participating in a mutiny at Fort Jackson in September. Jackson approved the executions and near Mobile on February 21 the six deserters were shot in front of a formation of 1,500 troops.

In February news was received that a treaty had been signed in Ghent, Belgium, on December 24, 1814. Captain Craig reported that the news was received on February 22 at Mobile. It had been ratified by the U.S. Senate, effectively ending all hostilities. On February 20 Gen. John McIntosh's militia arrived at Mobile, terminating Winchester's interim command. Coulter, arriving a few days later with his East Tennessee militia, was court-martialed for his delay and cashiered. With the war over, Brigadier General Winchester submitted his resignation, and Major General Jackson accepted it effective March 31.

At New Orleans Major General Jackson issued a General Order stating the soldiers were to be marched to their respective states, mustered for payment, and discharged. To reassure them, he added that "every arrangement will be made through the Department of War to have troops of Tennessee and Kentucky paid off the soonest possible after their return." A muster was taken by all the troops, as a result of General Jackson's General Order to return home. The muster roll taken by General Taylor's staff on March 20 reflects only General Taylor's immediate command at Camp Mandeville, Mississippi Territory. The muster roll was important, and care was taken to show the length of service and document the legality of their call up. This surviving muster roll states that his eighteen member staff served from September 20, 1814, until March 20, 1815.

There is no documentation currently available to suggest that Brigadier General Taylor was engaged in any military actions during the War of 1812. He was viewed unfavorably by Generals Winchester and Jackson, and whether he was entirely at fault is not always certain. First, he argued with Jackson over command of the First Brigade and lost the brigade command. Then his troops arrived too late to help Jackson protect Mobile. Jackson responded too late to be of any assistance in the controversy between Colonel Williams and Taylor. He marched his half armed force forward, although they were not effective as a fighting unit. His field command was plagued with a continual lack of supplies on the march, and his officers requested a delay until adequate provisions could be provided by the contractor. As Taylor moved into Creek Indian country where there was almost no European occupation, military roads had to be built and repaired. There were no farms to draw on for supplies. Various officers complained Taylor was not moving his troops fast enough to help Jackson protect Mobile. Captain Craig, departing from Reynoldsburg about the same time as Taylor, possibly with a smaller force, arrived at Fort Claiborne only a week before Taylor did.

Brig. Gen. Nathaniel Taylor's leadership ability had come under scrutiny before General Winchester's arrival from Nashville. Jackson had given Taylor and a regular army officer shared command of the Eastern District, suggesting a lack of trust in Taylor's ability. Jackson had heard earlier that Taylor had a drinking problem, and this may have affected his decision. After Winchester arrived in November, there were command and leadership issues. In an undated note, Winchester wrote General Taylor that he had found the picket on the Dog Run road withdrawn and wanted to know on whose order the decision was made. On March 18, 1815, Winchester was about to court martial Taylor for "intoxication, disobedience of orders and neglect of duty." When Winchester's comments are considered it appears that Taylor was not meeting his military responsibilities.

Returning Home to Carter County, Sabine Hill is Built

On March 21 Captain Craig left Mobile with his men, arriving home on April 14, 1815, after traveling a distance of 600 miles. It took Brigadier General Taylor and some, if not all, of his East Tennesseans until June 20, 1815, to reach their homes. The delay can partially be explained by family lore indicating that General Taylor was too sick to travel. The men were mustered in at Knoxville, Tennessee, and as required were discharged there.

Brig. Gen. Nathaniel Taylor was at his home, Sycamore Shoals Plantation, for eight months before he died on Tuesday, February 20, 1816. After Nathaniel's death, the May 1816 Carter County Pleas and Quarter Session appointed his widow, Mary Taylor, and their son, James P. Taylor, as executors of his will. At his death the general owned a vast amount of land and about twenty slaves.

In addition to settling the disposition of his personal wealth, there was an issue surrounding the general's military pay. On June 14, 1816, Assistant District Paymaster Joseph H. Winkle was in Cocke County, Tennessee, where the office for paying War of 1812 veterans was located. He paid the heirs of "Brigadier General N. Taylor of the Brigade of East Tennessee $657.87." Taylor was paid for subsistence for nine months and eight days of service, from September 20, 1814, to June 20, 1815. The muster roll of September 20, 1814, to March 20, 1815, for Taylor's command shows the general was ordered into service on August 4, 1814.

Nathaniel J.K. Taylor, the general's son, owned part of 381 acres that bordered Buffalo and Gap Creeks and included "the new houses (*sic*) barn which has been built by Mary Taylor since the death of Nathaniel Taylor dec'd." This description of the Sabine Hill property matches the property which Nathaniel purchased from Joseph Tipton Sr. for $2,282 on May 19, 1809. One can only wonder if Mary Taylor, Nathaniel's widow, used the general's pay from his military service to build Sabine Hill which was constructed by her sometime before May 1821. In 1981 James Patrick, writing in *Architecture in Tennessee 1768-1897*, determined a construction date for Sabine Hill of before 1820, and suggested 1818. He described Mary's residence as "a five bay-frame block with Federal details. The center bay was at some time made larger than the flanking bays to give the hall sufficient width. At the back of the house is the kitchen, an independent building placed close to the main block in the position which the ell would consistently occupy after about 1825."

Settling Brig. Gen. Nathaniel Taylor estate was a complicated process which took ten years. It was assumed that Nathaniel died intestate, and in Tennessee the descent of real property went to his children and heirs at law. On May 15, 1821, the heirs of Nathaniel Taylor conveyed to Nathaniel J. K. Taylor, youngest child of Nathaniel and Mary Taylor, the "tract of land lying on the south side of Watauga River including the new house [Sabine Hill], lately built by his mother Mary Taylor." It is not understood why the heirs agreed for the land to be placed in the hands of an underage son. Later, as the settlement process continued, Nathaniel J.K. Taylor's brother, Alfred W. Taylor, received Sabine Hill.

Mary Taylor, widow of Brig. Gen. Nathaniel Taylor, built her home Sabine Hill, with its Federal details, before 1821. It is one of the oldest homes in Carter County and is located on U.S. Highway 321, entering Elizabethton from Johnson City. The house stands on the side of a hill and overlooks Sycamore Shoals and the eastern portion of Happy Valley. The house is now part of Sycamore Shoals State Historic Area. This view was taken by W. Jeter Eason in the summer of 1936. Historic American Building Surveys, National Park Service.

The heirs continued to contest the settlement of the general's estate and had to go to the Tennessee General Assembly for assistance on this and other properties. A warrant for 300 acres of land had been issued earlier to Nathan Arnold who later assigned it to Nathaniel. The warrant was lost in the mail, and on November 5, 1819, the legislature authorized that a replacement be issued to the heirs. In another case that went to the general assembly, it was proven that Nathaniel Taylor transferred 400 acres of land to John Scoggins. On July 28, 1820, they authorized a grant for Scoggins.

In 1826 the settlement of the estate of Nathaniel Taylor was filed in the Carter County Court where another issue was also solved. James Patton Taylor, Nathaniel's son, declared his father had conveyed the "Sycamore Shoals Plantation" of 361 acres to him as a gift. When the H.T. Spoden & Associates historical report was concluded in 1974, it showed that on February 15, 1815, Nathaniel Taylor had sold 361 acres of the property alongside the Sycamore Shoals of the Watauga that he had purchased of John Scoggins to his son James Patton Taylor.

When the estate was being settled, James Patton argued he owned the land. Why he did not show the deed is unclear, and it may have been that he owed money on the property. Whatever the circumstances, in the July 1, 1826, settlement, he agreed to pay six dollars per acre for the property to obtain a clear title. To recapitulate, the property originally went to the child Nathaniel J.K. Taylor, then to Alfred W. Taylor, with James Patton Taylor finally obtaining ownership. In this sequence of events concerning the Taylor homes, it is important to note that about 1840 the original Andrew Taylor log home was torn down, and the logs used for other purposes. Mary Patton Taylor retained the right, in the estate settlement, to make Sabine Hill her home until her death which occurred on August 2, 1853. Her estate was probated December 19, 1853.

Decades after Sabine Hill was built, W.D. Peters of the *Bristol News*, Bristol, Virginia, visited the home site of Mary Patton Taylor, thinking incorrectly that her husband Nathaniel Taylor had built the house. Correspondent Peters made the trip in early spring and wrote his newspaper article about the house on Tuesday, December 20, 1892. To our knowledge, this is the first early description of Sabine Hill, other than what appeared in the deed of 1821. Peters wrote that the old frame house was located four miles from Johnson City on a knoll, and that it was deserted, abandoned, and going to decay.

The house, finished in 1821, was built on the site of a huge log structure. The doors were barred but he made his entrance through a window in the ell. The front door was made of panels of heavy oak with scroll work facings. There was a wide hallway with doors opening into rooms on either side, and the parlor was an immense room with wainscoted walls and frescoed ceiling. The brass-tipped andirons were still in the cavernous fireplace just as they had stood years ago. The sitting room finished in oak, with closets and cupboards galore, adjoined the dining room which was as large as the ground floor of an ordinary cottage. There were cupboards and closets set in the walls.

Upstairs there were four large bed rooms and a small room containing a baby's cradle and some toys. A ledger (location unknown) left in the house apparently showed that Mary's husband Nathaniel was a merchant. John Smith had purchased whiskey from him at fifteen cents a quart and fifty cents a gallon. Smith paid for his whiskey with bearskins and beeswax. Peters discovered a note which N. Swan of Dandridge, Jefferson County, Tennessee, had written to Nathaniel informing him that the boat load of iron shipped to him "had failed to arrive and he feared it was at the bottom of the river ... along with the five gallons of apple brandy" which Nathaniel had sent as a Christmas present. This would have been between the years of 1803 and 1816. If this was iron from Carter County, Nathaniel may have had it transported by wagon to the Nolichucky River which flowed into the French Broad River and then by Dandridge.

Nathaniel and his wife, Mary Patton Taylor, are buried together on a hill behind Sabine Hill in perhaps the oldest cemetery in Carter County. Nathaniel and Mary had nine children, and James Patton Taylor was the oldest.

Chapter 3

James Patton Taylor
1792-1833

James Patton Taylor was born Monday, November 5, 1792, in Washington County, Territory of the United States, South of the River Ohio. The eldest of nine children, his parents were Brig. Gen. Nathaniel Taylor and Mary Patton Taylor. On Thursday, August 22, 1816, Rev. Jonathan Mulkey performed the marriage ceremony for Mary Cocke Carter and James Patton Taylor which united two prominent families. Mary, born on May 5, 1799, in Washington County, Tennessee, was the daughter of Col. Landon Carter and Elizabeth Maclin Carter, for whom Carter County and Elizabethton were named. Mary Carter Taylor was one of the founding members of the Elizabethton Presbyterian Church founded circa 1819. Dr. J.J. Alexander states in *A Brief History of the Synod of Tennessee 1817-1887* that there was an earlier church and whether it dissolved or not is unknown. He states that in 1797 Elizabethton Presbyterian Church with a constituency of forty-nine families was listed with no known date of founding or no known founder.

Brigadier General Nathaniel Taylor gave his son James Patton the "Sycamore Shoals Plantation." James probably built his house after 1826. The site is located

on the southeast edge of present Sycamore Shoals State Historic Area. Nathaniel Greene Taylor also lived here, and this was the birthplace of his sons, Alf and Bob Taylor. Archives of Appalachia, East Tennessee State University.

Good transportation was on the minds of everyone in these early frontier days. Three years after James Patton was born, the wagon road from Nashville to Knoxville was opened, and in October the wagon road from South Carolina was completed. The road came through North Carolina and passed the mountains at Warm Springs on the French Broad River. This road opened markets and increased settlements along its length. In just over twenty years, much growth had taken place, and by the 1790s Cherokee attacks had virtually ceased.

By 1815 James Patton had purchased the "Sycamore Shoals Plantation" property, but did not obtain clear title until the 1826 estate settlement. It was here that he and Mary built their home, probably after the 1826 settlement of his father's estate. The house was situated on a rise of land on the southeast edge of the present Sycamore Shoals State Historic Area property. It was not too far from where his mother, Mary Patton Taylor, lived at Sabine Hill.

At age twenty-one, James Patton Taylor had become a successful attorney. As a trial lawyer, he was very good at convincing a jury to see things his way. Later, as prosecuting attorney, he had no equal in the state. When his father Nathaniel died in 1816, James Patton was the attorney for his estate. His father had established quite a prosperous iron business which included Vaught Creek Iron Works, Carter-Elizabethton Iron Works, O'Briens Forge on the Doe River, and the Roan Creek Iron Works. The Taylors were ranked third in importance of those families connected with the iron industry in Carter County. In 1820 they had thirteen employees working at Roan Creek, including a woman. The machinery used in the Roan Creek Iron Works consisted of "one hammer wheel, one hammer and anvil, one stamper wheel, and four stamps, two water blasts, two bloomery fires, and one drumbum and robit." At that time they had mined 200 tons of iron ore, using 1,200 cords of wood, at a cost of $2,000. An equal amount was also paid out in wages. The iron products they made were wagon tires, bar iron, scallop iron, and plow moulds amounting to $6,000 in sales. The net profit to the heirs was $2,600. It was divided among the children, each receiving a one-eighth share. These shares were eventually purchased by David Waggoner who became the sole proprietor.

In 1819 James Patton "was a lawyer of distinction and became Attorney-General of the First Solicitorial District (later changed to First Judicial Circuit) of Tennessee that encompassed Carter, Greene, Sullivan, and Washington Counties." It was the governor's duty to appoint the district attorney general and Gov. Joseph McMinn (1815-1821) selected James Patton who practiced law in the first courthouse built in Elizabethton around 1799 as well as in the second courthouse completed in 1821. Continuing the Taylor's interest in and support of education, James Patton Taylor, along with Alfred M. Carter, William B. Carter, James L. Tipton, and William Graham, was appointed as trustees of the Duffield Academy in Elizabethton, Tennessee, in 1819. James was a slave owner, and in 1821 he purchased a thirteen year old girl for his household for $400. In 1824 he bought a slave named Henry for $600, probably selected for the iron works.

James Patton had a grist mill on the Watauga River. This river begins high on Grandfather Mountain in North Carolina and flows sixty miles through some of the most beautiful mountains in America. It is only navigable between Sycamore Shoals and the point where it joins the Holston River. According to the language of a legislative act passed on July 3, 1820, Alfred M. Carter and James Patton Taylor of Carter County were authorized to keep up their mill dams on the Watauga River. The act also cautioned them not to obstruct the boating channel nearby.

James Patton with his entrepreneurial skill took advantage of the resources available, including the Watauga River upon whose banks his home was located. He added a fish trap to his grist mill "at the tumbling [Sycamore] shoals in [the] Watauga River." Fish traps, like mill dams, were regulated by the state, and the Tennessee General Assembly authorized the fish trap for James Patton on August 23, 1822, provided "that in so doing he shall not impede boats in descending said river."

An often repeated family story is told about James Patton Taylor, his grist mill, and David Haynes. Haynes, the father of Emeline Haynes who would later marry one of James Patton Taylor's sons, engaged James Patton as his attorney. Taylor submitted a bill to Haynes for $75.00 which irritated Haynes who was known to be tight with a dollar. Haynes wondering why a small task cost so much, requested an itemized receipt. Attorney Patton obliged listing his expenses as $5.00 for "drawing a bill in chancery [court]," trying the case $20.00, and for his knowledge of the law $50.00. Haynes paid the bill.

Later when Taylor wanted to build a mill at Sycamore Shoals, he employed Haynes to locate the race and mill site. Haynes submitted a bill to Taylor for $75.00. In his itemized invoice he listed the cost as follows, for "leveling and locating the race and site of mill $3.00," walking up and down the stream to conduct the work, $2.00, and for the benefit of his knowledge of engineering, $70.00, which just happened to equal Taylor's earlier attorney fees.

East Tennesseans desired good roads and watched with interest and anticipation as North Carolina built a "public road" from Wilkesborough toward Jonesborough, Tennessee. As they watched the progress of North Carolina's road building efforts toward the volunteer state, they were spurred to action. Accordingly, Tennessee passed legislation on November 14, 1821, to appropriate money and appoint commissioners to improve that part of the road needing the most work from Elizabethton east to the North Carolina line. On November 15, 1823, the Tennessee legislature selected James P. Taylor and four other commissioners from Carter County who they "authorized to draw from the Treasurer of East Tennessee Five Thousand dollars to be [used] in clearing out, and putting in good repair, that part of the public road from Jonesborough by way of Elizabethton to North Carolina." From this and preceding legislation, we conclude that James P., with the other commissioners, marked the future U.S. Highway 19 in Carter County.

The state did not have the money to complete the road project so on October 12, 1824, they authorized "a lottery in Jonesborough to raise money to finish the public road leading from Jonesborough through Elizabethton to the North Carolina line." James P. was still involved, and he and seven others were approved to raise by lottery no more than two thousand dollars to be applied to completion of the road. Since this was a considerable undertaking, the legislature explained how the lottery was to be conducted. They wanted the drawers, clerks, examiners, and all other persons engaged in the lottery to take an oath from a justice of the peace that they would act fairly and impartially. It was specified that if the lottery was not drawn within eighteen months from the passage of the act, the purchasers of tickets could demand and would receive as a refund the money they had paid for tickets. We trust the lottery went as proposed.

On Saturday, September 27, 1828, James P. Taylor and John A. McKinney announced their partnership to practice law in the counties of Carter, Greene, Hawkins, Sullivan, and Washington. They took cases in the Courts of Chancery at Rogersville and Greeneville and in the court of appeals and the federal court at Knoxville. This partnership did not embrace the state's business in James P. Taylor's district, where he was prosecuting attorney, or the United States business in the federal court. This was a huge area for them to cover in the days of horseback travel and poor roads.

In the early morning hours of January 12, 1833, tragedy struck when James Patton Taylor died of scarlet fever at his residence in Carter County after two weeks of illness. At his death, James Patton was forty years old and left his widow, Mary, with four children. Mary inherited the Sycamore Shoals property. On Monday, January 14, Alfred W. Taylor (1798-1856), with great sadness wrote to Governor William Carroll that his brother had died. He mentioned that James P. had been serving as attorney general since 1819, and as the governor would obviously have to fill the vacancy of attorney general in the First Solicitorial District, he recommended Thomas A.R. Nelson of Elizabethton for the position.

As Alfred W. Taylor suggested, Thomas A. R. Nelson, who had recently received his license to practice law, was selected as the replacement attorney general by Governor Carroll. T.A.R. Nelson, born March 19, 1812, was educated at Knoxville and moved to Elizabethton in 1828. Nelson was well thought of, and the Knoxville Bar Association endorsed him, saying he was "a young man of fine talents, sober industrious business habits, and considerable legal information." John Williams of Knoxville, regarded as a hero of the Battle of Horseshoe Bend and nemesis of General Nathaniel Taylor, had known Nelson since infancy. He considered Nelson one of the finest young men of the state.

After Taylor's death, the high esteem in which he was held was evident when his name was suggested for a new county being formed. In 1835, after at least two attempts to create Johnson County out of Carter County, the name Taylor was inserted in the legislation for the county's name. In 1836 a compromise was arranged, the new county became Johnson County, with the county seat named Taylorsville for James P. Taylor. At Taylorsville, on July 20, 1836, the Commissioners of Public Buildings for Johnson County advertised in September lots would be for sale. The commissioners stated that Taylorsville had one of the healthiest climates in the world and was located on the stage road halfway between Ashe Courthouse, North Carolina, and Elizabethton. As an inducement to potential buyers, the village site was described as having beautiful scenery and was contiguous to plenty of iron ore and water power. In 1866 Taylorsville was incorporated, but in 1885 the name of the town changed to Mountain City, the present county seat of Johnson County.

On Tuesday, August 2, 1844, Mrs. Mary C. Taylor, forty-five years and two months old, died at the residence of her sister in Jefferson County. Mary, the widow of James Patton Taylor, died of cholera "of but thirty hours duration [which] was extremely painful . . . during her illness; but to the last, she maintained that composure of mind, which words cannot purchase, and which Christianity alone can give." She "was a lady of a vigorous intellect, polished manners, and a kind heart."

When James Patton Taylor was born in 1792 and throughout his life, events were already occurring that signaled the growing difficulties between the United States government and Native Americans. The tribes in the Southwest Territory were selling their land to white men. Trade was established as an aid to controlling and civilizing the tribes. Treaties were violated as white men moved onto Indian lands. Nathaniel Greene Taylor, the oldest of James Patton and Mary Cocke Carter Taylor's children, was destined to become a major player in trying to control the tide of events which led to such tragedy for the Native Americans.

Chapter 4

Nathaniel Greene Taylor
1819-1887

The Whigs

Nathaniel Greene Taylor was born on December 29, 1819, at Happy Valley located in Carter County, Tennessee. His parents were James Patton Taylor and Mary Cocke Carter. Nathaniel was educated in private schools, and reportedly attended Washington College, Salem, Tennessee. Known as one of the oldest educational institutions in Tennessee, Washington College was created on July 8, 1795, by the Territory of the United States of America, South of the River Ohio. When Nathaniel was barely thirteen years old his father died.

Nathaniel Greene Taylor standing beside a table with a bible that reflected his Christian life. Presumably his beloved Happy Valley is in the background. He was named for his grandfather, Nathaniel, and for the revolutionary war hero Gen.

Nathanael Greene. He was an ardent member of the Whig Party. This portrait is thought to be by Samuel M. Shaver (1816-1878). B. Harrison Taylor Collection.

The year after his father's death, the Tennessee Constitution was revised, creating three "grand divisions" of the state, West, Middle, and East Tennessee. East Tennessee, including the county where Nathaniel lived, bordered Kentucky and Virginia on the north and North Carolina on the south. The Unaka Mountains were within this boundary where there was not much arable land, but the region's biggest deterrent to economic well being was the lack of transportation.

Two men from Carter County who would have a role in the emerging Whig Party that would be associated with Nathaniel Greene Taylor were Thomas A. R. Nelson who had replaced Nathaniel's father as attorney general of the First Judicial District, and William Gannaway Brownlow who began publishing the Elizabethton *Whig* in 1836. The next year he moved to Jonesborough and started publishing *The Whig* newspaper.

The Whig Party which played such a major role in the early political life of Nathaniel G. Taylor can trace its beginnings to the winter of 1833-1834. Andrew Jackson had been president since March 4, 1829, and was running for a second term, although some of his fellow Democrats were growing dissatisfied with him, and believed a new party was needed to compete for the presidency. Henry Clay of Kentucky who joined the Whigs recalled that during the American Revolution those who opposed the King were antimonarchists, called Whigs. Jackson was being derisively called "King Jackson" in the newspapers so those who opposed him decided on Whigs as the name for their party. The Whigs were for liberty, the common man, and more practically, for strong banks, business growth, and internal improvements. As the party grew in the 1830s, members worked to build a base, in order to win state and national offices. William Henry Harrison, a veteran of the War of 1812, was the Whig's candidate for the presidency in 1840 and won for them their first presidential race.

In 1840 Nathaniel graduated from New Jersey College, chartered in 1746 and renamed Princeton in 1896. He studied law and was admitted to the bar in 1841, practicing in Elizabethton, Tennessee. On May 5, 1842, Maj. Gen. William Brazelton, 1st Division Tennessee Militia, announced that he had appointed Nathaniel Greene Taylor of Carter County as one of his aides with the rank and title of colonel. Nathaniel used this title throughout his career.

An unexpected tragedy tore at the Taylor family on Sunday night, August 7, 1842. A lightning strike at a "Camp Meeting [killed] Miss Mary Taylor, daughter of the late James P. Taylor, . . . and John C. Miller" from Rutherford County, North Carolina. Both were students at Washington College. Mary, only fourteen years old, was Nathaniel's sister. She had lived with their mother at Sycamore Shoals Plantation. This camp meeting, known as Brush Creek Campground, was established in 1811 on Knob Creek, Washington County, Tennessee. It was adjacent to Nelson's Chapel, the second Methodist Church founded in Tennessee.

In 1828, Andrew Johnson, a new political player, won his first political office, that of alderman in Greeneville, Tennessee. He eventually won a seat in the Tennessee General Assembly. He opposed internal improvements, and in 1837 this brought about his defeat in East Tennessee by Brookins Campbell. Johnson, a States' Rights Democrat, defeated Campbell in 1839 and from 1840 on was an Andrew Jackson man to the core.

On February 22, 1843, running as a Whig, "Nathaniel G. Taylor, Esq." at age twenty-four, announced that he was "a candidate to represent Carter and Johnson counties, in the popular branch of the next Tennessee General Assembly." This may have been his first bid for public office. Unfortunately for the Whig Party, he was unsuccessful. In that same year, Democrat Andrew Johnson of Greeneville was elected to the U.S. House of Representatives for the First Congressional District of Northeast Tennessee, where he served until 1853. Although Johnson and Taylor were rivals in politics they would be drawn together during the Civil War because of their support for the Union. In 1843 Nathaniel established a law practice with Robert Love.

On May 10, 1843, Nathaniel Greene Taylor and Robert Love advertised their Carter County law practice in Jonesborough, Tennessee. Attorney Robert Love was the friend and prosperous partner of Nathaniel after whom he would name his third son. The name Robert Love would thus be preserved and passed down through the generations in the Taylor family. The Jonesborough Whig and Independent Journal, Jonesborough, Tennessee.

On Tuesday evening, January 30, 1844, Rev. J. Whitfield Cunningham, Jonesborough Presbyterian minister, presided at the wedding of Nathaniel Greene Taylor and Emeline Haynes. Emeline was born in April 1822 at Mt. Pleasant, Buffalo Valley, Carter County, Tennessee. Her father, David Haynes, was a farmer, trader, and millwright who lived about ten miles west of Elizabethton. Educated at Elizabethton and Jonesborough, Emeline was intelligent and an accomplished pianist with a wonderful voice. She loved poetry, liked a good sermon, and was helpful and considerate of others. She was called Emma by Nathaniel and the family. After their marriage, she and Nathaniel most probably moved in with Nathaniel's mother at the Sycamore Shoals Plantation in Happy Valley, three miles southwest of Elizabethton. Nathaniel's mother died on August 2, 1844. The H.T. Spoden & Associates historical report states that Nathaniel built a home on the property before 1848. On August 8, 1844, Nathaniel, a member of the Presbyterian Church at Elizabethton, requested to be dismissed by the Session in order to join the Methodist Episcopal Church. This was granted, and he later became a Methodist minister.

In 1844 Nathaniel's Whig Party was campaigning to elect the popular Henry Clay of Kentucky as president while the Democrats were trying to elect James Knox Polk, from Tennessee. On January 1, 1844, the Carter County Whigs assembled at Elizabethton to nominate delegates who would attend the Whig State Convention on February 22 at Knoxville, Tennessee, and the Young Men's National Whig Convention at Baltimore, Maryland, in May. At this meeting a committee of five, including Nathaniel, was chosen to draft resolutions. The resolutions, which Nathaniel read to the group, called for a sound national currency to be secured by a United States bank regulated by the nation, an adequate revenue such as a judicious tariff to supply fair protection to American industry, restraints on executive power with restriction on the exercise of the veto, an equitable distribution of the public domain and the sale of it among all the states, an honest and economical administration against improper interference in elections, and lastly, an amendment to the Constitution limiting the office of the president to one term.

Those elected to attend the Whig State Convention at Knoxville were Robert Love, Nathaniel Greene Taylor, Carrick W. Nelson, John Jobe, John W. Hyder, Samuel W. Williams, Christian E. Carriger, Hamilton C. Smith, and Abraham Tipton. Those elected to attend the Young Men's National Whig Convention at Baltimore were Nathaniel Greene Taylor, Robert Love, Samuel P. Carter, David L. Stover, Hamilton C. Smith, Samuel W. Williams, and William Dean. At the East Tennessee convention in February 1844, the Whigs appointed delegates to represent their three congressional districts at the national convention. At the Baltimore convention in

May, they nominated the candidates for president and vice president. The District Elector for the First Congressional District was Nathaniel's friend, Thomas A.R. Nelson of Washington County. Among the assistant electors were Nathaniel Greene Taylor of Carter County and Robert Love of Johnson County. William G. Brownlow of Washington County was the First District's delegate to Baltimore. Nathaniel was there in attendance at the national convention when the Whig Party chose Clay to run for president. It was against this national backdrop that Nathaniel became passionately involved in politics.

In April Thomas A.R. Nelson called on the party faithful to organize a countywide Clay Club. Following Nelson's instructions, on May 6 Colonel Nathaniel Taylor was among those meeting to form a Clay Club in Carter County. Vigilance committees were appointed in each of the counties ten civil districts. Nathaniel was responsible for the 6th Civil District, along with J. Cooper and Thomas P. Enson.

On August 27, 1845, Editor William G. Brownlow, a Methodist who despised Presbyterians, favorably reported that "Rev. N.G. Taylor, a newly licensed local preacher, [who was formerly a Presbyterian] and a young man of a liberal education, surpasses the expectations of his friends, and is destined to make a successful preacher. He addresses his appeals to the strongest feelings of the heart, and is admired for his animating fervor." We are not sure how much Rev. Taylor supplied the churches near his home as he was so heavily involved in politics and business, but he may have filled in for other ministers.

On July 8, 1848, in preparation for the upcoming presidential election, Whigs from different counties gathered in Jonesborough, and Nathaniel Taylor was there representing Carter County. At this meeting the members recognized that the Whig Convention in Philadelphia had nominated Gen. Zachary Taylor and Millard Fillmore as candidates for president and vice president of the United States. They also selected General Thomas D. Arnold of Greene County as the elector for the district.

In 1849 Nathaniel Taylor, a Whig from Carter County, ran for the First Congressional District. Brookins Campbell and Landon Carter Haynes, Emeline Taylor's brother, were also running against Democrat Andrew Johnson in this election, but Johnson's major opponent was Taylor. Johnson was reelected for his fourth term, although Taylor ran a very active campaign and had good newspaper coverage. Nathaniel went back home to Emma and their two sons at his Sycamore Shoals Plantation in what he called Happy Valley.

On February 3, 1850, the Tennessee General Assembly passed an act to establish the Emme Female Academy in Carter County. Nathaniel Greene Taylor, always interested in education, was named a trustee along with Alfred W. Taylor, James P. Tipton, Peter Emmert, M.N. Fulsome, James Price, and Dr. J. Powell. The female academy was short lived, perhaps due to a lack of funding since an act was passed in 1852 that required any academy receiving state aid to accept both male and female students. It is thought that the established Duffield Academy began receiving female students and siphoned off the Emme Female Academy school population.

In 1850 the Seventh Census of Carter County showed Nathaniel G. Taylor, age thirty, living in the Sixth Civil District. His occupation was listed as preacher and farmer, and his property was valued at $12,000. Supporting the census record showing his occupation as a minister, we find that on January 2, 1851, he took time out of his schedule to perform a wedding.

A story, often repeated in the Taylor family, is that Nathaniel exclaimed one day "this is a Happy Valley" and the name stuck. What he said and when he said it may not actually be known, but there is some indication that he named the post office. The Dividing Ridge Post Office was discontinued on August 5, 1850, and the Happy Valley Post Office was established shortly thereafter. Nathaniel was the first postmaster, starting on December 1, 1850. He was replaced by James Hickey on March 31, 1854, but soon afterwards, on December 22, 1854, Nathaniel resumed the position. The Happy Valley Post Office was discontinued on May 18, 1900, and patrons began to receive their mail at Elizabethton on May 31, 1900.

On January 23, 1848, the General Assembly authorized The East Tennessee and Virginia Railroad Company (ET&VA) to be built from Knoxville to the Virginia state line. Dr. Samuel Cunningham of Jonesborough was the driving force toward its completion, which occurred on May 14, 1858. In Knoxville the ET&VA connected to the East Tennessee and Georgia line. It then became possible for passengers to travel to Chattanooga, to eastern cities, and to make connections to Nashville, Atlanta, and New Orleans. Nathaniel was very much interested in railroads and other ways to improve transportation in Carter County, as was his father James Patton Taylor before him. On October 15, 1851, he traveled to Abingdon, Virginia, to attend the great railroad convention. There were several hundred people from Washington County, Virginia, in attendance; various counties of Tennessee and Virginia were represented, as well as the states of North Carolina and Alabama. All were working to complete the railroads in their respective states.

President Zachary Taylor died suddenly on July 9, 1850, and as Millard Fillmore, the vice president, assumed office, Whigs began to speculate about the effect of his death on their Party. Fillmore inherited the controversy over the extension of slavery and he facilitated passage of the Compromise of 1850 which Henry Clay had designed and championed. Under Fillmore's administration, federal land grants encouraged the construction of new railroads, and settlements continued to move across the prairies, which would have a bearing on Nathaniel's life years later. The compromise did not settle the debate over slavery.

In the late fall of 1851, the National Union Party was being revived for the presidential election. In April 1852 many southerners left the Whig Party, and there was a question of whether the slave states would attend the convention. At the Democratic National Convention on June 5, Franklin Pierce of New Hampshire was nominated as a candidate for the presidency and, as a compromise to the slave states. William R. King of Alabama was nominated for vice president. In the 1852 election Pierce won a stunning victory which foretold the demise of the Whig Party.

Andrew Johnson was elected governor of Tennessee and served from October 17, 1853, to November 3, 1857. His old nemesis, Brookins Campbell, now had a chance for the congressional seat in the First District. Campbell, from Washington County, was a graduate of Washington College (now Washington and Lee) at Lexington, Virginia. He served in the Tennessee General Assembly five different times and finally, with Johnson out of the way won a congressional seat in 1853. Unfortunately, he died on December 25, 1853, once again leaving an open field for his seat in Congress.

On February 11, 1854, the Whigs of Carter County met at the courthouse in Elizabethton for the purpose of appointing delegates to the Greeneville convention where a candidate was to be nominated to fill the congressional seat of the recently deceased Brookins Campbell. A friend of Nathaniel's, Dr. Abraham Jobe, was on the committee. About 100 Whigs were present at the convention, and after some deliberation, Nathaniel Greene Taylor of Carter County received the nomination. Taylor, an opponent of Governor Johnson, defeated Johnson's friend Sam Milligan in the First Congressional District race. The Thirty-third Congress to which Nathaniel was elected had convened on March 4, 1853, but because of the special election, Taylor did not arrive to take his seat until March 30, 1854. He finished out the session on March 3, 1855.

One of the most important pieces of legislation to come up while Nathaniel was in the House of Representatives was the Kansas-Nebraska Act which was supported by Senator Stephen A. Douglas of Illinois. It would repeal the Missouri Compromise that allowed for the states of the Louisiana Purchase with the exception of Missouri to enter the union as free states. This bill provided that Kansas and Nebraska be organized as territories on the basis of popular sovereignty. Under the doctrine of popular sovereignty, settlers of U.S. federal territories were allowed to decide whether to enter the Union as free or slave states. The southern states believed this was a concession to them.

On May 18, 1854, Rep. Nathaniel Greene Taylor of Tennessee rose before the House and addressed his colleagues. He said that his position and that of his constituents demanded that the Kansas-Nebraska Act be defeated to protect the union of the states. Taylor supported the territories coming into the Union as free states. Yet despite the opposition of Taylor and three other Tennessee congressman, on May 22 the Kansas-Nebraska bill passed the House by 112-100 votes. Southern Whigs were split in the vote, and they saw their fellow Whig's position of slavery in the new territories as a move to create sectional party differences. This sounded the death knell of the Whig Party. When the Kansas-Nebraska Act passed, Nathaniel appeared to be independent and reached out to the northern Whigs for the sake of the party. As the Know-Nothing Party, who opposed both the Whig and Democrats, grew in popularity, many Whigs joined it.

Emeline Taylor and her brother Landon Carter Haynes (1816-1875) were the children of David and Rhoda Taylor Haynes of Carter County. Landon was a newspaper publisher, lawyer, Tennessee Assemblyman, minister, and a pro southern Democrat who served as a senator (1861-1865) in the Confederate Congress. In debates between the two about issues of the day Haynes called his sister a "Lincolnite." When he was captured at the end of the war, the family story states that Emeline, who was living in Washington, D.C. (or perhaps still in New Jersey), appealed to Haynes' former political enemy President Johnson to pardon him. Haynes settled

in Memphis where he supported Johnson's brand of Reconstruction. B. Harrison Taylor Collection, Johnson, City, Tennessee.

In East Tennessee the First District became a Know-Nothing battleground for two old Whig antagonists, Nathaniel G. Taylor and Albert G. Watkins. Both men joined the Know-Nothings, needing their endorsement, and when Taylor received it "the vindictive Watkins castigated the local Know-Nothings . . . and secured the Democrat's endorsement by running as an independent." With the combined support of the Democrats, anti-Know-Nothings, and Whigs, Watkins narrowly edged out Taylor and began his congressional term on December 3, 1855.

Taylor was back home in Tennessee, probably contemplating his next run for congress, when in March 1857 the U.S. Supreme Court, in compliance with the Dred Scott decision, declared that slaves and free blacks were not and could not become citizens of the United States. The court also ruled that slavery was legal in all territories. The case brought slavery to the attention of the nation and made abolitionists angry. The importance of this decision entered the political arena in the Abraham Lincoln and Stephen A. Douglas debates in 1858 for the Illinois U.S. Senate seat. Although Lincoln lost the election, he gained national prominence for his position against slavery. It was Lincoln's belief that the United States could not survive with half free and half slave states.

In East Tennessee the 1859 congressional race in the First District signaled the coming political trends. From his home in Jonesborough, Thomas A.R. Nelson traveled, as a delegate, to the Whig district convention on February 15. Thomas B. Alexander, in his book, states that Nelson went, planning to nominate Nathaniel Greene Taylor, but he was nominated instead. Nelson, former attorney general of the First Judicial Circuit and a strong supporter of the Union, ran against Democrat Landon Carter Haynes. In the election Haynes received 3,484 votes while Nelson received 2,897 votes in the northeast counties of Carter, Johnson, Sullivan, and Washington. Yet Nelson won the First Congressional District. "N.G. Taylor sent his best wishes to Nelson on the occasion, stating that 'Colonel Haynes is my brother-in-law and esteemed personal friend . . .. [I] sympathize with him and am sorry for him personally in his defeat.'" Haynes later became a senator of the Confederate Congress. Thomas A.R. Nelson served in the Thirty-sixth Congress of the United States from March 4, 1859, to March 3, 1861. When the Civil War broke out he was very much against secession, as was Nathaniel Taylor.

This full length portrait of Emeline Haynes Taylor and her twin daughters, Mary Eva (left) and Rhoda, was probably painted about 1858 by portraitist Samuel M. Shaver, after the family left Washington, D.C., for East Tennessee. Photography did not reach the United States until the 1840s. Before and after that date portrait painters traveled throughout the states seeking patrons. Often they had the canvas prepared and all they had to do was add the face as may have been the case with Emeline and her daughters. B. Harrison Taylor Collection.

Pride, Poverty, Patriotism and the East Tennessee Relief Association

There were four candidates in the November 1860 presidential election. On the ballot were John C. Breckenridge of Kentucky, a Southern Democrat, Stephen M. Douglas of Illinois, a Northern Democrat, and Tennessean John Bell, Constitutional Unionist Party. All ran on a "save the union" platform. The Republican candidate, Abraham Lincoln of Illinois, was not on the ballot in Tennessee. Nathaniel Taylor, presidential elector on the Constitutional Union ticket was a strong supporter of John Bell from Tennessee. So intense were the feelings that in 1861 Thomas William Humes, rector of St. John's Episcopal Church in Knoxville, a Unionist, resigned his position. In 1888, he stated that his friend Nathaniel G. Taylor, during a debate in the presidential election of 1860, "spoke with almost prophetic tongue of the civil war and its train of dreadful ills, which he alleged, the malcontent politicians of a great party were preparing to bring upon the country if Mr. Lincoln were elected. So vivid was the picture which he then drew of those evils, that . . . some of the hearers wept."

In 1859 the successful American industrialist Peter Cooper founded the Cooper Union in New York City (Manhattan). They offered full-tuition scholarships and became one of the nation's leading colleges for artists, architects, and engineers. It was here in the Great Hall on February 27, 1860, that Abraham Lincoln made his famous speech to 1,500 spectators about slavery, saying simply that it was wrong. This "position statement," declaring where he stood, was widely reported in the press and reprinted throughout the north. This compelling speech probably did more to gain him the nomination for the presidency than any other effort he made. Since 1860 many presidents, recognizing the historic value of this venue, have made speeches in the Great Hall at Cooper Union. Nathaniel was at this famous venue as one of the early speakers in 1864.

When Lincoln was elected president on November 6, 1860, events signaling war began in rapid succession. On December 20 South Carolina seceded from the Union and six other states followed by February of 1861. These seven states were called the Confederate States of America. Lincoln was inaugurated on March 4, 1861, as the sixteenth president of the United States. On April 12 with the bombardment of Fort Sumter in South Carolina by the Confederates Civil War began. In late April the General Assembly of Tennessee met in special session and passed "A Declaration of Independence," withdrawing from the Union and authorizing a military league with the Confederate government. The Union leaders were canvassing East Tennessee to gain supporters, and "one of the most influential was Andrew Johnson of Greeneville." Another was Nathaniel Greene Taylor who spoke in Elizabethton on May 15 to defend the Union and oppose secession. Before the election on June 8 to vote on whether or not to separate from the Union Confederate troops were stationed throughout East Tennessee. The outcome of the June election statewide was decidedly for secession, but the East Tennessee counties remained in the majority with their support for the Union.

Historian Noel C. Fisher, in his book about partisan politics and guerilla warfare, notes that he and other historians, since just after the Civil War, have tried to determine why East Tennessee was loyal to the Union. Possible explanations are patriotism, relatively few slaves in the region, party affiliation, lack of a staple crop, and a variety of other factors. They generally agree that wealth and slavery were not issues in voting for secession in Tennessee. It has been suggested that loyalty to the Union was, because of the region's isolation and sense of uniqueness, the lack of transportation links, and its economic and cultural differences. Nathaniel fairly well fit this description as he was patriotic, owned slaves, was a Whig and an 1860 elector for the Constitutional Unionist Party, did not have a large cash income from a staple crop but was wealthy, and lived where transportation and access to markets was not adequate. Fisher, in comparing a number of economic and social factors, along with other influences, showed that "statistical results support two common interpretations of East Tennessee's Unionism, the relative absence of slavery and the influence of the Whig Party." Nathaniel may have been more influential in keeping the region loyal than he imagined. East Tennessee was also a region of mixed loyalties. To illustrate how the war divided families, we give one example. Alfred E. Jackson of Jonesborough, married to Seraphina C. Taylor, Nathaniel's sister, became a general in the Confederate army.

On July 26, 1861, Gen. Felix K. Zollicoffer, a Union supporter, switched sides and was assigned to Knoxville to command all Confederate forces in East Tennessee. They took over operation of the East Tennessee and Virginia Railroad. The Confederates began to tighten their grip on the area, and in August 1861, when Thomas A.R. Nelson was reelected to the Thirty-seventh United States Congress, he was arrested and imprisoned by the Confederates and never got to serve.

The Burning of the Bridges

In November the Confederates were shocked by an incident which later became known as the "burning of the bridges." Dr. Abraham Jobe of Carter County, a Union supporter, recounted how William A. Carter, a Presbyterian minister, of Elizabethton slipped out of the county and proposed a plan to President Lincoln and other leaders to deliver East Tennessee to the Union Army. Carter's plan was to cripple the Confederate transportation system by destroying nine railroad bridges between Bristol and Chattanooga. During the same time frame, a Union army would invade East Tennessee. Lincoln approved the plan, and as a result, in November 1861, area Unionists successfully destroyed five of the bridges. Unfortunately for the East Tennessee Unionists, Union forces did not invade East Tennessee as promised, and in the aftermath, five of the bridge burners were executed, and 200 were sent to a Confederate prison.

In the excitement, over 1,000 Union men, unorganized and poorly armed, gathered at Elizabethton, planning to march for Cumberland Gap in order to rendezvous with the Union army. First though they crossed the Watauga River at Taylors Ford and marched towards Carter's Depot, in hopes of capturing the rebel force. The hastily put together Union force was no match for the rebels, and Dr. Jobe, upon realizing this, persuaded them to return to the south side of the river where "they went into camp with headquarters in Col. N.G. Taylor's large barn, which stood a short distance from the banks of the Watauga River." A large Confederate force came into Carter County and captured several Union men, but many retreated into the mountains where they hid for about six weeks. Citizens of the area, including Dr. Jobe's friend and neighbor Nathaniel Taylor, provided food for them. The rebels were looking for Dr. Jobe, who was suspected of being involved in the bridge burning. To avoid the searchers, he hid in his cellar for six weeks. Fleeing for his life, he left his home late at night. Nathaniel took him to Elizabethton; from there he crossed the mountain into the Carolinas, on his way to relatives in Georgia. He was unable to return home to Tennessee until after the war.

Before this incident, the loyalists had been treated leniently. Afterwards, however, many people were arrested. Confederate authorities began to refer to East Tennessee loyalists, as enemies, and they employed increasing force in an attempt to subdue, imprison, or drive out the rebellious Unionists. Partisan warfare erupted, and the conflict now truly was a Civil War. The bitterness became personal and spilled over into whipping people, stealing, and destroying homes and crops. On March 3, 1862, President Lincoln selected Andrew Johnson as military governor of Tennessee. Johnson arriving in Nashville on March 12, 1862, was not able to exercise any control over East Tennessee until late 1863 and only served until 1864. Johnson was a firm leader and later used Tennessee as a model for Reconstruction.

There is some question as to whether Nathaniel moved to Knoxville during the Civil War. The answer lies in his earlier movements which help illustrate the difficulties suffered by many people loyal to the Union, difficulties that were never acknowledged and for which they were never compensated. Earlier in 1844 Nathaniel moved to Happy Valley, Carter County. One account states that he moved to his father-in-law's (David Haynes) estate in Buffalo Valley about 1851 or so. At this time Nathaniel reportedly purchased 1,000 acres from Haynes, but we do not know if it included the Haynes farmstead. As Nathaniel was postmaster at Happy Valley from 1850 to 1854, it is unlikely he moved ten miles away to the Haynes property. Dr. Abraham Jobe places him in Carter County in 1861. From the family collection, an abstract from the official 1860 Carter County Census shows Nathaniel Taylor, age forty, listed in the Peoplesville District, with the value of his real estate at $63,500 and his personal estate valued at $47,900. His wife Emeline (Emma) was thirty-eight, and his children were James P., fifteen, Alfred A., twelve, Robert L., ten, Nathaniel W., eight, twins Rhoda Emma and Mary Eva, five, David Haynes, three, and Hugh L. M., five months. Living with them was Julia Trusseller, a twenty-eight year old seamstress, and William Wickerson, age twenty-five, who was a miller. Also in 1861 Nathaniel purchased the O'Brien Ironworks on the Doe River, Valley Forge Community.

Nathaniel, writing in March 1865, said the rebel press had labeled him as an instigator and leader of the bridge burners. After a rebel friend informed him that he was to be shot on sight, he fled into the mountains where he was hunted on a daily basis. Scott and Angel in their book state that Col. Nathaniel Greene Taylor was among the refugees who hid at the home of David Stout in the wilderness on Buck Mountain, Carter County. This was near the Tennessee and North Carolina border close to Roan Mountain. Nathaniel wrote that he sought asylum at the headquarters of Col. R.B. Vance where he was tried and acquitted of bridge burning. In 1880 Hugh McClung of Knoxville wrote to Lyman C. Draper saying that in 1863 Col. Taylor owned and lived at his home at Sycamore Shoals. By the end of 1863, the Union army was in control of East Tennessee, except for bands of guerrillas and brigands. It was during this time in 1863 that Nathaniel went through the Confederate lines to Union controlled Knoxville.

As someone who had devoted his life, through politics, to the citizens of upper East Tennessee, Nathaniel could not stand idly by when not only his survival but that of his fellow citizens was at stake. While at Knoxville, according to his March 1865 letter, he stated unequivocally that he had conceived the idea of the East Tennessee Relief Association and organized it along the lines in which it was to function. He added that the founding committee, without his giving any input to the proceedings, voted on an annual salary of $4,000 for him. He declared that with that sum he had to clothe his almost naked family of twelve, pay their transportation to New Jersey, and pay for their education. He was also given traveling expense of $2,100 related to his relief work.

On November 17 General Burnside's Union army was placed under siege in Knoxville. During the siege many homes and properties were destroyed. For this and other destruction in late 1863 by both armies, Nathaniel, seeing the near famine in East Tennessee, decided that he must travel to the nation's capital to describe the East Tennessee Relief Association's plans, and seek assistance for his friends and neighbors by fundraising in the north. Historian William C. Harris, writing in the *Tennessee Historical Quarterly*, quoted Taylor as saying he wanted "to secure some action of the Federal Government which would furnish prompt relief to the sufferers." Taylor, with letters of introduction from William G. Brownlow and others, met with "President Lincoln and key members of Congress." On December 14, 1863,

Nathaniel wrote from Washington, D.C., to Tennessee's Military Governor Andrew Johnson at Nashville, telling of his meeting and saying "all seemed to sympathize with our people-and the president promised that everything the Executive could do should be done to succor them. . . . Taylor asked Johnson to use his 'powerful influence with the president-with Congress-and with the country [to] command prompt and efficient action by the Government for the salvation of our people from the horrors of Destitution which are now assailing them.'" Both Johnson and Lincoln failed to deliver, but Nathaniel had done what no other Tennessean had, in going to the president of the United States to seek aid for, as he refers to his fellow East Tennesseans, "our people." In this remarkable effort he demonstrates his compassion for the people of East Tennessee.

By 1864 both armies had marched back and forth over East Tennessee. Farms were ransacked, and food and clothing were scarce. Unable to raise food crops with so many men away in the army, a food scarcity was created, and prices soared, making goods virtually unobtainable. The loss of homes and property in other East Tennessee counties was driving refugees to war torn Knoxville. Housing shortages fast became a problem in Knoxville, which was already reeling under the burden of occupation and the lack of the basic necessities. While Nathaniel was away fundraising, the East Tennessee leadership organized the East Tennessee Relief Association on February 8, 1864, in Knoxville.

The desperate and extraordinary length applicants for relief, usually wives of soldiers who were in service or ill, went to for assistance may be illustrated in the following examples. In the summer of 1864, seven ladies, having been robbed of all they had by Confederate soldiers, were desperate for clothing and food. They walked sixty-five miles to Strawberry Plains, just outside of Knoxville, for assistance, which the relief organization provided. Upon learning of their success, nine ladies in similar circumstances who had forty-one dependents beside themselves walked eighty-five miles to Knoxville for clothing, and, since no clothing had arrived at the relief association, they had to walk home empty handed.

In such desperate times, prominent civic minded leaders, predominantly from Knoxville, came forth to provide leadership for the East Tennessee Relief Association. Nathaniel, representing the relief association in the northeastern states, had already initiated an appeal for funds from private citizens and state governments. Taylor was a natural candidate for this role for a number of reasons. He was a minister with great oratorical skills and powers of persuasion, and as a former member of Congress, he had stature among those with whom he would be working. Rev. Thomas H. Humes, chairman of the East Tennessee Relief Association, writing in 1888, said that Nathaniel Taylor went to Cincinnati where he raised several hundred dollars. There were many refugees from East Tennessee in Cincinnati, as in other cities, and a Refugee Relief Commission was established there.

It was announced by the Academy of Music, Philadelphia, Pennsylvania, that on the night of January 29, 1864, two well known witnesses would give addresses about the suffering of Union people. It was further stated that "our citizens are fully aware of the great destitution and suffering endured by the Union families in East Tennessee." One of the featured speakers was former Confederate Brig. Gen. Edward W. Gantt of Arkansas who had been pardoned for treason by President Lincoln in December 1863. The other speaker, Col. Nathaniel Greene Taylor, addressed as colonel by virtue of his being appointed colonel in the Tennessee militia in 1842, was described as "a distinguished and able gentleman . . . and he comes warmly recommended by Governor Andrew Johnson." Both Gantt and Taylor had spoken previously to a full house in Harrisburg, the state capital. It was added that their families were "now held as prisoners within the Rebel lines." Over $26,000 was contributed due to Taylor and Gantt's efforts, and "the Pennsylvania Relief Association for Tennessee with former Pennsylvania Governor James Pollock as president was organized."

In New England Taylor was also a success with one person saying it was their "sacred duty to sustain the East Tennesseans in their struggle." On February 5 Nathaniel addressed the Massachusetts Hall of Representatives, who were so aroused by his speech that they formed a committee to relieve the suffering in East Tennessee. This committee was headed by Edward Everett who had been a vice presidential candidate in the 1860 election and had shared the stage with Lincoln at Gettysburg. Nathaniel had been a Tennessee presidential elector for the Constitutional Union ticket of Bell and Everett, and Everett arranged a meeting for Taylor to speak at Faneuil Hall.

At Faneuil Hall on February 10, 1864, Everett, who was governor of Massachusetts and recognized as one of the greatest orators of his day, gave a wonderful summary of Nathaniel Greene Taylor's speech. Commenting on Nathaniel in his 1888 book, *The Loyal Mountaineers of Tennessee*, Thomas W. Humes, a colleague of Taylor, wrote that he gave "a fervent and impressive address, in which he briefly related the historical events in East Tennessee from the beginning of 1861, told of the wrongs inflicted upon its people, of the voluntary exile of its men and their enlistment in the United States Army, of the desolation their homes and fields had suffered from the war . . . and appealed on their behalf to the prosperous people among who he so stood, to send them help." The contributions in the months that followed amounted to $100,000. In Maine Colonel Taylor raised $11,000, and saw the beginning of a relief organization there.

On February 20, 1864, prominent citizens of New York City wrote to Nathaniel assuring him that they recognized "the important mission with which [he was] charged . . . namely, the relief of the suffering" in Tennessee and asked him to speak at a public meeting on March 10. Among those issuing the invitation was Peter Cooper of the Cooper Institute. Four years earlier Abraham Lincoln had made a speech at the institute which helped propel him to the presidency. Nathaniel and Lincoln were among the first well known speakers at the Cooper Institute which still hosts speakers today. Nathaniel was introduced by Gen. Hiram Walbridge, the presiding officer of the meeting. Walbridge recalled that the East Tennesseans were settlers from the "Old North State who inherited their convictions of popular liberty from the men who fought at Kings Mountain." He also made reference to those who came to the Watauga and "early engendered in [East Tennessee her] first distinct political organization." In correspondence Nathaniel was referred to as the "former Representative from Tennessee" and General Walbridge introduced him as such, saying "driven from his country, by the persecution of the rebels, he comes to represent to you the sufferings of his countrymen."

In his address in the Great Hall, Nathaniel told of the mountain beauty of East Tennessee, and throughout his remarks he was received with much applause. The war, he reported, had rolled over East Tennessee leaving it in ruins, "having nothing left her but pride, poverty, and patriotism." Addressing the history of East Tennesseans, he said they had ever "kept time to the music of the Union." East Tennessee had voted against secession in the February convention. He painted a scene of distress among the civilian population as armies marched over the land, exhausting supplies, taking livestock, blankets, corn, and wheat with thieves following behind them. Taylor stated that East Tennesseans had "drunk the full cup of suffering . . . and had sacrificed everything but loyalty and honor." He referred to the victories of the military in 1863 and stated that the "impetuous Sherman, along the slopes and summit of Mission (*sic* Missionary) Ridge, led his brave legions to victory at the cannon's mouth." Although a few years later Taylor may have offered a different assessment of William T. Sherman, his speech at Cooper Union was impressive, patriotic, passionate, and favorably met. In conclusion and perhaps theatricality, Nathaniel and General Walbridge shook hands, agreeing that slavery should be swept from the Union.

The East Tennessee Relief Association fulfilled its mission as they distributed food, clothing, and even seeds for gardens to the people of East Tennessee. They purchased foodstuffs and competed with the army for trains to transport and distribute the supplies equitably. Much of the relief efforts went to Knoxville and, as transportation improved, to other parts of the area.

Judging by the apparent ages of the children, it is estimated this image was taken about 1864, when the Nathaniel Greene Taylor family was living in Haddonfield, New Jersey. From left to right: Alfred Alexander (1848-1931), Mary Eva (1855-1916), Nathaniel Winfield Scott (1852-1904), Emeline Haynes (1822-1890), in her lap Sanna McClung (1862-1941), Robert Love (1850-1912), Hugh Lawson (1860-1935), Nathaniel Greene (1819-1887), David Haynes (1858-1890), James Patton (1844-1924), and Rhoda, (1855-1943) twin of Mary Eva. B. Harrison Taylor Collection.

Nathaniel's family was reportedly sent through the Union lines to join him in the North in the fall of 1863, arriving in February 1864. After meeting with the president and other cabinet officials in late 1863, Taylor was giving a speech in Philadelphia on January 29, 1864, where a newspaper stated that his family was not with him. Nathaniel was anxious for Emeline and the children to join him, leaving behind the strife and tension of a war ravaged land. Decades later, Alfred A. Taylor, Nathaniel's son, stated that he had accompanied his father to Faneuil Hall in Boston in February 1864 where they met Edward Everett. That same month Nathaniel moved his family to Haddonfield, New Jersey, located about six miles east of Philadelphia. In 1864 while Nathaniel was getting settled, Lincoln was reelected with Andrew Johnson as his vice-president.

Nathaniel Aids a Confederate Prisoner

Nathaniel was not one to forget his friends or those who had helped him. One person, Robert B. Vance who had probably saved his life, was a Confederate prisoner who had been incarcerated for over a year at Fort Delaware Prison just below Philadelphia. On March 1, 1865, while raising funds for the East Tennessee

Relief Association at Nashua, New Hampshire, Nathaniel wrote Maj. Gen. Ethan Allen Hitchcock at Washington, D.C. Nathaniel included a note from President Lincoln, written on his behalf, recalling for General Hitchcock that in the autumn of 1861, by the direction of Union military authorities in Kentucky, the citizens of East Tennessee burned several bridges on the East Tennessee and Virginia Railroad. Failing to receive the promised military assistance, this loyal Union militia fled to the mountains. Confederate Colonel (later Brigadier General) Vance had been among the Confederate troops sent to guard East Tennessee railroad bridges in the days following the attempt by Unionists to destroy those bridges in 1861.

According to Nathaniel, Vance and other Confederate men, "concealed [themselves] in our mountain fastnesses for weeks." Colonel Vance later assured Taylor that if he would turn himself in, he would protect him "and all other citizens not shown to be bridge-burners." In Taylor's words: "A company of cut-throat rebel horsemen on the lookout for me, with the avowed intention [as I was credibly informed] of hanging me to a tree or shooting me down on sight, got on my track, came near intercepting me, and pursued me to the very headquarters of Colonel Vance. He most kindly and magnanimously protected me and saved my life." By his "moderation and clemency"

Nathaniel was satisfied that Vance "had saved the lives and property of hundreds of . . . Union fellow-citizens of Carter and surrounding counties." Nathaniel requested that Brigadier General Vance be paroled or released in exchange for a prisoner of similar rank. He added that he had not had the honor of meeting General Hitchcock and for reference he gave the names of Andrew Johnson, Green Clay Smith, and Maj. Gen. Ambrose E. Burnside. On March 6, 1865, General Hitchcock forwarded the request to the attention of Commissary-General of Prisoners William Hoffman with the note from President Lincoln, stating that he "understands it to be the [president's] wish that this exchange be made." Vance was paroled on March 14, 1865.

Reconstruction, Emigrants, and Native Americans

Events that occurred during the Thirty-ninth U.S. Congress which convened on March 4, 1865, and closed on March 3, 1867, are some of the most momentous, collectively, that has ever occurred in our nation. They began at Appomattox, Virginia, on April 9, 1865, when Gen. Robert E. Lee surrendered to Union Gen. Ulysses S. Grant, bringing major hostilities of the Civil War to an end. It was on April 14, 1865, that Abraham Lincoln, while attending a play at Ford's Theatre, was assassinated by John Wilkes Booth.

Lincoln died the following day and Nathaniel Taylor's former political opponent and fellow Tennessean, Andrew Johnson, became the seventeenth president of the United States. Crucial issues faced the nation, including what should be done about the former slaves. Black voting rights was viewed by moderate Republicans as a practical problem not as an opportunity to impose social revolution on the South. A gradual approach was favored by the Republicans who saw civil rights legislation and creation of the Freedmen's Bureau as a necessary solution. For example, before the Civil War ended, congress passed the Thirteenth Amendment, abolishing slavery, and freeing about four million slaves who were mostly illiterate. This was sent to the states for ratification which occurred on December 8, 1865. If the slaves were to transition into society, they needed to be educated quickly. On March 3, 1865, the Freedmen's Bureau was created to do this but was vetoed by President Johnson. In 1866 his veto was overcome and over 1,000 schools (some sources state 3,000 schools) were built to meet this deficiency. Teacher training institutes were created, black colleges established, and hospitals built. Congress refused to seat the Tennessee delegation until the state ratified the Fourteenth Amendment, granting citizenship to those born in the United States which they did on July 19, 1866.

Nathaniel, who was re-elected to the First Congressional District on the National Union Party ticket, took his seat on July 24, 1866, the day Tennessee was readmitted to the Union. From Washington, D.C., on August 1, 1866, he addressed his constituents in a published letter, showing his support for President Johnson and stating the country was in a great national struggle. Although he had his differences with Johnson before the war, he now viewed him as one of the greatest intellects in the nation and as a strong defender of the Constitution. Nathaniel supported President Johnson and appealed to his fellow East Tennesseans to support a white government elected by white voters.

On February 18, 1867, while speaking on the House floor against the radical's plan for reconstruction, Nathaniel supported the president, saying he believed "the distinguished patriot, now President, who has been maligned and traduced, perhaps more falsely and fiercely than any man who ever lived in the United States, will shine brightly and tower conspicuously in history as a great and good man, as 'the noblest work of God-an honest man,' when the names of his traducers with their bodies shall have perished in the earth and been forgotten." Taylor's support and enthusiasm for Johnson seems to be out of the ordinary, even for a fellow Tennessean. It appears that Taylor realized his political career in Washington or in Tennessee could best be served if he was tied to the coattails of the president. His reward, perhaps, was his appointment by Johnson as Commissioner of Indian Affairs.

Many significant events that had their beginnings in the 1840s had an effect on Taylor's career in the post-war years. First and foremost was the 1803 Louisiana Purchase with its 825,000 square miles of land west of the Mississippi River. This purchase was endorsed by President Thomas Jefferson in part because he saw the West as an ideal place to relocate Indian tribes. In 1824 the Bureau of Indian Affairs was created under the War Department, and in 1832 President Andrew Jackson created the position of Indian Commissioner to head the bureau. On March 3, 1849, Congress, dissatisfied with the way the War Department was running the Bureau of Indian Affairs, transferred it from the War Department to the newly created Department of the Interior.

Also important to Nathaniel Taylor's future in the years after the Civil War was the construction of the transcontinental railroad, an idea that first surfaced in 1845 when Congress passed the Pacific Railway Act on July 1, 1862. On May 10, 1869, the nation's first transcontinental railroad was completed at Promontory Summit, Utah. The railroad connected the country with rapid travel, and less expensive shipment of freight. The telegraph, completed coast to coast on October 24, 1861, created a very important and fast communication system. Another piece of landmark legislation that transformed America most notably in the nineteenth century—and spelled doom for the Native American way of life—was the Homestead Act of 1862. The act gave 160 acres of land, out of the public domain in the western lands, to qualified emigrants.

These events, shaped by Congress, enabled settlement of the interior United States, as was their purpose, but they came into direct conflict with the Native American population's way of life. Even the Oregon Trail, which began in 1843 as an emigrant route through more than 2,000 miles of country beyond the frontier, was eventually assisted by Congress. In 1846 Congress authorized forts to be built along the trail to protect the travelers and ostensibly to ensure Indian rights.

> —A record has been kept at Fort Laramie of the emigration that has passed that point this season. Up to the 10th of August it numbered seven thousand seven hundred and eighty-four wagons, twenty-four thousand two hundred and twenty-seven men, women and children, and forty-four thousand two hundred and forty-three horses, mules and oxen.

The Oregon Trail that passed by Fort Laramie was well used, as this August 1864 list of travelers and stock shows. It was perhaps the best known of all the trails that emigrants followed west. Farmers, businessmen, and missionaries left home on an incredible and difficult journey across the nation to Oregon. It is estimated 400,000 people traveled the Oregon Trail. The Philadelphia Inquirer, Philadelphia, Pennsylvania, Thursday, September 8, 1864.

The large number of emigrants on the Oregon Trail caused severe problems for the Indian tribes. The emigrants' livestock consumed the grass along the trail, the emigrants cut the trees for firewood destroying habitat, and either killed or drove the animals away from the watering sources. In 1834, as part of the western fur trade, Fort Laramie was established at the junction of the Laramie and North Platte Rivers. In 1849 it became a U.S. military post for the protection of travelers on their way to Oregon. To keep the peace with the Arapaho, Cheyenne, Crow, and Sioux, the Fort Laramie Treaty was signed in September 1851 with about 10,000 Indians in attendance. A key provision of the treaty was that the military would continue to pursue "the right of the United States to establish roads and military posts in the Indian Territory."

Problems on the Indian Frontier

The Sand Creek Massacre that shocked Congress and the nation occurred on November 29, 1864, when about 150 Arapaho and Cheyenne were killed, scalped, and horribly mutilated by Col. John M. Chivington's Colorado militia troops. A commission led by Wisconsin Senator J.R. Doolittle was formed to investigate. The congressional instructions to the commission "were to establish a permanent peace between the Indians and whites and among the Indian tribes themselves." "The object of the commission was, for the first time, to define precisely the limits of tribally owned land and to compel the Indians to live within their own boundaries."

According to historian Henry G. Waltmann, cost was also a factor in addressing the Indian problem. The civil component stressed that it was cheaper to have treaties than to conduct war, but the military believed that the Indians must be whipped into submission. Even while treaties were ongoing, the [army's policy was to chase] hostile Indians. There was no declaration of war, but episodes or campaigns to fight the Indians for some wrong or perceived wrong." The Indians also fought the soldiers or attacked settlers for some wrong or perceived wrong.

In June 1866 a treaty was negotiated with the Oglala and Upper Brule Sioux, the Northern Cheyenne, and the Arapaho at Fort Laramie. This treaty was important because the favorite hunting grounds of the tribes were crossed by the shortest route to the Montana diggings. The Bozeman Trail, or Powder River Road, which ran from Fort Laramie northwest into the Powder River country, was about four hundred miles shorter than the route by way of Fort Hall and Virginia City. The Indians were upset that the commissioners planned to construct and garrison Forts Phil Kearny, C.F. Smith, and Reno through their country. Further exacerbating the problem, the Fort Laramie negotiators found that people were "interested in keeping up an agitation for the purpose of keeping freight at higher rates." Those non-military groups of freighters, contractors, and speculators wanted hostilities because they shipped army supplies. The Union Pacific Railroad profited, for example, as two-thirds of their business was with the War Department.

On August 6, 1866, the military changed the Division of the Mississippi to the Division of the Missouri with Maj. Gen. William T. Sherman commanding. One problem the military had in 1866 was being able to quickly respond to attacks on the emigrants by the Indians. Earlier in the year, representatives of territories in the upper Mississippi Valley demanded military protection for the routes to Montana, but Major General Sherman maintained that he could protect only the main routes. These included the Missouri River, the Platte River and Bozeman Trail, and the Fort Pierce Road through the Black Hills.

The military was facing a huge task. During the 1866 summer traveling season, it was estimated that as many as one hundred thousand people would be on the move. "Forty steamboats were already preparing to ascend the Missouri as far as Fort Benton, Montana." Emigrants, with wagons loaded with food and household goods and flanked by small herds of cattle, were traveling these roads, passing through Indian country. There would be Indians whose food supply was constantly diminishing watching furtively as the snakelike trains edged forward. In some cases the temptation would be too much, and the hungry natives would accost the trains; then there would be trouble."

In May 1866 newly promoted Lieutenant General Sherman went to see for himself what conditions were like in Indian country. He visited the railroad construction camps, Forts Riley and Kearny, and observed emigration along the various routes. Logistically, he was pleased by the construction of the railroad because he would be able to move men and materials much more cheaply than paying the current wagon freight rates. Sherman visited Col. Henry B. Carrington who planned to build three forts along the 550 mile route from Bridger's Ferry on the North Platte River, to Virginia City, Montana Territory. Treaty negotiations were ongoing at Fort Laramie on June 13, 1866, when the 18th Infantry, commanded by Col. Henry B. Carrington, arrived. Red Cloud, a great leader of the Sioux, left the negotiation in disgust upon learning Carrington was there to build forts. He vowed to make war on whites who used the trail.

William Tecumseh Sherman was born in Lancaster, Ohio, and graduated from West Point. he is perhaps best known for his Atlanta Campaign during the Civil War, and he played a major role in western affairs. In 1866 he was placed in charge of the Division of the Missouri. Library of Congress.

Effective July 27, 1866, President Andrew Johnson appointed Orville Hickman Browning as Secretary of the Interior. Browning, born in Kentucky, was a former U.S. Senator from Illinois, and served in Johnson's cabinet until March 4, 1869. "Browning's administration . . . covered a period in which important efforts were made to restrict the tribes to limited reservations where they were supposed to be protected and taught to become self-sufficient farmers and laborers." Browning called this the best, if not the only, policy that could be pursued to preserve the tribes from extinction.

On December 21, 1866, a wood gathering party of eighty one men commanded by Capt. William J. Fetterman were led into a well planned trap by the Arapaho, Cheyenne, Lakota Sioux, and annihilated. Reminiscent of the Sand Creek Massacre, the soldiers were stripped and mutilated, but this time the whites were the victims instead of the Indians. A national uproar was created in the press. Word of this successful attack spread quickly along the frontier, and Congress, the War Department, and the Indian Affairs office were called on to explain what happened. On January 3, 1867, the nominee as Commissioner of Indian Affairs, Lewis V. Bogy wrote Secretary Browning stating that the Indians were on a friendly visit to Fort Phil Kearny when attacked. Bogy, Nathaniel's predecessor, "commented that the policy of the military was 'to chastise the Indian when any white men were killed, regardless of the fact whether they were assailants or defending themselves.'" Bogy believed Sherman was wrong in his policy to deal "summarily with the tribesmen outside restricted areas." To Bogy "unmolested overland travel was essential, but the way to obtain this privilege was through treaties, annuities, and 'judicial management,' not military action." General Sherman was irritated and embarrassed, demanded an investigation, and recommended that Carrington be removed. He also said "we must act with vindictive earnestness against the Sioux . . . even to their extermination, men, women, and children."

On January 15, 1867, Secretary Browning wrote President Johnson that he was "disturbed [about the] state of the Indians" suggesting that war was coming in the spring with much destruction of life, property, and expense to the government. To ease tensions and to calm the situation, he believed a commission, consisting of four or five men from the military and civilians acquainted with the character of the Indian tribes, should be designated to confer with them to determine their needs and wants; to impress upon them the resources of the government and the certainty of their extermination if they started war; to assure them of the humane interests of the government toward them; and to provide them reservations for homes if they returned to peace. He added that with these measures which show "friendship, justice, and fair dealing . . ., we will have no further trouble." He strongly encouraged such a commission be convened.

On January 25, 1867, Senator Doolittle's belated congressional inquiry into "the conditions of the Indian tribes" was published just as Browning was reporting to the president. Doolittle found that the tribes were "declining in population because of the loss of land and the growing scarcity of game, and [were] progressively corrupted by whiskey, disease, and other white vices. Most Indian hostilities, the evidence showed, could be traced to white encroachment or white provocation. The reservation system was being offered as the only sound basis for policy. Its success depended on people who could civilize the Indians and teach them to support themselves by farming. Military officers possessed neither the skills nor the inclination for such a task, and therefore the Indian Bureau should remain in the Interior Department." Five boards of inspection were proposed to oversee the civilization progress and eradicate the evils of the existing system. Historian Robert M. Utley wrote that Doolittle's report was "a milestone in the unfolding of an Indian policy aimed at peaceful resolution of Indian difficulties."

On February 4, 1867, interim Commissioner Bogy suggested that in the coming summer they should study the possibility of "locating all tribes on one or two reservations where they could farm, raise livestock, attend school, and overcome uncivilized habits." At the same time General Sherman made preparations to defend emigration and overland transportation on four principal routes that he had designated in 1866. In meetings of the president's cabinet in the early months of 1867, Secretary of War Edwin Stanton urged vigorous military retaliation for the Fetterman Massacre, but Interior Secretary Browning opposed this and President Andrew Johnson plainly wanted some kind of peaceful handling of the Indian difficulties.

At the conclusion of the Thirty-ninth Congress on March 3, 1867, Nathaniel Greene Taylor, at age forty-seven was out of a job. Perhaps as many as seven of his children were living with him and Emeline, including his married son James Patton. Returning to Tennessee where money was scarce and reconstruction rampant was not a good option. The chances for any income in law or the ministry were probably remote. Further, he had a debt of thousands of dollars hanging over his head, stemming from the lawsuit brought against him by William H. Turley. His was not an enviable position. He saw better educational opportunities and employment for his children in the North.

The Civil War had crushed Nathaniel financially, but brought him closer politically and personally to the now serving president, Andrew Johnson. According to at least one Taylor family descendant, Nathaniel wrote President Johnson in desperation, asking for a job with an adequate income. Patronage among politicians was not uncommon. The Andrew Johnson Presidential Papers do not include such a letter, and there is no way to document that Nathaniel specified Commissioner of Indian Affairs in his request.

Nathaniel appointed Commissioner of Indian Affairs

During the time Nathaniel was seeking a position, President Johnson nominated Lewis V. Bogy as Commissioner of Indian Affairs on March 9, 1867. Bogy was a Missouri lawyer, state legislator, and businessman who had worked in the Indian Affairs office during the Civil War. In his home state, however, he had awarded several questionable contracts to firms that were operated by family members. For this reason and because of his criticism of radicals in the legislature, his nomination was rejected by the Senate. Johnson, needing to appoint someone quickly, passed over more qualified candidates and appointed Nathaniel Greene Taylor, whose selection obviously was based less on qualifications than on patronage.

Writing about Nathaniel's appointment as Indian commissioner, Robert M. Kvasnicka and Herman J. Viola stated that "few men assumed the office of Indian commissioner under more adverse conditions." Browning was upset and wanted to keep the businesslike Bogy. "The secretary was contemptuous of Taylor and did everything he could to maintain Bogy in a position of authority." Bogy was appointed by Browning to handle all of the Indian Office's contracting business. Nathaniel responded to this by saying that he should be able to decide who would be appointed to help him. The Senate Judiciary Committee ruled on March 29 that Browning had exceeded his authority, but Bogy was kept on until June, when Nathaniel wrote the president about the situation. Nathaniel, in a rather lengthy letter to President Johnson on June 15, discussed the "grave differences" between himself and the Interior Secretary, regarding his duties and responsibilities. Taylor pointed out that by law he should be allowed to make certain decisions about his operation even though they had been absorbed by the Interior Department. His appeal to the president was based on the "kind personal relations that have existed between us and the warm political fellowship for six or seven years past." Nathaniel, hoping that Johnson would have confidence in his integrity stated that he would discharge his duties to the credit of Johnson's administration. The outcome of this was that Browning and Bogy capitulated and Taylor could concentrate on the duties of his office.

Problems and Challenges

On Wednesday, March 27, 1867, Nathaniel Greene Taylor, President Andrew Johnson's nominee for Indian Commissioner, was confirmed by the U.S. Senate. While he was Commissioner of Indian Affairs, Taylor's family lived near Laurel, Maryland, just outside of Washington, D.C., and close to the Baltimore and Ohio Railroad which they used to travel into the city. Taylor's son, James Patton, age twenty-two, was married on December 28, 1865, to Mary S. George, and we suspect he was living at home with his parents. He worked in the patent office. Alfred Alexander Taylor, age eighteen, the next in line, worked in the Indian Affairs office, and Robert L., at a youthful sixteen, worked in the Treasury Department. This obviously helped the family financially.

Many issues faced Nathaniel Greene Taylor when he accepted the position of Indian Commissioner. The mindset of many people in the post Civil War period was the same as their ancestors who colonized America. The wilderness they faced was terrifying to them and had to be overcome along with any "savages" they met. Environmental Studies Historian Roderick Nash wrote "Safety and comfort, even necessities like food and shelter, depended on overcoming the wild environment." Progress, as viewed by

Europeans, was advancement from a primitive society to a civilized one. The tribes, different culturally and politically, were seen simply as Indian and labeled savage, or even more cruelly thought of as subhuman, which meant they were thought to be both culturally and morally beneath the standards of civilized Europeans.

Policy makers in the 1850s had yet to confront the problem of how to "civilize" the Indian, as the policy heretofore had been one of removal. By the 1850s most native tribes had been relocated west of the Mississippi River. The government thought of the Indians as wards and therefore treated them as children. Historian Henry G. Waltmann stated that problems caused by lack of a consistent approach to relations with the tribes were understandable. He cited that between 1865 and 1887, there were "ten different secretaries and twelve commissioners. [The] official responsibility for Indian relations resided with the Indian Bureau, but for practical reasons, the army exercised authority over the more uncivilized tribes [or at least those who were hostile]." Waltmann asked two vital and perplexing questions about the Indians: "what should be done with them, and which branch of the government should carry out the will of the government? Should the tribes be dealt with by negotiations as the Interior Department wished or by force as the War Department advocated? Discord between representatives of the civil and military branches was so persistent that, even while serving together on the noted peace commission of 1867-1868, they disputed the course to follow, especially toward the uncivilized tribes." The only civilized tribes, in their opinion, were the Cherokee, Choctaw, Chickasaw, Creek, and Seminole.

The settlement of the western plains obviously impacted the Indian tribes more than it affected any other segment of the population. The depletion by whites of the bison which was the tribes' main source of livelihood was cause for alarm. To stop or forestall settlement Native Americans, in their outrage, cut telegraph lines, attacked pony express riders, railroad survey crews, construction workers, stagecoaches, emigrant trains, farmsteads, gold seekers, forts, and soldiers. The Bureau of Indian Affairs had its hands full trying to establish treaties that the Indians, as well as the military and civilians, would honor. Conflict between Indians and emigrants continued unabated as western expansion increased. The United States "wanted to insure safe passage for its citizens and the safe construction of railroads to facilitate travel and trade between the two coasts." The War Department had politicians clamoring for more protection. Newspapers were vilifying the War Department, and reformers were castigating them for their harsh policies.

Also at issue was land. The natives believed in communal use of large areas of land with vague boundaries. Ownership of land was part of the European economic system, with the rationale that land could not be used unless it was legally acquired. By acknowledging the Indian's title to the western lands, treaties became the means for the United States to make a legitimate claim of ownership. The huge land acquisition gained as a result of the Mexican War had a great impact on Indian policy, as the government was forced not only to provide military protection for large numbers of emigrants but to work out some humane disposition of the Native Americans.

This task fell to the Bureau of Indian Affairs, Department of the Interior, which was headed by a Commissioner of Indian Affairs, with a staff in Washington, D.C., that "functioned mainly through a field force of superintendents and agents." Utley, in his book, *The Indian Frontier*, gets to the point of the problem, saying that the superintendents and agents were part of "the worst evils of the spoils system. Appointments usually went to men with no other qualification than faithful party service." In the angry debates over the Kansas-Nebraska Bill which Senator Stephen A. Douglas and Nathaniel were a part of, Douglas got to the core of the issue stating the railroad could never be a success without joining the two coasts together and settling the land in between.

The problems of the Bureau of Indian Affairs included not only physical but administrative matters such as "supervising thousands of diverse Indians at extensive reservations far from sources of supply, lines of communications, agencies of law and order, and the comforts of civilized life." Historian Henry G. Waltmann supported Utley's position by saying that to aggravate the situation, there were some [not all] underpaid, inexperienced, incompetent, or dishonest agents, unethical contractors, selfish settlers and miners, vituperative editors, critical and often uncooperative soldiers, overzealous reformers, humanitarians, and economy minded congressmen which did not help the situation. "Most agencies were set upon by predatory whiskey-peddlers, gun-runners, traders, hunters, thieves, gamblers, wenchers, and speculators."

The question was what to do with the Indians now that there was no good hunting land to which they could be removed. Utley said "the answer evolved out of a proposal" made in 1848 by Commissioner of Indian Affairs William Medill who suggested "colonies" to gather the Indians into "while the Whites filled in the country around them." By the 1850s the reservation system began to become policy. The whites desired that the Indians be taught farming in order to become self-sufficient. Those in favor of this policy thought it would meet both practical and moral objectives, as it would clear the Indians from the travel routes and settled areas while advancing what one official called the great work of regenerating the Indian race. Congress and the president and his Indian officials often disagreed on which lands to set aside and how much to pay for them, but the policy itself attracted broad and consistent support.

Utley stated that a treaty was "the mechanism for extinguishing title and defining all other relations between the United States and a tribe." The flaw was that the executive or legislative branch did not feel any scruples about violating the treaty nor did the tribes. "An insidious by-product of the treaty system was the annuity system-the practice of paying for land with cash dispensed in annual installments over a period of years." It was fraught with abuse. "Besides the army and the Indian Bureau, a third institution of government dominated Indian relations: the Congress." The former were in the executive branch of government, and were funded by legislation produced in Congress. Both the House and Senate had Indian committees that provided input as to how they thought these two departments should handle Indian relations. Further "the Senate had to consent to presidential notification of Indian treaties in the same manner as for treaties with foreign nations."

Historian Robert G. Athearn identified another factor that came into play, the newspapers, which did not always report the facts nor handle the news in a responsible manner. The western and eastern press argued about how to handle the Indian tribes. "The eastern papers sympathized with the noble savage and counseled kindness while the western press screamed 'kill him.' The army in the middle, managed to please neither side."

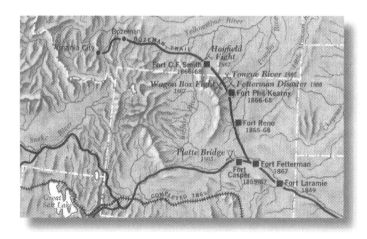

The Bozeman Trail or Powder River Road ran 550 miles from Bridger's Ferry northwest into the Powder River country, to Virginia City, Montana. Forts Phil Kearny, C.F. Smith, and Reno were constructed along the road inciting the Indians to war. From *Soldier and Brave*, National Park Service.

Forts built along the Bozeman Trail to protect gold seekers and emigrants incited the Indians to war. Permission to build forts on Native American lands came from a stipulation in the Fort Laramie Treaty of 1851. Historian Susan Badger Doyle, who edited the diaries of travelers on the Bozeman Trail, wrote that the tribes having "experienced game depletion and habitat deterioration along the main overland routes did not want to see this repeated in the Powder River Basin." The basin was occupied by the Sioux, Northern Cheyenne, and Northern Arapaho, and, according to Doyle, the "so called Sioux Alliance . . . focused its aggressive power on resisting [the] American invasion." Intertribal warfare was part of the culture of these particular Indians yet they were always in close alliance when it was for their common benefit. In Doyle's opinion the emigrant wagon trains provided the Indians attractive new opportunities. She said that in this clash of cultures, what the Americans viewed as stealing, the Indians considered capturing. She added that "to the emigrants an attack, fight, or victim was to the Indian a raid, contest, or target." Still the emigrants, aware of the hazards, chose to take the trail.

According to the Indian commission population report of 1868, with some figures based on estimates, the number of Indians residing within the United States in 1867 was 286,441 when Nathaniel became commissioner. Indian hostilities had continued during the Civil War, and Secretary of War Edwin M. Stanton reported that just over thirty million dollars had been expended for supplies and payment to some twenty five thousand troops engaged against the tribes during 1864 and 1865. For Nathaniel the tribes that were considered to be the crux of the "Indian problem" were the powerful, mounted, warlike, nomadic Apache, Comanche, Crow, Kiowa, and Sioux of the Great Plains and Southwest.

As a result of his congressional experience and his habit of reading newspapers, Nathaniel surely knew the Native American issues needed a better focus. When he took office in 1867, the Pawnee Fork Incident cast him as a major player in developing Indian policy. The incident began with the signing of a treaty in October 1865 in which the government was trying to persuade the Southern Cheyenne to leave the vicinity of the Republican and Smoky Hill Rivers. Although there were no problems in 1866, the presence of armed tribesmen in the path of railroad crews alarmed citizens and the military. Because of pressure from the frontier, Congress appropriated funding for a military expedition into the Central Plains. Accordingly, on February 18, 1867, Sherman directed Maj. Gen. Winfield Scott Hancock to put his troops in readiness. In the Indian Peace Commission's report written on January 7, 1868, it was stated that on March 11, 1867, Major General Hancock wrote Edward T. Wynkoop, the agent for the Cheyenne and Arapaho, "that he had about completed arrangements for moving a force to the plains." Hancock stated his objective was to show the Indians that he was "able to chastise any tribes who may molest people travelling across the Plains." He wanted Wynkoop to tell the Native Americans he was coming "prepared for peace or war." Hancock insisted the Indians keep off the main lines of travel where their presence might create hostilities with the whites. The Peace Commission reported this was a hunting ground for the Indians and was secured by treaty, indicating the tribes could go where they wanted.

Hancock marched 1,400 men to Fort Larned (1859-1878), arriving on April 7. About 1,500 Cheyenne and Sioux were camped thirty miles away at their village on the Pawnee Fork of the Arkansas River. They refused to travel to Fort Larned for peace negotiations so Hancock, on April 13, marched his force to them. The nervous Cheyenne and Sioux fled the village encampment because, as the Peace Commission reported, they remembered Sand Creek and were concerned about such a large military force camping near them. During the Indians exodus, an Overland Stage Company station was attacked and three men were killed. It was attributed to these Indians. Upon being informed about this Hancock ordered his men to burn the village consisting of 272 lodges, destroying in the process huge quantities of belongings and supplies. Following what came to be known as the Pawnee Fork Incident, General Hancock was severely criticized by the Indian Bureau and army officers alike, and a congressional investigation was instigated. In July Sherman considered a report Hancock filed "satisfactory," but General of the Armies, Ulysses S. Grant, thought the Cheyenne and Sioux should be reimbursed.

During the summer of 1867 when the Pawnee Fork Incident was making headlines, West Point graduate, Gen. Alfred Sully, who chaired the commission to investigate the Fetterman Massacre, reported that the Northern Plains Indians wanted peace. His recommendation was that the Bozeman Trail be abandoned, the Platte Route be defended with the military, and eighty thousand square miles of the Missouri and Yellowstone basins be set aside for the Indians. In addition the Indian Bureau should not be placed in the War Department but have its own cabinet level department. The Indian Affairs office favored these recommendations.

The burden of providing for a speedy peace was placed on both the War and Interior departments. On Monday, July 8, 1867, upon a resolution by the Senate, Interior Secretary Browning was asked to submit a report listing existing hostilities by Indian tribes on the frontier and "whether they are waging war as tribes or individuals." The Secretary was also asked to make suggestions that would "lead to the speedy termination of pending hostilities and prevent Indian wars in the future." Secretary of War Edwin M. Stanton was also asked by the Senate to transmit telegram orders that had been issued by the military when "conducting hostile operations against the Indians" and to communicate their reasons for waging war, and how the military had reacted. Secretary Stanton was to suggest the best way to "secure speedy and lasting peace with the Indian tribes." It is important to note that the Senate made a distinction between warring tribes and individual natives taking up arms, a fact which the army and many civilians ignored.

Nathaniel's Recommendations to the Senate

On July 13 Commissioner of Indian Affairs Nathaniel Greene Taylor responded to the Senate's request with his recommendations. He summed up succinctly what was already known, and it was a damning and dismal record of massacres and broken treaties. Taylor explained that the facts he had gathered came from the official records. He referred to the horrible December 1864 Sand Creek Massacre in which friendly Cheyenne and Arapaho in the Colorado Territory were killed. The war occurring in 1865 as a result of Sand Creek not only cost valuable lives but also $40,000,000. Peace was negotiated that year in October. When the commissioners met at Fort Laramie to treat with the Indians in June 1866 they asked them to grant the United States the right to establish posts in what turned out to be the only reliable hunting grounds of the Sioux. While this was being discussed a military command arrived to construct the forts and the Indians withdrew and soon went to war on the Montana Road or Bozeman Trail.

Taylor wrote that the Fort Phil Kearny Massacre, referred to as the Fetterman Massacre (December 1866), involving the Northern Cheyenne, the Arapaho, and the Sioux, and totaling from 1,600 to 1,800 warriors, was probably the cause of the present hostilities with the Indians. Nathaniel also submitted as documentation forty-five telegrams sent since February 21. This also served to illustrate the importance of the telegraph to both departments in communicating with their western employees and officers.

Maj. Gen. John B. Sanborn's report to the Senate gave credence to Taylor's account. As told by Historian Waltmann, Sanborn's report "on the treatment of the Sioux and Cheyenne at Pawnee Fork was a denunciation of General Hancock, western interest groups, and the war policy." Sanborn stated, "this 'revolting' war policy was not in the public interest . . . it [is] a mockery practiced by contractors, ranchers, and certain military leaders. The argument for war to safeguard travel and transportation was an 'absurdity,' for the prerequisite of safety was peace."

In conclusion, Taylor stated that there could be security on the frontier and in the territories without war and at a fraction of what it would cost to wage war. His method was to make right the wrongs committed. To do this, he proposed paying the Arapaho, Cheyenne, and Sioux for the trespass committed by emigrants, for the privilege of right of way, and for posts on their land. To the Southern Cheyenne, he thought the government should restore the property "we so wantonly and foolishly burned." His position, as quoted, was that the United States would only be "doing them justice, as established policy requires, and this makes them our friends at once, renders travel and transportation safe, and garrisons almost useless." He added that "it seems to me there are but two alternatives left us as to what shall be the future of the Indians, namely swift extermination by the sword and famine, or preservation by gradual concentrations on territorial reserves and civilization. . . . The sentiment of our people will not for a moment tolerate the idea of extermination. In my judgment, the Indian can only be saved from extinction by consolidating them as rapidly as it can be peacefully done on larger reservations. Here the natives could be educated, trained in the arts of civilization, and eventually gain citizenship." Thus Nathaniel began advocating for the reservation policy.

Creation of an Indian Peace Commission

Congress was impressed with Indian Commissioner Nathaniel Taylor's recommendations, which indicated he was "looking toward a peaceful resolution of the crisis on the plains, and ready to try a new peace initiative." On July 20, 1867, Congress passed an act called the "Creation of an Indian Peace Commission" with a $500,000 appropriation, which President Andrew Johnson signed on July 30. The act authorized President Johnson to appoint as members of the Indian Peace Commission, Nathaniel Greene Taylor, Commissioner of Indian Affairs, who was a former congressman, Methodist minister, and humanitarian, and a strong advocate for civilian control over the Indians; John B. Henderson, a Senator from Missouri who was sponsor of the legislation and Chairman of the Committee of Indian Affairs of the Senate; Samuel F. Tappan, a Bostonian who came west in 1856 and was a supporter of Indian rights who had headed the military investigation of the Sand Creek Massacre in 1864; and retired Maj. Gen. John B. Sanborn, who had served on the commission which investigated the Fetterman Affair. These four men were named explicitly in the legislation, and the act stated that three other military officers were to be selected. In his book Douglas C. Jones lists those officers, who were appointed by President Johnson. They were "Lieutenant General William Tecumseh Sherman, commander of the Division of the Missouri-he controlled all military troops and installations west of the Mississippi, from Canada to Mexico; Major General William

S. Harney, retired Indian fighter; and Major General Alfred H. Terry, commander of the Department of Dakota. Major General Christopher C. Augur, commander of the Department of the Platte, who at first substituted for Sherman [and later] became a regular member of the commission." Taylor, Henderson, and Tappan were supporters of civilian control of Indian Affairs and of peace. Sherman, Terry, and Augur favored a coercive policy. Seventy year old Major General Harney who had many friends among the Indians and Major General Sanborn who had condemned the military's action at Pawnee Fork held the swing votes. These commissioners were given the power and authority to call the chiefs of the warring tribes together to determine their reasons for hostility, to make treaties at their discretion under the direction of the president, and to establish security along the railroads being constructed in the frontier settlements and on the travel routes to the western territories that would most likely insure civilization for the Indians and peace and safety for the whites.

When discussing the Indian Peace Commission of 1867, Historian Utley stated in his book *Frontier Regulars* that the "Indian administrators and their political supporters held the short-term promise of restoring peace to the Plains and the long-term promise of a solution to the Indian problem." Jones, in *The Treaty of Medicine Lodge*, stated that the Henderson Bill for the peace commission included the phrase "Establishing a system for civilizing . . . [which] was a unique phrase that set the 1867 peace commission apart from the ones before it. It was a definite commitment to something new. No longer was the Indian to be pushed away into some remote corner in the hope that he would behave himself and stay clear of white men. Now he would be remodeled into a red counterpart of the white man."

Jones thought Taylor, of all the commission members, was perhaps the most interesting to the press. Jones' book, based on contemporary newspaper articles, described Taylor "as wearing gold-rimmed eye glasses and a wig, who would go to any lengths to pamper the Indians or curry favor with the president, and enjoyed poetry reading." Sherman, a friend of the frontiersmen, was also well known, and was often quoted in the press. Jones wrote that "reporters who came in close contact with him did not like Sherman personally-in fact, most of them despised him-but they showed a marked respect for him."

On July 22 Nathaniel met with President Johnson to discuss Indian negotiations and the commission's upcoming trip to the west. Shortly afterwards, Taylor, with commission members Tappan and Sanborn and other staff, departed Washington by train for St. Louis, Missouri. Accompanying them was A.S.H. White, a Department of the Interior employee who would assist Taylor as well as being a liaison for the Secretary of the Interior. As Nathaniel traveled west to begin the work of the peace commission, two incidents occurred involving Red Cloud who was opposed to soldiers on the Bozeman Trail. The first occurred on the morning of August 1 when a haying contractor, starting his work about two and one half miles northeast of Fort C.F. Smith, was attacked by Indians. The attack lasted several hours and was known as the "Hayfield Fight." It involved thirty one soldiers and civilians who, from a large fortified corral, held off a huge number of Sioux and Cheyenne. Two soldiers of the 27th Infantry were killed, and three were wounded, as was one civilian. The Indians lost about eight killed and thirty wounded. The second incident occurred on August 2 when woodcutters from Fort Phil Kearny were about five miles west of the fort with their soldier escort. Red Cloud, with about 1,000 warriors, attacked the party of six civilians and twenty-six soldiers who were armed with the new Springfield Model 1866 rapid-firing breech loading rifles. Commanded by Capt. James Powell, the group "took cover inside an oval of wagon boxes used as a stock corral" where three men were killed and two wounded. The Indians suffered higher casualties. It was an ominous beginning for the peace commission. Nathaniel's observation was that the United States in its negotiations failed to give Native Americans a means of redress. The only law the Indians knew was one of retaliation. How to seek legal action was important but difficult to get across to nomadic warriors.

In August and again in November 1867, the Indian Peace Commission met in Parlor No. 5 of the Southern Hotel in St. Louis, Missouri. The hotel, shown in circa 1910, was on Fourth and Walnut Street. It closed in 1912. Missouri State Archives.

On Tuesday, August 6, 1867, with the exception of Major General Terry, the civilian-military commissioners met in the Southern Hotel, St. Louis, Missouri. Here they made their plans and began to organize the Indian Peace Commission. On a motion by General Sherman, Nathaniel G. Taylor was selected as president of the commission, and A.S.H. White was elected secretary. On Wednesday they met at Sherman's headquarters at the military Division of the Missouri. It was agreed that Taylor and Sherman would notify their respective officers and agents to send out runners inviting the western Dakota tribes to meet with the peace commission. Taylor and Sanborn were to purchase all supplies necessary for the Indian visits, but it was Sanborn who actually handled this task.

On Monday August 12, the commissioners traveled to Fort Leavenworth, Kansas, on a fact finding mission. They first interviewed Major General Hancock at his headquarters of the Department of the Missouri which consisted of the states of Missouri and Kansas, the territories of Colorado and New Mexico, and the Indian Territory south of the Arkansas River. Hancock opened the interview by stating that he considered all Indians hostile. When asked why by General Sherman, Hancock responded in a prepared statement that he considered the present war with the Plains Indians due to the crowding of the whites from all directions onto the Indian's hunting grounds reducing the game upon which they depended for food, clothing, and shelter.

On Tuesday the commissioners reconvened at the Planters House, Leavenworth, Kansas. Nathaniel, as president of the commission, suggested that the testimony of those having knowledge of existing facts concerning the Indian difficulties, be taken under oath. This was approved. Those testifying were Col. Jesse H. Leavenworth, U.S. Indian Agent, Thomas Murphy, Superintendent of Indian Affairs, Central Superintendency, D.A. Butterfield, a licensed trader, and John E. Tappan, Fort Dodge, Kansas, a fort sutler.

While at Fort Leavenworth, Taylor met with Murphy to discuss agency business and the arrangements for the upcoming treaty. Superintendent Murphy, headquartered in Atchison, Kansas, had been in office since 1865. He had a large jurisdiction covering Kansas and the Indian Territory and had selected as the place where the Medicine Lodge and Elm Creeks joined, near the southern border of Kansas as the site of the peace talks.

The peace commissioners made plans to continue their fact finding tour on the upper Missouri River while the runners gathered the Indian tribes for the treaty meeting. They wanted to interview residents who knew about the land, its suitability for agriculture, possible sites for reservations, and about the Native Americans in the vicinity. At St. Louis they chartered the steamer *St. John* and purchased the goods they thought suitable as gifts to the Indians. On Friday, August 16, 1867, the peace commission met at 11:30 a.m. on the *St John*. Interest in their work was high, and Nathaniel shared telegrams from Secretary of the Interior Browning and President Johnson. General Sherman informed the commission that General Hancock would make arrangements for meeting the Indians at Fort Larned on October 10, with 50,000 rations being supplied. General Augur would have 100,000 rations at Fort Laramie for that assembly. Sometime after August 16, Nathaniel learned that a family member was sick. He rushed back across the country to his home near Laurel, Maryland. We do not know the details of his return trip, only that he returned west before September 12.

Steaming up the Missouri River on the *St John*, the commissioners arrived near Fort Sully on August 28. General A.H. Terry joined them on August 25, having arrived earlier on the steamer *Guidon*. John B. Sanborn was declared vice president of the commission and conducted meetings on the *St. John* in Taylor's absence. General Sherman informed everyone that, because the river was at a low state and slowing their progress, they would not be able to reach Fort Rice and return in time to keep the September 13 meeting with the Indians at Fort Laramie. The group decided to visit near the Big Cheyenne River and then return to Fort Sully to obtain testimony of Indians and whites about that region and also about the Black Hills.

At Fort Sully the commission met with the Sioux and Dakota Indians, and vice chair Sanborn stated that the president of the United States had sent them to examine the Indian country as to its fitness for a permanent reservation. They wanted to know if the tribes had any complaints, and if so, how their situation could be improved. Two Lance, a Sioux chief, said that they had maintained peace and wanted to keep their land which ran to the head of the Cheyenne River in the Black Hills. Their desire was to be able to move freely about and not be required to stay in one place. They had been practicing farming and were promised farming implements which they had not received. He complained that they were not receiving adequate clothing, and when the annuities reached them, someone had been removing articles beforehand. This was a common complaint among the Indians, and Commissioner Tappan wanted to get to the root of the problem. He recommended that they take the sworn testimony of the agents to the Indian tribes in order to understand their duties, how the goods were obtained, the quality of the goods, and how they were issued. Chairman Taylor of the peace commission had already asked that sworn testimony be taken, but apparently that did not include the employees of the Indian Bureau as evident from Tappan's request.

On Thursday the steamer, *St. John*, arrived near the Ponca Indian Agency where the commissioners met with the Ponca Chiefs to determine their present condition and their needs. Indian Agent J.A. Potter came with the chiefs, and one point they all stressed was the difficulty in raising enough food and having enough to store for the winter. Hard Walker, a Ponca chief, said he was satisfied with their agent. That evening, on board the steamer near the Santee Sioux Agency, the chiefs were told of a proposal to move them to a new permanent home. They reluctantly agreed to consider this.

A meeting was held at the Santee Sioux Agency on the west bank of the Missouri River on September 6. Santee chief Wabasha told how grasshoppers had destroyed their crops, as had others before him. They had been promised good land which they did not receive. They did not want to move, but Senator Henderson spoke, saying that they had come with the plan of settling, if possible, all the Indians between the Niobrara and Cheyenne Rivers. The government wanted them to move because they were on a state boundary, and also they did not believe the soil was good enough for farming. Henderson added that the commissioners had seen a place at White Stone Creek near Fort Randall that he thought the Santee would like very much. There was plenty of timber which they could cut and sell to the steamboats as a way of earning an income. The Santee agreed to examine the lands and give a reply within twenty-five days.

On September 12, Nathaniel joined the commissioners at the military headquarters, Department of the Platte in Omaha, having returned from his trip home. He and Sherman shared dispatches and letters they had received with the assembled group. Nathaniel announced the next day that Alfred H. Love, an influential member of the Society of Friends (Quakers) from Philadelphia, had offered the services of the Quakers to support the purposes for which the commission was organized. After the Civil War, the missionaries and reformers had begun to look into the conditions surrounding the Indians. As historian Utley stated when Nathaniel Greene Taylor and the peace commission began to popularize the idea of "conquest by kindness, the radical idea that the Indian had rights that for humanity's sake ought to be respected took hold." The commission was informed by scouts that the Northern Sioux were waging war on the Powder River and would not meet them at Fort Laramie at the time indicated. As a follow up to the commissioner's meeting with the upper Missouri River tribes, General Sherman agreed to consult with General Terry, commander of the Department of the Dakota, as to the best way to provide relief to the Native Americans whose crops had been destroyed by grasshoppers.

Nathaniel presented a paper from Governor Faulk at the Herndon House on September 14, giving estimates of what would be required to purchase supplies for the various tribes and bands of the upper Missouri River who had been deprived of their means of support for the winter by the destruction of their crops by grasshoppers. After a discussion, Senator Henderson proposed that Commissioner Taylor use the unexpended balance of the appropriated fund for the peace commission for the benefit of those Indians and the motion carried.

Nathaniel opened the September 18, meeting in North Platte, Nebraska. He introduced two long-time residents of the area, Todd Randall and Leon F. Pallaroy, traders with the Sioux in the Fort Laramie vicinity. Mr. Pallaroy was also U.S. Special Interpreter at the Upper Platte Agency. The men gave their views about the condition of the tribes, and whether they were friendly or hostile. Arrangements had been made to hold a council with Spotted Tail, a friendly Sioux of the Brule Band, and other chiefs of various hostile tribes.

On the nineteenth Taylor addressed the assembled Indians, saying the commissioners wanted peace and the great father (President Johnson of the United States) had heard of the troubles between Indians and whites. Testimony was taken from them. Nathaniel also introduced General Harney as the greatest war chief of all times and Sherman as the great warrior who led all the white soldiers on the plains, adding there were also other great war chiefs. He introduced, Senator Henderson, as a great peace chief, who helped make the laws in the great council in Washington. Last of all, he introduced himself as their friend who was speaking to them. He told them that he was the Commissioner of Indian Affairs and superintendent of everything that related to them. Taylor emphasized that the great father would not send all these big chiefs hundreds of miles just to converse with them, but that they were to find out what the trouble was between the white men and the Indians. He asked them to speak freely and to know that a record of the meetings was being kept.

Chief Spotted Tail was blunt and to the point saying the Sioux had put up the lodge, consisting of two teepees, for the big men to assemble in and had come there upon serious business. Spotted Tail said the Indians objected to the Powder River Road and the Smoky Hill Route because the country they lived in was being cut up by the white men who were driving away all the game. He wanted the two roads closed, as they ran through their bison country. He told the commissioners that there was plenty of game in their country at present, and they could not go to farming until that was all gone. They wanted the traders to stay among them. Others that followed reiterated his position, most specifically included the halting the "iron road."

Senator Henderson proposed that Commissioner Taylor, as president of the commission, prepare a paper in response to the Brule and Oglala Sioux, and also to the Cheyenne who were gathered in council. Other members of the commission were to prepare papers, at their option, to be submitted early on September 20 for the consideration of the commission. When they met, Sanborn, Sherman, and Taylor read the papers they had prepared. Tappan moved that Taylor's address be adopted as an answer to the proposition made by the Indians. Terry proposed that Sherman's paper be presented as the view of the entire commission, and a vote confirmed this. The commission agreed to meet the Indians in council at Spotted Tail's camp.

After Nathaniel opened the meeting, General Sherman spoke to the assembled Sioux and Cheyenne, telling them that the peace commission believed the principal cause of the present trouble was building the railroad up Smoky Hill and the wagon road by the Powder River. The government, he remarked, believed that the Smoky Hill Route had been agreed upon by the Cheyenne and Arapaho who owned that country more than five years previously, and had been traveled by stages and wagons ever since. Military posts and mail stations had been there more than two years and were not considered a cause of war when they were constructed. The government thought that the building of a railroad would be no different to the tribes, but to the government it was much quicker and more convenient and was very necessary for people who lived in New Mexico and Colorado. Sherman told the gathered assembly that the peace commissioners were to meet the Cheyenne the next month, and if they learned that the Indians were damaged by the railroad, they would make compensation, but the road must be built and they must not interfere with it. Sherman then moved on to the Powder River Road which had been established a year before, for the purpose of hauling flour, coffee, and sugar to people who were digging for gold in Montana. No white settlements had been made along the road, and the travel did not disturb the bison nor did it destroy the elk and antelope. The Indians were permitted to hunt them as usual. The commission supposed that the Indians in that country had consented to this road in the Treaty at Fort Laramie the previous spring. Sherman said that while the Indians continued to wage war about the road, the government would not give it up. If, on examination at Fort Laramie, they found the Indians were right, they would give up the road or pay them for it.

Sherman also gave the advice the chiefs asked of the commissioners. He was very direct and truthful, stating that the white men, as the chiefs knew, were advancing in all directions, and in spite of all that the tribes might do, the whites would soon have all the good land of the country, so that unless they chose a home now, it might be too late by the next year. If they interfered with the whites, they would be swept out of existence.

He told them that the government proposed for the entire Sioux Nation, them included, to select a country on the Missouri River, embracing the White Earth and Cheyenne Rivers, to be theirs forever. All whites would be kept out, excepting traders and agents. The commission proposed to help the Native Americans if they needed help.

Senator Henderson spoke to the chiefs and the assembly, informing them that the commissioners would meet at Medicine Lodge Creek on October 13, at North Platte on November 1, and at Fort Laramie on November 3. They should decide whether they wanted to meet, and join in the treaty making with other tribes. Afterwards, Swift Bear, Man That Walks Under the Ground, Pawnee Killer, and Big Mouth all spoke saying that they wanted peace, but they needed arms and ammunition to feed themselves during the winter. Nathaniel said he was pleased to hear their talk, and that they had smoked the pipe of peace together, and peace was what the commissioners wanted for both Indians and whites. Nathaniel told them that the commission did not have any ammunition, but they would send word by the "Long Tongue" (telegraph) and have some sent to them at once. He added that the commission would show that they were friends of the Indians by trusting them with ammunition. Ending his talk, Taylor said the commission planned to have a big council with the northern Indians on November 1, at which time they would make a treaty with them. At the conclusion of the meeting, G.B. Willis, the phonographer (one who recorded the talks), was authorized to proceed to St. Louis to make up the record of the testimony.

An 1867 map showing the Union Pacific Railway which stretched to Fort Harker, Kansas (present Ellsworth). The Indian Peace Commission traveled by train to Fort Harker which was a major supply center for military installations in the west. Almost thirty miles southwest was Fort Zarah on the Santa Fe Trail where they

also stopped. Medicine Lodge Creek, the treaty meeting site, was due south of Fort Zarah. They visited briefly at Fort Larned (misspelled on the map) located on the Pawnee River, a tributary of the Arkansas. This fort had also been established to protect mail coaches, freighters, and emigrants on the Santa Fe Trail. Profile Map of the Central Pacific Railroad (Omaha to San Francisco), 1867, *Harper's Weekly*, December 7, 1867, Bruce C. Cooper Collection.

In early October 1867 the commissioners left Fort Leavenworth for Fort Harker, Kansas, (1866-1872) traveling on a section of the Union Pacific Railway which was completed on July 10. The Thirty-eighth Infantry regimental band welcomed them, and the ladies of the fort served refreshments. The next day the travelers crossed the Smoky Hill River and camped on the wind-blown prairie two miles from the fort. As they settled down for the night, the camp was arranged into three parts, an arrangement that was repeated each night during the treaty negotiations. One area was set aside for the commission officials. The Kansas delegation, including Governor Samuel Crawford and Senator E.G. Ross with "secretaries, aides, ambulance drivers, commission cooks, interpreters, and the newspaper reporters," had their spot. The wagon park with the teamsters and picketed mules, which carried gifts for the Indians and the commission's supplies, was nearby. Major Joel H. Elliot was the commander of the military escort, and next day as they moved into unfriendly territory, he had armed troopers flanking their column on each side. Four companies of the Seventh Cavalry had been ordered to escort duty by General Hancock, but only two companies accompanied the peace commission. Also accompanying them were the horse-drawn rapid-firing Gatling guns of B Battery, Fourth Artillery.

On October 9 the expedition traveled about thirty miles and spent the night on Cow Creek near Fort Zarah (1864-1869) on the Santa Fe Trail. On October 10 a meeting of the commissioners took place at Walnut Creek. Nathaniel had received an alarming dispatch from Superintendent Murphy which he read to the other members of the commission. Murphy wrote that he had placed Col. C.A. Butterfield, who was a trader, freighter, and stage line operator on the Kansas frontier, as head of his task force at Medicine Lodge Creek. According to Butterfield, all the provisions for the camp had been issued, but Maj. Meredith H. Kidd, 10th Cavalry, Fort Larned post commandant, had been directed by General Sherman not to allow any more trains to leave for Medicine Lodge until the arrival of the commissioners. With food cut off to the Indians, the commission party was placed in danger from irate warriors and the peace talks were put in jeopardy. The army, from the time the Interior Department gained control of Indian Affairs in 1849, retained the task of feeding the Indians. For the meeting, Sherman ordered 50,000 rations which would provide 150,000 meals. Superintendent Murphy had ensured that the food was sent to Fort Harker at the end of the tracks, from which it was hauled by wagon to Fort Larned. Superintendent Murphy said he did not know what would be the result if they did not get the provisions released. Mr. Sanborn agreed to proceed to Fort Larned and have the Indian goods forwarded. Convening a treaty was not only expensive, but required considerable logistics in order to be maintained.

The commissioners stopped briefly at Fort Larned before going upstream about six miles and crossing the shallow water to the south bank of the Arkansas River. They were now seventy miles from Medicine Lodge Creek where the tribes had agreed to meet. When the peace commissioners arrived, newly hewn sandstone buildings had replaced the dilapidated adobe and wooden houses at the fort. The commission camped in deep buffalo grass one mile from the river and began their meeting with the Kansas delegation. Senator Henderson gave a long recitation on the history of treaties leading up to that time. Governor Crawford appeared to be concerned about the many Indians in his state and feared that Kansas lands would be taken for reservations. The governor submitted a written report, and in his remarks he said that he and the Senator "thought" there would be an Indian war, and they wanted to raise more troops for Kansas. Further, they wanted the already established Osage reservation returned to state control.

Newspaperman Milton Reynolds of the Lawrence *State Journal* was not buying into this charade, and in fact he may have wanted to cover the peace commission in order to get a better look into what the governor's intentions for Kansas really were. Governor Crawford and Senator Ross actually favored war because of the economic gain it would provide for Kansas. In 1867 a single army contract released in Fort Leavenworth "called for hauling supplies to various posts throughout the state. The rates ranged from $1.54 to $1.65 per hundredweight per hundred miles [and] this single contract involved about 1 ½ million pounds of supplies. One good cavalry horse cost an average of $159 . . . [and] a cavalry regiment needed one thousand horses." Reynolds was critical of the governor in his articles, but he never stumbled onto the governor's real motive, which was simply profit.

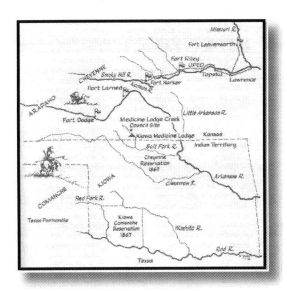

This map shows an approximation of the land claimed by the four major Indian tribes, Arapaho, Cheyenne, Comanche, and Kiowa. The Medicine Lodge Creek Council Site of 1867 was near the present Kansas/Oklahoma border. Fort Harker at the end of the railroad line is at the top of the map. This map "The Troubled Area of 1867" is from *The Treaty of Medicine Lodge* by Douglas C. Jones, Copyright © 1966 by the University of Oklahoma Press, Norman. Reprinted by permission of the publisher. All Rights Reserved.

U.S. Indian Agent Edward W. Wynkoop, Upper Arkansas Agency, was headquartered at Fort Larned, representing the Apache, Arapaho, and Cheyenne. On October 12, before the commissioner's party could depart for Medicine Lodge Creek, they had to wait for Wynkoop and U.S. Indian Agent J.H. Leavenworth who represented the Comanche and Kiowa. At noon the two agents arrived with "thirty additional wagons loaded with Indian gifts." In his book Jones stated that a company of Third Infantry along with a company of the Fifth Infantry were riding in ambulances. This was unusual, for as reported to us enlisted men almost never rode in the Rucker ambulances which held about twelve men. When they departed for Medicine Lodge Creek, newspaperman Reynolds reported 211 vehicles in the two mile long column with 1,250 animals and about 600 men. That night they camped at Rattlesnake Creek.

During the night of October 13, Maj. Gen. C.C. Augur and his aides arrived in camp, having ridden from Fort Harker. The general had with him a presidential order appointing him to serve in Sherman's place. The next day the column continued toward Medicine Lodge Creek, a sacred Indian site. The outriders were pulled back, and the infantry ambulances and troops were moved to the rear of the column. The purpose of this maneuver was to avoid any military pretense or stance that might incite the warriors

Arrival at the Medicine Lodge Creek Council Site

As they approached the site, a small group of painted Indians appeared before them. Nathaniel and the commissioners with their interpreters dismounted and met the welcoming Indians on foot, with embraces and many handshakes. Among the painted Indian leaders was Black Kettle whom Commissioners Sanborn and Tappan knew. Black Kettle had been at Sand Creek in November 1864 when Chivington's men charged into his sleeping camp, killing about 200 people. That Black Kettle could continue to seek peace was remarkable and showed him to be an outstanding statesman and peace advocate. His ability to forgive is almost beyond comprehension. As Taylor, Black Kettle, and other commissioners talked, a reporter, S.F. Hall, noted that Senator Henderson had a bright yellow nose, a red streak on one cheek, and green patches on the other. The colorfully painted Indians with their close hugs had unintentionally decorated him.

The Indian Peace Commission arrived at the northwest end of the basin close to the Arapaho tribe. In front of them, beside Medicine Lodge Creek, was the site where Butterfield dispensed rations. The Cheyenne camp was located across the stream with another site which dispensed rations. Beyond the Arapaho were camped the Apache from the plains. Across the creek from them were the Comanche, and downstream, on the south side, were the Kiowa. Black Kettle was camped near the commissioners, often talking to them each night. Black Kettle shocked the commissioners by suggesting that the Cheyenne camped on the Cimarron might attack the peace meeting.

As the peace commissioners' camp was prepared, the wagons were drawn into a circle. The encampment was closed at night, and no one could leave without a pass from General Harney. Tents were placed in the center near the cook fires. Superintendent Murphy estimated there were about 5,000 Indians present, which included the ones camped nearby and also those on the Cimarron.

On October 15 the first full day of meetings between the Indians and the peace commissioners, the peace council was held in a clearing near the center of a grove of tall elms. They had "casual, unhurried," deliberations, with much smoking and handshaking during the preliminaries. That afternoon Nathaniel called a small number together about a quarter of a mile from the commissioner's camp. A large tent fly had been constructed to provide shade. The reporters described the scene. Nathaniel wore a wide-brimmed felt hat, and dwarfed the camp stool on which he sat. Tappan, with his long drooping mustache, sat whittling on a stick, as he did throughout the conference. Harney, next to Taylor, was sitting stiffly as though at attention. Terry was prim and neat, with his flat stomach, and well fitted uniform. Augur, who sported muttonchop whiskers, sat smoking a cigar. Senator Henderson stood nearby, waiting impatiently for the Comanche to arrive. The Apache, Arapaho, Cheyenne, and Kiowa were already present. Once the Comanche arrived, Nathanial, as chairman, gave a short welcoming speech and then oversaw the distribution of presents of clothing to the Native Americans in attendance. The chiefs then made speeches of welcome, and the group began to discuss when the grand council should begin.

Alfred A. Taylor, the nineteen year old son of Nathaniel, was present at the treaty making. He was an employee of the Indian Affairs office, and this was the chance of a lifetime for him to be introduced to the west, to see Native Americans, and to observe the working relationships among different interests and politicians. He attested to all three treaties that were concluded, and one actually listed him as assistant secretary. Also present was Miss Julia Bent, fifteen year old daughter of the legendary Col. William Bent. Bent was married to Owl Woman, a member of the Cheyenne tribe. His two sons, George and Charles Bent, were also there and were used as runners and possibly interpreters. Mrs. Margaret Adams, a thirty-three year old French-Canadian who spoke fluent English, Kiowa, and Arapaho was brought to the council to interpret for Little Raven. Intelligent and refined, she was dressed in crimson, and wore a black cloth coat with "a small coquettish velvet hat, decorated with a white ostrich feather." Her daughter Virginia accompanied her.

The Indian Peace Commissioners meeting underneath an arbor in an elm tree grove with the Indian chiefs and onlookers in October 1867 at Medicine Lodge Creek. Kiowa Chief Sa-tan-ta (White Bear) is addressing them. This contemporary drawing was

made by Hermann Stieffel, a private of the Fifth infantry, originally from Wiesbaden, Germany, who was one of the guards. Smithsonian American Art Museum.

On October 19, 1867, after some delays and preliminary meetings, the council meeting got underway at the popular sun-dance ground with 5,000 of the Arapaho, Cheyenne, Apache, Comanche and Kiowa in attendance. Historian Waltmann wrote that Senator Henderson spoke to the assembled Native Americans, saying that it was the government's wish that they "settle down and farm on a three million acre reservation between the Red and Washita Rivers. . . . The Cheyenne and Arapaho were to occupy a reservation about half that size further north. This was the government's concentration policy being enacted which forced tribes into specified areas. The United States [it was explained] would provide beef, flour, coffee, sugar, blankets and clothing, farm tools and seed, teachers, carpenters, and blacksmiths—everything the Indians needed to become happy and prosperous like white men."

The tribesmen were not in agreement with this and objected to the terms offered. "Ten Bears, an influential Comanche, decried the loss of his prairie homeland. Santana, the Kiowa 'orator of the Plains,' complained about the wrongs suffered by his tribe before consenting to the government's demands." Black Kettle of the Cheyenne, Little Raven of the Arapaho and others made their speeches. Reluctantly, with winter coming on and with the prospects of presents, most of the tribesmen sought peace. Three separate treaties were signed by the tribesmen and the seven commissioners. Historian Robert M. Utley wrote that "in short, nomadic warrior-huntsmen were to be transformed into sedentary agriculturalists and inculcated with Anglo-Saxon values."

Signing of the Medicine Lodge Peace Treaties

The peace commissioners, representing the United States, signed the first peace treaty, later referred to as the original treaty, with the Kiowa and Comanche. The Indians agreed to the treaty in exchange for land which would be set aside as a reservation for them where no whites, other than employees of the U.S. Government, could enter. The government promised to construct buildings for their use and gave the heads of families exclusive possession of 320 acres of land if they took up farming. "To insure the civilization of the tribes" the tribal leaders recognized education was needed and pledged "themselves to compel their children, male and female, between the ages of six and sixteen years to attend school." The commissioners promised that the annuities named under the treaty of October 18, 1865, at the mouth of the Little Arkansas, would continue to be delivered annually on October 15 for thirty years.

On the basis of these promises, the tribes agreed to relinquish their claim to all other lands outside the proposed reservation but retained the right to hunt the bison, as long as they remained south of the Arkansas River. They also agreed to withdraw all opposition to the railroads being constructed and to not attack emigrants. "The Medicine Lodge treaties embodied the principles of the concentration [or reservation] policy. . . . With the laying out of reservations, the tenets of concentration as applied in the Medicine Lodge treaties" was urged as the foundation of future U.S. Indian policy."

As president of the Indian Peace Commission, Nathaniel Greene Taylor signed the treaty along with fellow commissioners, Wm. S. Harney, Bvt. Maj. Gen. Alfred H. Terry, Brig. and Bvt. Maj. Gen. John B. Sanborn, Samuel F. Tappan, and J.B. Henderson. Signing with their mark for the Kiowa, were Santank, or Sitting Bear, Sa-tan-ta, or White Bear, Black Eagle, Kicking Eagle, Stinking Saddle, Woman's Heart, Stumbling Bear, One Bear, The Crow, and Bear Lying Down. Ten Bears, Painted Lips, Silver Brooch, Standing Feather, Gap in the Woods, Horse's Back, Wolf's Name, Little Horn, Iron Mountain, and Dog Fat signed for the Comanche. Those that attested to or affirmed their names were James A. Hardie, Inspector-General, U.S. Army; Samuel S. Smoot, U.S. Surveyor; Philip McCusker, Interpreter; J. H. Leavenworth, United States Indian agent; Thomas Murphy, superintendent Indian affairs; Henry Stanley, correspondent; Alfred A. Taylor, assistant secretary; William Fayel, correspondent; James G. Taylor, artist; George B. Willis, phonographer; and C. W. Whitaker, trader. This treaty, signed on October 21, 1867, was ratified by the U.S. Senate on July 25, 1868, and proclaimed on August 25, 1868.

The second treaty, also dated October 21, 1867, included the Apache who wanted to be confederated with the Kiowa and Comanche in order to be placed on equal footing with them. This treaty was signed by the same commissioners and chiefs of the Kiowa and Comanche tribes as in the first. Signing for the Apache were Wolf's Sleeve, Poor Bear, Bad Back, Brave Man, Iron Shirt, and White Horn. Those affirming the treaty were Ashton S. H. White, secretary; George B. Willis, reporter; Philip McCusker, Interpreter; John D. Howland, clerk of the Indian Commission; Samuel S. Smoot, United States surveyor; Alfred A. Taylor; J. H. Leavenworth; United States Indian agent, Thomas Murphy, superintendent Indian affairs; and Joel H. Elliott, Major, Seventh U.S. Cavalry. This treaty was proclaimed on August 25, 1868.

The third treaty which was consummated on October 28, 1867, was with the Cheyenne and Arapaho. It was essentially the same as the original treaty, with the exception that the reservation assigned was different. Bull Bear, Black Kettle, Little Bear, Spotted Elk, Buffalo Chief, Slim Face, Gray Head, Little Rock, Curly Hair,

Tall Bull, White Horse, Little Robe, Whirlwind, and Heap of Birds signed for the Cheyenne. Little Raven, Yellow Bear, Storm, White Rabbit, Spotted Wolf, Little Big Mouth, Young Colt, and Tall Bear signed for the Arapaho. Those affirming the treaty were C.W. Whitaker, interpreter; H. Douglas, Major, Third Infantry; John D. Howland, clerk for the Indian Commission; Samuel S. Smoot, United States surveyor; Alfred A. Taylor; John S. Smith, United States interpreter; George Bent, Interpreter; and Thomas Murphy, superintendent of Indian affairs.

After signing the third treaty the commissioners made their way to Fort Laramie, Dakota Territory, where they agreed that a treaty should be prepared and signed by the chiefs of the Sioux and Cheyenne who were camped on the Republican River at North Platte. Red Cloud, a Sioux leader, would not attend the council meeting so Nathaniel met with the peaceful Crow, but treaties were not signed. The disappointed commissioners rescheduled their meeting for the spring. The work of the peace commission was being commented on in the press, and the *Nation* indicated it was cheaper to treat with the Indians than to coerce them. The *Nation*, in its October 31, 1867, issue, estimated that it would cost $70,000 to kill each Indian. Major General Henry H. Sibley who had been Secretary Browning's choice for Indian Commissioner when Nathaniel Greene Taylor was chosen, was not for "purchased peace," and he demanded a full scale war, thinking that spending eight to ten million dollars would "suffice to close the war within two years."

On December 11-12, 1867, the Indian Peace Commission on Indian Affairs met in the U.S. Senate Committee Room in Washington, D.C. The report that was to be made to the president of the United States was among the topics of discussion. Senator Henderson, General Sherman, and Indian Commissioner Taylor were selected to write the report. They discussed whether or not to abandon the Powder River Road, but no decision was reached. A delegation from the Society of Friends, who wished to express their views about the welfare, education, and improvement of the Indians, made a presentation.

On January 7, 1868, the commissioners met in Taylor's office of Indian Affairs in Washington, D.C. They passed a motion made by Mr. Sanborn which paid them ten dollars a day, plus five dollars per day for personal expenses, and ten cents per mile for traveling expenses. The report to the president was considered, further amended, and unanimously adopted and signed. The commission delivered the report to President Johnson at the Executive Mansion the next day with accompanying journals, treaties, statements, and documents, comprising the record of the commission.

In the report to the president and Congress, the commissioners "reviewed the causes of the Indian hostilities and severely indicted white treatment of the Indians."

Nathaniel was compassionate, lamenting that "no one pays any attention to Indian matters." He believed race, customs, manners, and language were the factors that kept the Indians and whites apart. The committee's recommendation was one of acculturation. Nathaniel visualized white and Indian neighbors having an understanding whereby they could live in harmony.

The report, showing the influence of Taylor, highlighted the fact that white men only wanted the Indian lands. It indicted those men who had profited by the taking of those lands by force or fraud and who refused to support peace. To secure the frontier settlements and the building of the railroad, and to maintain peace, the settlers should, according to the report, treat the Indians with humanity. The railroad directors had to make sure that the Indians were not shot down by railroad employees in wanton cruelty. The tribes must be seen as deserving their sympathy and care instead of as wild beasts. The commissioners did not want to put an end to the development of the frontier, but they condemned the widespread lies, violence, and broken treaties. It was likely that memories of the bipartisan bitterness of the Civil War contributed to Taylor's sympathy for the Indians.

Results of the Medicine Lodge Negotiations

There were eleven recommendations made by the commissioners towards improving relations and suggesting policy with the Native Americans. These touched on trading, deciding whether the bureau should be in the civil or military department of government. They wanted to prohibit governors of the territories from allowing settlements on Indian lands before treaties were signed. The governors would not be able to call up troops for war against the Native Americans. The government also noted that the tribes must be protected from unscrupulous traders. They also recommended that either a new commission be appointed or that they be authorized to meet with the Sioux the next spring with authority to conclude treaties with those tribes confessedly at peace.

The War Department and Bureau of Indian Affairs spent the winter planning for the coming summer with the tribes. Accordingly, Nathaniel wrote traders and interpreters, including Rev. Pierre Jean De Smet, a Jesuit missionary, asking that they invite the Arapaho, Northern Cheyenne, and Sioux to Fort Laramie for a council meeting in April 1868. The Union Pacific Railroad had reached Cheyenne, Wyoming Territory, and General Sherman was pleased on two accounts. The forts on the Bozeman Trail could be closed, and he now had transportation in order to move troops further and more quickly than ever before.

In 1867 an annual pass was issued for Col. N. G. Taylor and his son, with the title of Commissioner, Indian Peace Commission, on the North Missouri Railway and branch line. At St. Louis prior to the 1874 completion of the Eads Bridge for railroad traffic across the Mississippi River, passengers and goods had to be ferried across. Located on the St. Louis side of the river, the North Missouri Railway continued railroad service, running northwest across the Missouri River toward Allen and Macon, Missouri. B. Harrison Taylor Collection.

On March 14, 1868, the Indian Peace Commission met in Nathaniel's office of the Commissioner of Indian Affairs in Washington, D.C. where Nathaniel moved that the commission meet in Omaha at the Cozzen Hotel. They met on April 1, and in addition to the peace commissioners, Governor Faulk of the Dakota Territory and Father DeSmet, both invited guests attended. Nathaniel was not present, and Senator Henderson had been detained in Washington because of the impeachment trial of Nathaniel's benefactor President Andrew Johnson. General Sherman announced that he had been summoned to Washington by the president, and left the next day. General C.C. Augur filled in for him at the meeting. The commissioners prepared a letter, urging General Sherman, Senator Henderson, and Commissioner Taylor to go before both houses of Congress to argue for the approval of a bill setting apart two "Grand Reservations" for use of the tribes, with an appropriation of two million dollars to be used by the governors and general superintendents to provide for the Indians who settled within those reservations. Before he left Sherman stated he was convinced that over the coming years all the Indians east of the Rocky Mountains should be gradually assembled in the two territories that had been defined and that, through gradual influences, this would lead to their ultimate civilization. He added he would vote against giving ammunition or any arms to the Indians who resided beyond these boundaries.

Spring was approaching as the commissioners traveled to Fort Laramie where they hoped all the tribes would be gathered for their prearranged meeting. "The way had been paved for this meeting by the government's willingness to withdraw the posts from the Powder River country." The tribes slowly came in, and a treaty was signed on April 29. The treaty pledged peace, "fixed the boundaries of the Sioux reservation in what became South Dakota; closed the Bozeman Trail and withdrew the military posts to protect it, authorized the natives to hunt north of the Platte and in the Republican and Powder River regions" for as long as the bison lasted. Financial and technical assistance "was provided to those taking up farming," rations were promised to those who settled on the reservation, and "an annual clothing allowance with cash-equivalent annuities for thirty years" was promised. On May 7 the Crow signed a separate treaty, and on May 10 the Cheyenne and Northern Arapaho signed.

Before the summer was out, the commission had a full plate in terms of signing treaties with various tribes. Francis Paul Prucha writing in his classic, *American Indian Treaties*, says "the treaties of 1867 and 1868 signed by the United States Indian Peace Commission were the most important of the final Indian treaties, and they epitomized the radical reformist Indian policy that emerged in the years immediately following the Civil War. The treaties of 1865 on the southern and northern plains" were proven ineffective. The deteriorating condition of Indian tribes and their hostility was a cause for alarm and needed to be solved. Historian Prucha said the action of the 1867 peace commission "crystallized in a firm recommendation for a reservation scheme by which the plains Indians would be moved out of the way of the whites [and was an] absolute necessity . . . in order to save the Indians. The Indians should be made to move to the reservations, where they would be given livestock, agricultural implements, and spinning and weaving equipment to enable them to move toward self-support; schooling in letters and industry; and missionary instruction in Christianity. There they could be isolated from all whites except government employees and some others who would be permitted on the reservations."

Nathaniel's objective was to bring the Indian tribes together to keep the peace with the whites, to provide for them a suitable reservation, and a means to obtain an education and become "civilized." He divided the commissioners and gave out assignments to each because they had a great deal of negotiating to do before summers end. At Fort Laramie, Harney and Sanborn waited on Red Cloud and Man-Afraid-of-His-Horses. Harney and Sanborn treated with other Missouri River tribes. Generals Augur, Sherman, Tappan, and Terry left for Cheyenne. From there, Augur proceeded to Fort Bridger where the Shoshone were waiting. Terry went to Forts Randall and Sully to treat with the Sioux.

On May 13 after arriving in Cheyenne, Sherman and Tappan traveled to Fort Sumner in eastern New Mexico to meet with the Navajo on May 28. The treaty Sherman and

Tappan concluded was part of the major reformist policy advocated by Taylor. About 8,000 Navajo were captured in the 1863-1864 military campaign led by Col. Christopher "Kit" Carson and moved from northeastern Arizona to the Bosque Redondo Reservation in eastern New Mexico on the Pecos River. The treaty Sherman and Tappan signed at nearby Fort Sumner with the Navajo Nation on June 1, 1868, allowed the imprisoned Navajo to relocate to a six-million acre reservation that included their ancestral homeland at Canyon de Chelly, Arizona. They continued their work and "in mid-June the two peace-makers, Sherman and Tappan, conferred with Ute leaders north of Fort Union.

Between mid-February and April 6, 1868, Nathaniel wrote Interior Secretary Orville Browning, expressing the need for a quick appropriation "to keep the faith of the government and the promises of the Indian Peace Commission." Nathaniel was alarmed and insisted that his bureau not "be held liable for hostilities or depredations by needy red men." The annual appropriation was not passed by Congress until July 27, and $500,000 of that amount was to be disbursed under the direction of General Sherman. Sherman realized the funding for the Indians should be disbursed quickly. "Superintendent Thomas Murphy some time earlier reported the Cheyenne, Arapaho, and Apache of the Southern Plains [were] near starvation and in a state of unrest." Of this fund, about which Nathaniel was so concerned, $150,000 was owed for outstanding claims against the commission and had to be paid. The remainder was allocated and handled through the Army's quartermaster and commissary departments.

The Indian Peace Commissioners signed the Treaty of Fort Laramie, Wyoming, on April 29, 1868. In the treaty the United States agreed to quit the Bozeman Trail, abandoning the military forts on it. Although not known at the time it also designated

the gold rich Black Hills of South Dakota as a reservation. Shown here negotiating with the Sioux from left to right are: Unknown, Maj. Gen. William S. Harney, Lt. Gen. William T. Sherman, Unknown, Maj. Gen. Christopher C. Augur, Maj. Gen. Alfred H. Terry, and Unknown. The individual on the far right has often been incorrectly identified as Nathaniel Greene Taylor. Alexander Gardner, 1868, National Archives.

General Sherman issued General Order No. 4 to department, district, and post commanders on August 10, 1868, enabling them to move tribes to their new homes, using the funds he had been allocated. "Major General W.S. Harney relocated the Sioux Nation [to what amounted to the western half of present South Dakota]. Major General W.B. Hazen relocated the Cheyenne, Arapaho, Kiowa, and Comanche [to Oklahoma]. Major General George W. Getty relocated the Navajo, Major R.S. LaMotte the Crow, and Major General C.C. Augur the Shoshone, and allied tribes." Once the tribes arrived on the assigned reservations and were settled, civilian agents were appointed to care for them, and the army's authority ceased. The Interior Department then had charge of the reservations.

On August 10, 1868, about two hundred Cheyenne, along with a few Arapaho and Sioux, attacked settlers between the Solomon and Saline Rivers in northwestern Kansas. They killed "fifteen men, [raped] women, captured children, and destroyed property." This, of course, violated the Treaty of Medicine Lodge. Civil and military authorities could not agree on why the Cheyenne perpetuated these attacks. Commissioner Taylor did not defend the Indians, but he believed the attacks were based on revenge because the supplies, including arms and ammunition, promised by the peace commission were not delivered. General Sherman believed the Cheyenne had learned of the government's concession to the Sioux concerning the abandonment of the Bozeman forts, and they wanted to achieve the same goal for the Smoky Hill region. Later investigation did prove that the whites had not provoked the Indians. Sherman's patience ran out and he ordered "[Major General Philip] Sheridan to herd the Indians south of the Kansas line at once, killing those who resisted. 'This amounts to war,'" he reported. As a result of the effort to move the Indians to reservations, many young warriors became hostile, and across the western frontier, seventy-nine deaths were attributed to the Cheyenne in August and September.

Abraham Jobe, Special Agent to the Chippewa

In August 1868 while Dr. Abraham Jobe was on a trip to Washington, D.C., Secretary of the Interior, Orville H. Browning, met with him. Nathaniel had no doubt informed the secretary of Jobe's past experiences with Indians. Dr. Jobe, born in Carter County, Tennessee, was Nathaniel's lifelong friend. Jobe had lived among the Cherokee and Creek Indians and held many of the same beliefs as Taylor. After the Civil War, he worked as a special agent for the post office department in Raleigh, North Carolina. Dr. Jobe's Indian experience and Taylor's job as Indian Commissioner reinforced their friendship. Browning requested that Jobe visit the Chippewa, a problem area for Nathaniel, adding that it was a dangerous mission. Jobe accepted the job and requested and received a two month leave from the postal department.

Jobe led the diplomatic mission to the Chippewa Indian reservations in northern Minnesota. His memoir of this trip, as historian and biographer David C. Hsiung explains in *A Mountaineer in Motion*, that when the U.S. Government in Minnesota tried to "civilize" the Chippewa Indians, one faction of the tribe accepted this, but they still wanted to pursue the age old practice of subsistence hunting. Another faction, consisting mostly of young warriors, resisted the government's attempt to settle and Christianize them. In 1863 the Chippewa sold their land along the Mississippi River to the government and relocated to the Leech Lake region. An 1867 treaty allocated lots to individual Indian families, which created problems with whites who were taking advantage wherever they could. Historian Bob Moore of the National Park Service states that the Indian "family allotments were smaller than tribal allotments and could be purchased or swindled away from an individual, unlike tribal grants which needed the concurrence of the entire tribe to be sold." Lack of land for hunting was a major issue for the Indians, leading to the assassination of one chief by a rival group. In 1868 part of the Chippewa Indians moved to the White Earth Reservation, while the others remained at Leech Lake.

Hsiung wrote that "from the United States Government's perspective, the treaties offered a consistent package of promises of money, goods, services, reservations of land and rights to resources, all in return for cession of specific Chippewa lands. . . . The government faced difficulties during the treaty negotiations. One problem arose from the organization of Chippewa society, which was separated into different regions. . . . The second problem . . . [was that] each land cession brought greater numbers of Americans, increased commercial logging, and triggered the arrival of additional missionaries. . . . The third issue was that many Chippewa opposed these treaties because the United States fell behind in making the annuity payments and because fraud often whittled down the size of those payments. In the debate over how to respond to these challenges, the Indians split into two competing groups."

In September 1868, Jobe, as Special Agent of Indian Affairs, left Washington, D.C. for Chicago with Nathaniel, and his wife Emeline and their oldest son James Patton Taylor. Also on the trip was Sue Gillespie, James' fiancée. After three and a half days in Chicago, they departed for Milwaukee and Prairie du Chien, crossing the Mississippi River at McGregor. At St. Cloud, the farthest they could go by train. Jobe "left St. Cloud in a buggy . . . with Joel B. Bassett, the local Indian agent, arriving at the Indian Agency, a distance of sixty-five miles, just after dark." The rest of the party arrived at the agency on September 15.

Dr. Jobe quickly became aware of the discontent and ill feeling among the Chippewa Indians while visiting the Chippewa or Ojibwa Nation. Several days were spent with the Indians, and Nathaniel held one council meeting with them. Nathaniel and Dr. Jobe parted ways at Little Falls, Minnesota. Taylor and his party went to Michigan to visit another tribe. Jobe left with his party for a hazardous undertaking. The War Department furnished Dr. Jobe with thirty soldiers and an officer, as guards, plus fourteen wagons carrying supplies for the Indians. Included in his party were three clergymen, representing the Methodist, Presbyterian, and Roman Catholic faith. The main objective of Jobe's trip was to look into the many complaints of prominent Minnesota citizens who were fearful of war. He was to determine the situation and to make recommendations to Secretary Browning. We do not have the results of his report. Jobe was trying to draw the two competing groups (White Earth and Leech Lake) together hoping to establish a working relationship with them and the U.S. Government. In late September, when he met with the White Earth group, they complained about the government's treaty stipulations, which Jobe painstakingly explained that they misunderstood. He assured them that the government would carry out the treaty in good faith. The Leech Lake Indians were very hostile and Jobe feared for his life. He had little success drawing them out or establishing any sort of mutual trust with them. He thought the annuity payments were a mistake and we assume this was included in his report. The Indians were making more demands than could be met for annuity payments; in addition, he thought that their dependence on those payments kept the Indians from hunting and supporting themselves. On October 20, 1868, Dr. Jobe turned in his report and was paid $1,057 for his service.

The Chicago Meeting, Final Recommendations

On October 7, 1868, members of the peace commission convened in Chicago to review their work and to make final recommendations to the president. Samuel F. Tappan, a member of the commission, was urging Sherman not to go to war but to take a more conciliatory tone. There was support for Sherman's position from an unlikely source, the *New York Times*, which in an editorial praised his vigorous measures. Senator Henderson was not present in Chicago while the commission deliberated for three days, leaving only Taylor and Tappan opposed to the use of force. General Grant, commander of all the armies, was in Chicago and sat in on the meetings, supporting Sherman.

The Indians, in the Medicine Lodge Treaty, had been given the right to hunt outside their reservations, but a resolution proposed by General Terry, passed by the commissioners stated that only when peace was restored could the natives leave the reservation. The military was empowered to force any Indian back to their lands. By October 9 the commission had reversed the stance which they had assumed in the Medicine Lodge Treaty. The war advocates now had the votes to pass six resolutions that were significant. The first was that provision and supplies only be furnished to the eleven tribes who had settled or would soon settle permanently on agricultural reservations. "The second proposed recognition of only those treaties, ratified or pending, which affected these same tribes. The third called for an end to the recognition of Indian tribes as 'domestic dependent nations' . . . and the application of civil law to Indians. This meant the end of negotiating treaties. The fourth recommended that, because of treaty violations, tribes under the Medicine Lodge Creek treaties would no longer be permitted to roam and hunt outside their reservations. The fifth proposed the use of military force to compel unwilling natives to move to reservations after due notice and provision for rations and protection. Significantly, the last resolution stated. ' . . . in the opinion of this commission the Office of Indian Affairs should be transferred from the Department of the Interior to the Department of War.'" Now the policy of confinement had been confirmed.

These resolutions were the beginning of a major shift in the United States policy toward the Native Americans. Historian Francis Paul Prucha, an authority on Indian affairs, stated that the treaties of Taylor's Indian Peace Commission "epitomized the reformist Indian policy" that emerged in the following years. The tribes were placed on reservations and efforts were made to provide them an education, teach them good agricultural practices, give them the necessary agricultural implements, and "civilize" them. A significant change was that the tribes were not recognized as independent nations as they had been from colonial times. This would shape the 1871 policy which led to the abolishment of treaties.

The October resolution, suggesting the Office of Indian Affairs be transferred to the War Department, irritated Nathaniel so much that when he submitted the commissioner's 1868 annual report in November, he devoted sixteen pages to why the office of Indian Affairs should not be transferred out of the Interior Department. His reasoning and logic were sound. He listed eleven reasons and expounded on each. Nathaniel insisted that the successful management of his Indian Affairs agency was too important to be transferred to the War department. He believed the transfer would promote war and that the War department's earlier attempt to manage Native American affairs was a failure. Nathaniel's remarks were passionate with a caring attitude for Native Americans as he tried to protect his own agency.

Indian Peace Commissioner Samuel F. Tappan wrote to Nathaniel from Washington, D.C., saying that from a newspaper account of December 4, 1868, he had learned about "an engagement . . . between a detachment of United States troops and a company of Cheyenne Indians, near the Washita River, Indian Territory." He feared that the Indian tribes would unite in war against the army and settlers unless the present war policy was immediately abandoned and all treaty stipulation with the tribes guaranteed. In his long letter, Tappan stated that Nathaniel should not respond "to the oft-repeated assertion that the efforts of the Indian Peace Commission" had proven a failure. As far as the commission itself was concerned, Tappan said its mission and its laborers had been pre-eminently successful; for wherever the commission had been enabled to carry out its plans, and fulfill its promises, its efforts for peace and settlement of Indian troubles had succeeded, and none of the Indians had disappointed them. The Indians the peace commission met with at Medicine Lodge Creek in 1867 had "remained at peace for nearly a year and were compelled to go to war in self preservation." Tappan voiced his concern about the delay of Congress in making its appropriations and the subsequent annuity payments, as well as the way some military officer's aggressiveness with the Indians forced them into war. He reminded Nathaniel that those Indians the commission met in 1868 numbering "from 75,000 to 100,000 [were] at peace and carrying out the plans and purposes of the commission."

After the October peace commission meeting, "Sherman and Sheridan were determined upon a winter campaign to drive the tribes to their reservations and to harry and kill those who refused to settle down, with none too great care to separate those who were actually hostile from those who hoped to remain at peace." The Battle of the Washita in the 1868-1869 winter campaign was the result of Lieutenant

General Sherman's goal, to clear the land between the Arkansas and Platte Rivers of Native Americans. Sherman wanted the southern Plains tribes to be concentrated southward toward the Indian Territory "and locked to the institutions of control and acculturation envisioned by the [Indian] Peace Commission of 1867." This winter operation, led by Maj. Gen. Philip H. Sheridan, Department of the Missouri, contributed toward forcing the Indians to accept reservation life.

In August Sherman had "created two military districts, one for the Sioux under Gen. William S. Harney, and another for the Cheyenne, Arapaho, Kiowa, and Comanche under Hazen. They were to act as 'agents' for the Indians not on reservations." Black Kettle confessed that he could not keep the young warriors from going out on raiding parties. Although informed that not all the Cheyenne were hostile, Hazen chose not to use this information. About mid-November 1868, Cheyenne Chiefs Black Kettle and Little Robe went to Fort Cobb, Oklahoma Territory, on the Washita River, seeking a peaceful solution from Bvt. Maj. Gen. William B. Hazen, but Hazen refused to meet with them.

Historian Utley stated that during this operation, Camp Supply, Oklahoma Territory, on the North Canadian River, was established 100 miles south of Fort Dodge. It was near Camp Supply that a trail in the snow left by one hundred warriors returning to Black Kettle's camp was discovered, alerting the army to the presence of the Indians. Sheridan ordered Lt. Col. (brevet major general) George A. Custer to take 800 men of the Seventh Cavalry to pursue the Cheyenne. Custer remembered that in an incident at Pawnee Fork in April 1867 the Cheyenne and Sioux escaped, and he was not about to let this happen again. In that battle he had chased the departing Indians, at times becoming the pursued, without success. His loss of animals and equipment and the toll on his men was devastating. At Washita he was determined to bring the Indians quickly to battle.

Cheyenne Chief Black Kettle (Moke-tavato) for years had sought peace with the whites because he thought an accommodation could be reached whereby they could live peacefully together. Toward that purpose he signed the Fort Wise Treaty in 1861. Black Kettle survived the attack on his sleeping village by the Third Colorado Cavalry on November 29, 1864, where his wife, Medicine Woman, was horribly wounded. Still determined for peace in October 1865 he signed the Little Arkansas Treaty and in October 1867 the Medicine Lodge Creek Treaty. He and his wife were killed on November 27, 1868, in a predawn attack by the Seventh U.S. Cavalry at their Washita River campsite near present Cheyenne, Oklahoma. Drawn from a photograph of Black Kettle by John Metcalf. Research Division of the Oklahoma Historical Society.

On November 23 there was a foot of snow on the ground when Custer left Camp Supply with his troopers and a long supply train. For four days they searched for the Indians and finally found them in camp on the Washita River. On Friday, November 27, Custer's Seventh Cavalry attacked the camp of Chief Black Kettle, who perhaps unknown to him, held four white captives, two of whom were killed by the Cheyenne when the attack began. The warriors fought desperately to defend their families. Maj. Joel H. Elliott, with fifteen men, chased a fleeing group downstream and was wiped out by the Indians.

In the attack on the fifty-one lodges, Custer reported killing 100 men, women, and children, but the Cheyenne only claimed losses of thirteen warriors, sixteen women, and nine children. Custer lost twenty-one killed and fourteen wounded. Among the Cheyenne casualties were Chief Black Kettle and his wife, Medicine Woman. Later, Custer ordered the slaughter of all the Indian livestock which consisted of about 875 animals. The lodges, with all their winter supply of food and clothing, were burned and destroyed. The Cheyenne were devastated by the loss of their foodstuffs and transportation. This action insured all out war and was compared to the Sand Creek Massacre.

The capable Edward W. Wynkoop, agent to the Cheyenne and Arapaho, wrote the eastern newspapers of his displeasure at the attack on peaceful Indians (although they did harbor hostile ones) and resigned in protest. The job of Taylor's commission, which laid the ground work for the peace that Congress sought, was made more difficult by Sheridan's winter campaign. However, President Grant's administration later pursued the reservation system Taylor advocated, but abandoned the treaty system recommended by the peace commission.

Taylor as a Reformist

When Nathaniel was appointed Commissioner of Indian Affairs he faced a monumental task. Policy makers had struggled for years with how to treat with the Native Americans. The tribes, different culturally and politically, were seen as savages. The government did not know what to do with them. After the Civil War thousands of white emigrants went west seeking land for a better life and in the process destroyed the way of life of the Indians. This led to conflict and the United States responded by building forts along the emigrant routes and increasing the size of the military. There was no more land for them. Native Americans believed in communal use of large areas of land based on animal migration. Europeans believed in land ownership. Treaties became the means by which the government could make a legitimate claim of ownership.

Commissioner Taylor responded to a request by the U.S. Senate on how to treat with the tribes, and he made recommendations they were favorably impressed with. His approach toward Native Americans was one of conciliation. He advocated payment for the wrongs the Native Americans had suffered at the hands of the whites, payment for rights of way across their property and for military forts on their land. He encouraged friendship with them. He favored the reservation policy, in part, to avoid extermination of the tribes. The Congress responded in July 1867 by creating an Indian Peace Commission that he would lead.

The Indian Peace Commission had as its charge to restore peace on the prairie and find a long term solution for the Native American problem. It was a unique commission, and in late July 1867 Nathaniel and the seven other commissioners went west to begin their work. This commission was of such significance that nine newspapermen reported on its every activity. Nathaniel's peace commission made many important recommendations toward improving relations and policy with the Native Americans. Noted historian Frances Paul Prucha wrote that the treaties under Nathaniel's tenure were the most important to the final Indian treaties that "epitomized the radical reformist Indian policy" after the Civil War. They crystallized the need for a reservation system in order to save the Indians.

The Indian Peace Commission was a major effort by the government to treat with the Native Americans. Taylor's commission began a reformist movement and a major shift in the United States policy toward the issue. A significant part of this policy was the freeing of some 7,200 Navajo held in eastern New Mexico who were allowed by an 1868 treaty to return to their homeland in northern Arizona. In the following years, historian Frances Paul Prucha noted that while the tribes were placed on reservations, efforts were made to provide them an education, and to teach them good agricultural practices leading to self sufficiency. In August 1868 Commissioner Taylor signed the last treaty (with the Nez Perce tribe) between the United States and the Native Americans. This event marked a major change in dealing with the tribes because they were no longer recognized as independent tribes or sovereignties, which eventually led to the abolishment of treaties in 1871. As mentioned earlier, Taylor and the reformists did not support the change.

On March 4, 1869, Ulysses S. Grant, at age forty-six, entered the White House as president. The next day Jacob Cox was appointed as the new Secretary of the Interior, and even though Nathaniel wanted to stay on as Commissioner of Indian Affairs, he reluctantly had to resign on April 21, 1869, as it was customary for each new secretary to choose his own Indian Commissioner. Leaving his home in Maryland, he returned to Tennessee, where it was said he moved to his father-in-law's (David Haynes) estate in Buffalo Valley.

Back Home to East Tennessee

Nathaniel, the statesman, returned home to East Tennessee and Carter County and spent his remaining years. On June 11, 1870, when the United States Census was taken, Nathaniel, age fifty, and his wife Emeline, age forty-eight, were living in Carter County Civil District No. 5. Their post office was Cave Springs which was open from 1855 until 1884. The value of Nathaniel's real estate was $148,200, and the value of his personal estate was $5,000. This value for land is deceptive as land was not selling, and to our knowledge Nathaniel did not have a position with a salary. The children listed in the census for Nathaniel were: Alfred A., twenty-one, a lawyer; Robert L., nineteen; Nathaniel W., eighteen; twins Rhoda E. and Mary E., fifteen; David H., thirteen; Hugh S., ten; Laura M., eight; and the eldest son, James P., twenty-five, with his wife Mary S., also twenty-five, their son Nathaniel F., age three who was born in Washington, D.C., and their younger son, James P., age one, who was born in Maryland. Rachael C. Bell, (perhaps their cook/housekeeper) age twenty-five, and Jennie, age seven, presumably her daughter, were also living with Nathaniel and Emeline.

There is very little documentation of Nathaniel's life after he returned to Tennessee. About 1870, probably through his Methodist connections, he secured a position at East Tennessee Wesleyan College, Athens, Tennessee, as professor of Belle Lettres (literature). Formerly the Odd Fellows Female College, chartered on January 2, 1854, it became Athens Female College in 1857 under the auspices of the Methodist Church. On April 13, 1867, Athens Female College became the struggling East Tennessee Wesleyan College and today is Tennessee Wesleyan College. There were only ten graduating students in 1871. Nathaniel moved his family to Athens where he lived and worked until 1874.

The Taylor Battery Gun

The eldest son of Nathaniel and Emeline, James Patton Taylor (1844-1924), was named for his grandfather, Nathaniel's father. On July 4, 1871, he obtained a patent for a rapid firing weapon. Five more patents quickly followed for the same invention, all issued to James P. Taylor of Elizabethton, Tennessee. James was trying to compete with the Gatling gun, the first successful rapid firing rifle (machine gun), which received its patent in November 1862. In probably the 1870s, the Taylor Repeating Ordnance Association was formed with George Andrews as president and H.H. Taylor as vice president. Charles H. Brown was secretary and treasurer. On August 25, 1874, James P. Taylor entered into a contract with E. Remington & Sons to manufacture and sell the "Taylor Battery Gun" as it was called. In February 1875 the board of directors of the Taylor Repeating Ordnance Association voted to cancel the contract with Remington and were released on April 15, 1875. However, the manufacture's data plate on the Taylor gun shows J.P. Taylor had three patents for the gun, which were issued in 1876 and 1877. This suggests that Remington made one or more weapons for them. Of more than eighty patents issued for machine guns between 1862 and 1883, only one other justified the ordnance trials undertaken for the Taylor weapon on May 16, 1878, at Sandy Hook, New Jersey. The army rejected the Taylor gun because of its feed of bullets into the weapon, but they did say it was an ingenious and promising machine.

Taylor's Debt to Turley

On February 19, 1863, Nathaniel had unwittingly set the stage for a tremendous financial setback when he borrowed $9,000 from William H. Turley of Carter County to pay debts he owed in Richmond and to support his iron manufacturing business. There were two stipulations with the loan. First, Taylor had six months before beginning to repay the loan, and secondly, the total amount was due in two years in current bankable funds. When the loan became due in February 1865, Taylor had not made any payments. The parties disagreed as to whether it should be paid in U.S. or Confederate currency. In 1869 Turley sued Taylor in the Howard County Circuit Court in Maryland, and Taylor appealed to the court of appeals. When compared to gold it took seven Confederate dollars to pay one U.S. dollar. Using a 7:1 ratio, the loan that should have amounted to $12,633 with interest was only worth $1,804 when paid in Confederate money. Both parties had agreed the loan would be repaid "in current bankable funds." At the time Taylor obtained the loan the Confederacy occupied Carter County, but Taylor was ordered to repay $12,633 which had increased, probably due to interest.

On January 9, 1874, from Carter Depot, Carter County, Nathaniel wrote to former President Andrew Johnson at his home in Greeneville requesting a loan. Earlier in the September 1873 Term of the Tennessee Supreme Court the justices ruled that Taylor would have to sell his land to pay his debt to William H. Turley. Nathaniel was instructed that by February 19, 1874, he had to pay Turley about $17,000. He was desperate, as it would force him to sell "an important part of his Happy Valley farm." If the amount could be raised in cash he would avoid a quick sell of his property. He was willing to offer his real estate of 500 acres, his iron works and mills, including "nearly 800 acres of river lands of his home farms, as security for a loan of six or twelve months. Nathaniel added that he thought in ordinary times this would be worth more than $50,000. He offered this security saying his son James would buy "the property-since the success of his gun-enterprise is already assured" and it would avoid the sacrifice of his property. On January 16, 1874, President Johnson replied to Taylor stating he "sincerely [regretted]" that it was out of his power to come to his relief. "My financial affairs have taken a turn that makes it impossible for me to furnish the amount of money needed by you. I most earnestly hope that you may succeed in some other quarters in raising the means which will relieve you from your present embarrassment. . . . Please accept assurance of my high esteem for yourself and tender my regards to Mrs. Taylor." The outcome of this financial disaster is unknown, but presumably Nathaniel had to sell his land to settle the debt as the court ordered.

Nathaniel returned to the ministry, and a few years later on February 16, 1879, Emeline (Emma) wrote to Sallie, the wife of her son Bob Taylor, who lived in Jonesborough. From Knoxville, Tennessee, Emma said that she and Nathaniel had "a cozy little house, a grand cook, and [were] getting along very nicely, plenty of friends." Nathaniel's financial outlook must have improved somewhat. She wrote that Nathaniel, a Methodist minister, had a large church with two hundred members. "I have to call upon all of them . . . all the other churches call to see me. [and I] have to return calls . . . so you see that I can do but little else than visit and make calls." Emeline added that Nathaniel "preached one of his soul stirring sermons today."

While in Knoxville Nathaniel, a short term professor at East Tennessee Wesleyan College, was honored when the local leadership addressed him as Dr. Nathaniel Taylor. As Dr. Taylor he was one of the vice presidents of the Knoxville library. Knoxville, the place Nathaniel helped so much when working for the East Tennessee Relief Association was gaining some of its pre-war prosperity. The library organized by the public on March 6, 1873, had been supported by Nathaniel's Relief Association in 1877 with a $360 donation. In 1879 the name was changed to the Public Library of Knoxville and incorporated. Shares which Nathaniel purchased sold for $3.00 in lots of from three to ten.

According to an abstract of an 1880 Carter County census for District 6, Nathaniel was back in Carter County. He was sixty years old, and his occupation was listed as a minister. His wife Emeline was fifty-eight years of age. In the household were their sons Alfred A., a politician. Robert L., a lawyer and his wife, Sarah, twenty-three years old. David H. worked as a clerk in the U.S. Treasury, and Hugh L. was a teacher. There was also a Sannie R. age eighteen. Mary McInturff, age fifteen, was listed as a servant, as was William McInturff, age twenty-five, but we do not know their relationship. Dema Gordon and Josephine Straly, age fourteen, were African American servants. To round out the household was Burten Stuart, age fourteen, a female African American servant.

On March 10, 1886, Nathaniel, still referred to as Dr. Taylor, helped fellow Methodists, Peter M. and Matilda Reeves, celebrate their fiftieth wedding anniversary near Johnson City. Dr. Taylor "announced the doxology hymn, 'Praise God From Whom

All Blessings Flow.'" He was still an eloquent speaker and was described as giving an address as good as could have come from Henry Clay or Patrick Henry. William Bailey writing in 1999 said that as Nathaniel spoke "the eyes of speaker and hearers would well up with tears, and then sparkling good humor would paint all faces with smiles." Reportedly, from 1872 to 1887, Nathaniel served one year terms as a Methodist minister at Johnson City, Elizabethton, Greeneville, and possibly other locations.

It was a great loss, when on April 1, 1887, Nathaniel Greene Taylor passed away in Happy Valley, Carter County, Tennessee, at sixty-seven years of age. Reverend J.J. Manker, D.D., of Chattanooga University officiated at his funeral, assisted by Rev. George Cox, Rev. Schrence, and President Josephus Hopwood of Milligan College. The 1,200 people attending the service were evidence of the esteem in which Nathaniel, one of Carter County's most famous citizens, was held by his contemporaries. He loved his family, and supported education, both for his children and the community at large. Nathaniel was a patriot and was compassionate and strong in his convictions. Dr. Taylor was buried with Masonic honors by Dashiell Lodge of Elizabethton in the Old Taylor Cemetery, Sylvan Hill Road, Elizabethton, Tennessee. On November 16, 1890, Emeline Haynes Taylor died in Johnson City, Tennessee, and is buried beside Nathaniel in the Old Taylor Cemetery.

1867-1868
Ratified Indian Treaties
in which
Commissioner of Indian Affairs Nathaniel Greene Taylor participated.

Number and Date	Tribes	Place	Commissioners	Citation
357 [364] Oct. 21, 1867	Kiowa	Medicine Lodge	Nathaniel G.	Taylor Kappler, 972-82;
Proclaimed Aug 25, 1868	Comanche	Creek	William S. Harney, C.C. Augur Alfred H. Terry, John B. Sanborn, Samuel F. Tappan, J.B. Henderson	15 Stat. 581-87
358 [365] Oct.21, 1867 Proclaimed Aug. 25, 1868	Kiowa Comanche Apache	Medicine Lodge Creek	As for no. 357	Kappler, 982-84 15 Stat. 589-92
359 [366] Oct. 28, 1867 Proclaimed Aug. 19, 1868	Cheyenne, Arapaho	Medicine Lodge Creek	As for no. 357	Kappler 984-89 15 Stat.593-99
360 [367] Mar. 2, 1868 Proclaimed Nov. 6, 1868	Ute, Tabeguache, Muache, Capote, Wiminuche, Yampa, Grand River, Uintah	Washington	Nathaniel G. Taylor, Alexander C. Hunt, Kit Carson	Kappler, 990-96 15 Stat. 619-27
361 [368] Apr. 27, 1868 Proclaimed June 10, 1868	Cherokee	Washington	Nathaniel G. Taylor	Kappler, 996-97; 16 Stat. 727-29
362 [369] Apr. 29, 1868 And later,	Sioux: Brule, Minneconjou,	Oglala, Fort Laramie	William T. Sherman, William S. Harney	Kappler, 998-1007 15 Stat. 635-47

Proclaimed Feb. 24, 1869	Yanktonai, Hunkpapa, Blackfoot, Cuthead, Two Kettle, Sans Arc, Santee, Arapaho		Alfred H. Terry, C.C. Augur, J. B. Henderson, Nathaniel G. Taylor, John B. Sanborn, Samuel F. Tappan	
363 [370] May 7, 1868 Proclaimed Aug. 12, 1868	Crow	Fort Laramie	William T. Sherman, William S. Harney, Alfred H. Terry, C.C. Augur John B. Sanborn, Samuel F. Tappan	Kappler,1008-11, 15 Stat. 649-53
364 [371] May 10, 1868 Proclaimed Aug. 25, 1868	Northern Cheyenne, Northern Arapaho	Fort Laramie	As for no. 363	Kappler, 1012-15, 15 Stat. 655-59
365 [372] June 1, 1868 Proclaimed Aug. 12, 1868	Navajo	Fort Sumner	William T. Sherman, Samuel F. Tappan	Kappler, 1015-20, 15 Stat. 667-72
366 [373] July 3, 1868 Proclaimed Feb. 24, 1869	Eastern Shoshone; Bannock	Fort Bridger	Nathaniel G. Taylor William T. Sherman, William S. Harney John B. Sanborn, Samuel F. Tappan, C.C. Augur	Kappler, 1020-24 15 Stat. 673-78
367 [374] Aug. 13, 1868 Proclaimed Feb. 24, 1869	Nez Perce	Washington	Nathaniel G. Taylor	Kappler, 1024-25; 15 Stat. 693-95

Francis Paul Prucha, *American Indian Treaties* (Reprint, 1994; Berkeley, Calif.; University of California Press, 1997).

Chapter 5

Alfred Alexander Taylor
1848-1931
and
Robert Love Taylor
1850-1919

The Pennington School and the 1867 Medicine Lodge Creek Treaty

Nathaniel Greene Taylor and Emeline Haynes Taylor had ten children, including a set of twins. Two of the children became governors of Tennessee, Alfred Alexander Taylor and Robert Love Taylor. In the history of the state there has been only one other set of full-brothers and one set of half-brothers who have been governors of Tennessee. In 1848 Nathaniel and Emeline Taylor were residing at the old family farmstead called the Sycamore Shoals Plantation in Happy Valley. Their second son Alfred Alexander was born on August 6, 1848, on the beautiful Watauga River just west of Elizabethton, Tennessee. Alf, as he was known throughout his life, first attended a subscription or old field school which was funded by parents of students and was often conducted in a home or a farm building. If the weather was pleasant, the schoolmaster held classes outdoors, thus the name field schools. Alf later attended the Duffield Academy in Elizabethton where his great-grandfather had been a trustee in 1806.

Following the Civil War, the devastation in East Tennessee was harsh, with many people destitute and hungry. Nathaniel, in his position as a fund raiser, traveled to the northern states. He and Emeline subsequently rented out their farm in early 1864 and took the family to Haddonfield, New Jersey. Possibly because they were Methodists, Nathaniel and Emeline enrolled their children in the Pennington Seminary and Female Collegiate Institute, a well regulated school for both sexes founded in 1838 as the Methodist Episcopal Male Seminary at Pennington, New Jersey. Originally founded as a college preparatory school for boys and young men, it officially became coeducational in 1854. The Taylor children boarded at the school which was about thirty-three miles from Haddonfield. After September 1864 Nathaniel moved the family to Longacoming, New Jersey. The older Taylor children, James Patton, Alfred Alexander and Robert Love were still attending the Pennington School, and Nathaniel Winfield Scott Taylor who would have been about twelve years of age may also have attended.

Nathaniel moved his family from Longacoming to East Tennessee in May or early June of 1865, where he was elected as congressman, representing the First Congressional District, from July 1866, to March 1867. The family moved to Laurel, Maryland, where, after serving as congressman, Taylor was appointed Commissioner of Indian Affairs by President Andrew Johnson in March 1867. While the family lived in Maryland, James Patton obtained employment in the Treasury Department, and his brother Alf, as indicated previously, took a post in the office of Indian Affairs with his father.

On July 20, 1867, Congress created the Indian Peace Commission which was signed into law by President Andrew Johnson. Nathaniel would eventually be named president of the commission, and in late July a group of peace commissioners, including Nathaniel and his son Alfred, left Washington by train for the West. On August 6 the commissioners met in St. Louis, Missouri, to organize the work of the Indian Peace Commission. For young Alf Taylor, the trip west provided new experiences. From the bustling riverfront town of St. Louis the party traveled up the Missouri River by steamer, meeting with Native Americans along the way. In September as they concluded this part of their trip, they returned to St. Louis, and caught the Union Pacific Railway for Kansas.

On October 7, 1867, the commissioners and journalists left the train and boarded wagons for Fort Harker, Kansas. Joined there by two Indian agents, two companies of infantry, and thirty wagons containing presents for the Indians, the party set out for their eventual destination, Medicine Lodge Creek, Kansas. On October 12, the peace commission's wagon train was crossing the grassy prairie toward a campsite at Rattlesnake Creek when outriders spotted bison, and the men decided to hunt. Alfred Taylor and John Howland of the *Harper's Weekly* scrambled onto horses. They discovered that the hunters were killing the bison and only taking their tongues and the hump steaks from the fallen animals. A number of the men just shot the bison for sport and left the bodies lying on the prairie. Newspaper correspondent George C. Brown described the scene as young Taylor and Howland returned "with bloody hands and the red tongues of their victims hanging from their saddle pommels." He also told of their prowess with a rifle. Kiowa Indian chief San-tan-ta was furious with the hunt and complained loudly to Maj. Gen. William S. Harney who ordered that the shooting stop and some of the hunters arrested. Nevertheless, on that cold night at Rattlesnake Creek, many of the newspaper men ate bison tongue and hump steaks.

A youthful Alfred Alexander Taylor, born in 1848, lived in what would become known as Happy Valley, Carter County. He attended the Duffield Academy in Elizabethton, Tennessee and the Pennington Seminary and Female Collegiate Seminary at Pennington, New Jersey. He accompanied his father on the trip west when the Medicine Lodge Creek Treaty of 1867 was signed. Archives of Appalachia, East Tennessee State University.

On October 27, after days of treaty negotiations, a sight-seeing expedition was organized down Medicine Lodge Creek to where the Kiowa Sun Dance of 1866 had been held. In his book, *The Treaty of Medicine Lodge*, Douglas C. Jones stated that at that time the Medicine Lodge still stood, and the group "was anxious to see . . . a traditional religious ceremony site of one of the Great Plains tribes." Another account of their departure for Medicine Lodge was left by Henry M. Stanley, a British journalist, who wrote in 1867 that "about a dozen young fellows, composed of two artists and a wild, hair-brained correspondent, the Washington papoose [Alf

Taylor], and other bloods disposed for a lark, determined to travel to see the famous Medicine Lodge." Jones states that the party left Sunday morning and rode about twelve miles to the Sun Dance lodge.

According to Stanley, they found the Sun Dance Lodge, consisting of a vast circle surrounded by boughs tied together by rawhide, about three miles from camp (this differs from Jones mileage). "Long poles extended all around and were tied in the center with strong lariats, forming beams to bear a roof made of branches." In 1924 Alf, writing about his youthful adventure, gave a clearer description, saying "this lodge was simply a grove of cottonwood trees, bushes and various under growth, all planted in circular form, with open spaces in the center, more or less shaded." Alf said they saw the brightly colored trinkets tied with rawhide strings to the bodies of the trees and limbs. Stanley wrote that the party dismounted and went inside where they found other talismans on walls and ceilings. Feathers, arrows, beads, and brightly painted gourds hung there, and a decorated bison skull covered with a blue cloth was tied high on the center pole. The temptation to take away a few souvenirs was too great to resist, and most members of the party took decorations from the walls.

In his book, Jones elaborates on the story, writing that Alf and his sightseer friends rode away from the religious site, nervously passing by the Kiowa and Comanche camp, fearing that the Indians would spot the pilfered sacred objects. As they neared camp, Interpreter McCusker heard bursts of gunfire and shouting an alarm, he dashed into the stream with the others following. As they forded the stream, they threw their souvenirs into the water. As it turned out, the shooting was a mock attack on horse thieves staged for the commissioners by the Arapaho. Also complicating the issue, the Cheyenne delegation was just arriving for their treaty negotiations. The sightseers were very frightened men and extremely embarrassed at having charged into the camp just as the Cheyenne peace delegation arrived. Their interest in Indian mementos waned considerably after that.

In late October 1867 three treaties were signed at Medicine Lodge Creek with Alf attesting to the signatures of the commissioners and Native Americans. Alf and his father arrived back in Maryland in November. Already, at nineteen, experienced the partisan activities of the Civil War, moved to New Jersey, then to Laurel, Maryland, worked in the nation's capital, and participated in the Indian Peace Commission's work of 1867.

Nathaniel's son, Nathaniel Winfield Scott Taylor, at age fifteen poses on the far right with unknown Indian Chiefs in, probably, Washington, D.C. To his right in the center of the photograph is Indian Commissioner Nathaniel Greene Taylor. B. Harrison Taylor Collection.

From Maryland to East Tennessee and Brother Bob

Nathaniel served as Commissioner of Indian Affairs until April 21, 1869. Five long, hard years after leaving the homestead on the banks of the Watauga River in Carter County, he returned with his family to Tennessee. The June 1870 Carter County census shows the family living in Civil District No. 5 of Carter County. Alfred age twenty-one was living at home, and his occupation was listed as lawyer. Although it is more likely he was studying law since his official biography in the congressional directory states he "studied law; was admitted to the bar in 1874 and commenced practice in Jonesboro, Washington County, Tenn."

Alf's brother, Robert Love Taylor, was born on July 31, 1850, and was also living at home in 1870. The story of Alf can hardly be told without including the story of his brother, Bob. From the book, *Life and Times of Robert Love Taylor*, written in 1913 by his three brothers, we learn that after the Taylors' long absence from their farm, they found the tenants had left the home "a virtual wreck." During the war and afterwards, thieves, and probably the tenants, had stolen for fuel the wooden fences, outbuildings, shingles, and weatherboarding. The family had thought that because of its isolation, the farm buildings would perhaps be saved. They "all went to work to restore the old home as best [they] could and retrieve, as far as possible, [their] shattered fortunes . . . By the autumn of 1869 [they] had partially succeeded in making [the] old place habitable, and had made crops and accumulated live stock sufficient for [their] immediate and most pressing needs."

As was their wont, they next turned their attention to the education of the children, especially the older sons. In Alf's congressional biography he is listed as having attended Buffalo Institute, which later became Milligan College. No date is given which makes it difficult to document whether he ever attended school there. Bob would have been nineteen that autumn of 1869 and may have briefly attended Buffalo Institute. In the book, *Life and Times of Robert Love Taylor*, there is an account of Bob acting in the play "Horatio Spriggins, a comedy in three acts." which was performed at Elizabethton, Jonesborough, and other towns. The Jonesborough *Herald and Tribune* documents Bob's role in this play, illustrating his interest in dramatics and acting. In 1871 the play was performed at 107-109 East Main Street in Jonesborough where John F. Grisham and Horace Lampson had just constructed a three-story brick building that housed offices and an entertainment hall. The hall was rented by the Methodist Episcopal Church, South to raise funds for repairs to the church, and the play was part of this effort. The newspaper reported on the performance stating that the actors eclipsed anything ever brought before a Jonesborough audience. In one of those performances, Mr. Robert Taylor's Horatio Spriggins was described as the 'brick' upon the occasion, and his reference to Confederate General Alfred E. Jackson, a kinsman from Jonesborough, brought much applause.

Nathaniel obtained a teaching position for the 1871 fall term at East Tennessee Wesleyan, Athens, Tennessee. His reason for going to Athens was that he needed to educate his children, and with him working and living there, they would not have to pay room and board, making college more affordable. Bob attended East Tennessee Wesleyan, but in the summer of 1874, as reported in his biography, "circumstances compelled the family to leave Athens and return to the old Happy Valley home." These circumstances no doubt included the huge debt due Turley which Nathaniel owed from 1863. Afterwards, Bob entered the business world but failed at each enterprise. In 1877 he visited his brother Nat in Asheville, North Carolina, and there he met Sarah (Sallie) Baird and fell in love.

Bob wrote to Sallie often and many letters survive. One is dated September 22, 1877, from Greeneville, Tennessee, apparently written shortly after they met, expressing his affection for her. On November 22 Bob was in Jonesborough, according to the letterhead on his letter which reads "Office of S.J. Kirkpatrick, Attorney at Law." Samuel J. Kirkpatrick lived at 301 West Main Street, and Bob boarded with him as indicated in a letter dated May 2, 1878. The law office was upstairs in the

Grisham and Lampson building, 107-109 East Main Street, number five. In a letter written to Sallie on February 23, 1878, Bob referenced his engagement. He was studying law under Kirkpatrick and the February letter indicates he had proposed to Sallie and that she accepted. With his study of law apparently on his mind Bob wrote in lawyer terms to Sallie that "You needn't think that because your father does not own you now, you are free. No, no, I have in my possession a deed in fee with his signature and a good witness conveying all of his right, title and interest in you to me. See? You are mine, and I wouldn't take a million $ for you. You see now, how highly I value you . . . How much I love you now . . . I swear to you that my heart, my life, my future are yours."

These letters provide the first documentation of the financial misfortune that befell the Taylor family during the Civil War. In a letter dated March 14, 1878, Bob suggests the pain it caused them. He said, "my chief trouble and bitterest reflection is that I will not be able to surround you, my darling wife [to be], with the blessings and comforts of wealth. I don't intend to conceal anything from you when you marry me. It shall be done voluntarily with all the light before you. You shall know everything. When the war commenced, my Father was worth 150 thousand $. In the goodness of his heart he went every body's security [and] it robbed him of his fortune. He and his sons have been struggling for years to save $30,000 worth of Real Estate [which is] the remnant of our fortune. We are still en—with debt! [At the time the court ordered Nathaniel's to pay Turley the country was in the financial Panic of 1873 and would not climb out of it until 1879]. But I feel sure that a brighter and better day will dawn in the near future. So you see, you are about to marry poverty. . . . I thank God I have a future." Bob was active in the Jonesborough Literary Club and enjoyed debating. In early May he wrote Sallie with enthusiasm, reporting that they were preparing for the East Tennessee Sunday School Convention to be held in Jonesborough on May 16 and 17. Bob said that he might not be able to attend the Sunday School Convention because the Democratic Convention was to be held in Greeneville at the same time. From Jonesborough, on June 7, 1878, he proudly wrote that "I am now, a full-fledged lawyer." Elaborating on political activities in May, he said that Kirkpatrick was a candidate for judge at the Greeneville convention on the coming Thursday, and he had been giving all his effort for his selection. He felt sure Kirkpatrick would be nominated and elected and that the next fall he could "step into the best kind of practice." Bob wrote that his brother Alf, a Republican, was a candidate for Congress, and he had "been trying to help him too."

Robert Love Taylor, was born on July 31, 1850, in Happy Valley, and went with the family in 1864 to New Jersey where he attended the Pennington Seminary and Female Collegiate Institute. When his father was a congressman and Commissioner of Indian Affairs he lived with the family near Washington, D.C. After his father obtained a position in 1871 at East Tennessee Wesleyan, Athens, Tennessee, Bob apparently attended school there until 1874. This photograph shows Bob when he was twenty years old. Adapted from the Life and Career of Senator Robert Love Taylor.

Alf, living with his parents, was practicing law at Jonesborough. He entered politics and from 1875 to 1877 was a member of the 39th Tennessee General Assembly. This was an exciting legislative session in Nashville as ex-President Andrew Johnson was running against four other candidates for the U.S. Senate. At that time U.S. Senators were selected by the Tennessee legislature. The situation became desperate as promises were made, alliances forged, and candidates dropped out. When Johnson won the senate seat on the fifty-sixth ballot the General Assembly rose in cheers. A biographer of Johnson, Hans L. Trefousse, wrote in 1989 that House member Alfred A. Taylor ran to the Maxwell House where Johnson awaited the outcome and breathlessly rushed into room five, shouting, "Mr. Johnson, you are elected," and then fell into a faint. "The new senator was dashing water in his face," wrote Trefousse, when the slower E.C. Reeves arrived with the news. Alf had voted for Johnson as payback for the position that Johnson had given his father, Nathaniel, in 1867. Alf, in Delong Rice's book, *Old Limber*, tells the same story but does not mention that he fainted.

Alf was very proud that he was the one to introduce the legislation to create Unicoi County, which became law on March 23, 1875. When he became governor, Alf liked to comment on "his county." He told the *Johnson City Press* in 1923 that Unaka had been suggested for the county's name, but he knew it would be called Unaky so he "held on to the name he proposed [Unicoi]." He said, "I am the Daddy of that county, and I exercised a dad's province. I named it."

In 1878 Alf was in a tough race with Major A.H. Pettibone of Greene County for the Republican Party's nomination for Congress. The Republican executive committee of the First Congressional District met in Jonesborough to make the nomination. They called for Republicans from the twelve counties in the district to meet and appoint delegates to the general convention. Each county instructed its delegates to vote for Alf, thinking he would have the majority of votes. At the convention, however, Major Pettibone won by a slight majority, and Alf and his supporters were indignant at losing in the primary. Bob, in Kirkpatrick's law office, mourned over brother Alf's defeat. On August 26, 1878, he wrote to his fiancée Sallie Baird that the defeat was regretted by many and had been procured by fraud, money, liquor, and lies.

Bob, early in life, proclaimed he was a Democrat. He and Alf spend their youth debating about a variety of subjects to the entertainment of field hands, friends, and neighbors. They gravitated to the political issues of the day, and since Bob had declared as a Democrat Alf represented the Republican side of issues. In 1878 when Alf lost his bid for congressman the Democratic nominating committee meeting in Jonesborough recognized a split in the Republican Party and suspected that Bob could garner the votes his brother might have had. A week before Alf's loss to Pettibone, Bob won the Democratic nomination. In a letter to Sallie, he described how he first became interested in politics, saying that while he was "in Kirkpatrick's law office, much to his surprise, "people from every quarter and of all parties began to call upon me to be their standard bearer in the coming campaign."

The Democratic Convention had met in Jonesborough on August 21, and to his amazement "the enthusiasm, especially among the young men was very great." Several candidates were on the ballot in the election until "finally the race narrowed down between Charles R. Vance of Bristol" and Bob. At midnight Bob was seated a block from the Washington County courthouse with his friends when a shout and "one continuous yell followed which was caught up all over town." Everyone grabbed him, shook his hand, patted his back, and propelled him into the courthouse. William B. Carter, a kinsman, was the president of the convention, and he introduced him to the crowd as the victor, and Bob made a short speech accepting the nomination. He had received ninety-six votes out of the 108 cast. With supreme confidence, he shared with Sallie that his election was a foregone conclusion. Bob added "This nomination is the greatest compliment ever paid to a young man of my age [twenty-eight] in Tennessee." With his steadfast preparation, knowledge of politics, and enthusiasm, he won the First Congressional District seat to the Forty-sixth Congress.

In October 1878 Bob married Sallie, but she stayed home when he first went to Washington. He served from March 4, 1879 to March 4, 1881. On the first day of Congress, he wrote Sallie, saying that Congress adjourned without passing an appropriations bill, and President Rutherford B. Hayes called for an extra session to begin on March 18. Bob's plan was for Sallie to join him, with George G. Dibrell of Sparta escorting her to the nation's capital. Bob had previously instructed Sallie to shop at James H. Dosser's or Hoss and Johnson's in Jonesborough as he had made credit arrangements with them. He told her "you will have to put on a little style here to keep up appearances. I mean you will have to dress a little more elegantly than people do in the country and country towns." He further advised Sallie to "buy a dress and have it made before you come" but added that she could get her hat and other dresses in Washington.

In 1879 Jonesborough celebrated its centennial on October 2-3 as part of the annual Washington County Agricultural and Mechanical Society Fair. The celebration was held at the fairgrounds two miles east of town, and Alfred A. Taylor, ever the politician, was among the "distinguished visitors." Alf's reasoning was good, as a huge crowd was expected. About 10,000 people attended; it was the largest crowd to be gathered up to that time in Washington County. Alf kept his hand in politics during the presidential election of 1880, serving as elector for the state at large on the Republican ticket of James A. Garfield of Ohio. Garfield was elected, but was assassinated in his first year of office. In that same election year, Alf supported Republican Alvin Hawkins who was elected Tennessee governor. Bob was defeated in the First Congressional District race in Tennessee due to A.H. Pettibone rallying the Republicans against him.

The 1880 Carter County census, District 6, shows Alf as a thirty year old politician, and Bob as a lawyer married to Sallie. They all lived with Nathaniel. On June 22, 1881, Alf, at thirty-two years of age, married Florence Jane Anderson, who was just shy of her fifteenth birthday. Jennie, as she was called, was the daughter of John A. and Mary Ann Jones Anderson. She was an accomplished young lady, having attended the Buffalo Institute. As a wedding present, her well-to-do parents gave her eighty acres of land on the south side of the Nolichucky River, just a few hundred yards east of the present Alfred A. Taylor Bridge on Tennessee Highway 81.

The house, located in Washington County, still stands. A descendant, Jennie Taylor Rogers, in probably the 1990s, wrote a small essay titled "Mama's House at Taylors Bridge" stating that "the farm house on the south side of the Nolichucky River at Taylors Bridge was known in the Taylor family as "Mama's (Jennie's) house." On March 7, 1890, for the amount of $5,000 Alf bought an additional seventy-two acres adjoining the land he and Jennie Taylor owned. Mrs. Rogers stated that the big brick farm house (no longer standing) to the west of Mama's house, also on the south side of the river, was known as the "Big House" and was owned by Alf Taylor.

Taken in May 1994, this view shows the two story clapboard home on the Nolichucky River that Jennie Anderson Taylor received from her parents as a wedding present. It is located near present Tennessee Highway 81 and the Alfred A. Taylor Bridge in lower Washington County. Larry and Yanah Sullins restored the interior of the house. The Sullins also added three front gables to the exterior, shortened the porch, and installed two windows on the lower level. Jennie Rogers Taylor.

The Johnson City and Carolina Railroad built a branch line from Johnson City to Embreeville a distance of ten miles which serviced the Embreeville iron works. It was completed in 1891 and operated until November 1894. The line had difficulties, and the Southern Railway purchased it in April 1903, beginning service in January 1904 which continued with passenger service until 1935. It was this railway line, despite its erratic schedules, that enabled Alf to live on the Nolichucky, for it provided transportation to Johnson City and connections elsewhere. Freight trains stopped running in 1939.

Bob had tried his hand at business between 1874 and 1878 but was unable to succeed. He tried again on March 15, 1884, investing in the *Comet*, a weekly newspaper in Johnson City. Nat C. Love was the publisher, and Bob Taylor and Robert Burrows, Bob's fellow investor and boyhood friend, served as editors. Bob was unsuccessful in this endeavor, although the newspaper continued until 1919. In 1884 Bob was a presidential elector for the Democrats and campaigned successfully to win the election for Grover Cleveland (1885-1889). Bob left the paper and in 1885 was living in Knoxville where, as a result of his work for Cleveland, he was appointed United States Pension Agent, a patronage position that was intended to last four years. In 1884 while Bob was involved with the newspaper business, Alf challenged Pettibone for the Republican seat in the First Congressional District nomination, but he was soundly defeated.

The War of the Roses, 1886

In the 1886 gubernatorial election, Alf and Bob placed an indelible mark on Tennessee's political history. In a campaign that came to be known as the "War of the Roses," the election captured the imagination of the entire nation. It began on June 18 when the Republican Convention chose Alf as the party's candidate for governor. The Republicans thought that if they had Alf as their nominee, the Democrats would not want to select Bob. Another reason for selecting Alf, who won on the first ballot, was that he was the best choice to win the independent vote as well as the vote of discontented Democrats. The opinion of the public was that the phenomenon of relatives running against each other for political office was unnatural.

In Tennessee, since before the 1886 election, the Democratic Party had been separated by feuding factions, sectionalism, and apathy among the rural voters. A candidate was needed to help reorganize the party and instill harmony in order to win elections. In a move that surprised many, Robert L. Taylor was nominated and gained the support of the younger voters, most of them from rural areas. Daniel Merritt Robison in his 1935 book, *Bob Taylor and the Agrarian Revolt in Tennessee*, said Bob was "recognized as an outstanding leader among the younger men of the party" and as someone who could bring the party together. Bob became the Democratic nominee for governor on the fifteenth ballot at the August 11 Democratic Convention in Nashville.

The gubernatorial campaign, with the two brothers running against each other, soon captured the attention of the country's newspapers. The friendly brothers traveled on the same trains, stayed at the same accommodations, and ate at the same table. The dignified, but sometimes contentious, contest began in Madisonville, Tennessee. Robison stated "that their debates were filled with thrusts and anecdotes directed at each other, but in them there was not the sting of bitterness." Bob was described as being taller than Alf, with a bland face, dealt in generalities, and spoke with more ease and fluency. Alf, on the other hand, was more knowledgeable of the topics being discussed. "Both had a keen sense of humor and used a liberal supply of anecdotes." Bob was the professional speaker. Alf would laugh while telling his stories. Robison, in his book states that "the debates between the brothers were not profound and were almost devoid of serious discussion of state issues." They did touch national issues but not in much depth. Robison wrote that "many editors entered into the spirit of the campaign and substituted wit, ridicule and satire for the usual campaign abuse." It may have been this type of coverage that first caught the attention of newspaper readers and voters who turned out to hear them for the entertainment value. As the crowds continued to increase in size, it was apparent that as expected, Bob was the favorite of the young men.

Robison states that the campaign came at a transitional time in Tennessee's history. The previous twenty-five years had been traumatic as the Civil War and Reconstruction, with all the accompanying problems, had created a huge state debt by the 1870s, forcing the state to undergo economic and social changes. The Taylors' campaign was different from recent campaigns, where appeals to war prejudices were common. Tennessee was a rural state, and for the farmers the Taylor's debates were free entertainment. Two brothers battling in the gubernatorial race had a certain appeal. Alf and Bob's folksy way of poking fun at each other and telling stories contrasted sharply with the droll campaigns in previous elections.

Forty-one debates between the two brothers were scheduled throughout the state. The first, on September 9, 1886, was at Madisonville where Bob's speech inadvertently "immortalized in Tennessee's history the War of the Roses." After Bob went on the lecture tour in 1891, he wrote his speech titled "Visions and Dreams," and in 1899 when he was governor of Tennessee, he shared, in his "Visions and Dreams" lecture, how the story of the war of the roses came about. To quote from Bob's speech, he said, if I "could only reach the exalted position of governor of the old Volunteer State I would then have gained the sum of life's honors and happiness. [Yet] another son of my father and mother was dreaming" the same dream. "Fate had decreed that 'York must contend with Lancaster' in the War of the Roses; and with flushed cheeks and throbbing hearts we eagerly entered the field, his shield bearing the red rose, mine the white. It was a contest . . . a white rose on every Democratic bosom, a red rose on every Republican breast, in the midst of a wilderness of flowers. . . . But when . . . I looked upon the drooping red rose on the bosom of the vanquished knight . . . the white rose triumphed." This is the first mention of the "War of the Roses" between the Taylors and would often be recited and written about in differing ways. The analogy Bob referenced is more correctly called the "Wars of the Roses" which occurred in England and was a series of civil wars fought between the House of Lancaster and the House of York from 1455 to 1487. The title came from the badges worn by the two opponents, red for Lancaster and white for York, although the term Wars of the Roses was not used by them.

Newspapers, hungry for a story, picked up on Bob's reference to the War of the Roses. In the Taylor brother's 1913 book about Bob, they began the myth of how, after reading about this, an elderly landlady in Bridgeport, Alabama, greeted her gubernatorial guests with red roses for Alf and white for Bob. She thus became the originator of another legend saying 'Now I want you boys to take these flowers for the sake of your mother. I know she must be proud to have sons who can be political opponents and can still be brothers."

Another myth surrounds the fiddles carried by the brothers on the campaign circuit. On September 14, 1886, a *Chattanooga Times* correspondent interviewed the two brothers in the Read House Hotel. He reported that when he met them, out came two fiddles which they played for him in perfect harmony. "Thus the reporter set about interpreting the fiddling as the symbol of fraternal harmony." An artist from *Frank Leslie's Illustrated Newspaper* picked up on this story, and in the October 2, 1886, issue showed the two brothers sitting on a lecture platform, each playing a fiddle. This never happened. The brothers, never ones to shy away from publicity, began to carry their fiddles on the campaign as props but stuck to their regular speech making.

In October the brothers arrived in Blountville near Happy Valley, the ancestral home, where they concluded the long tiresome campaign. Robert Love Taylor won the election and was Tennessee's governor from 1887 to 1889. He was then reelected and served from 1889 to 1891. Robert E. Corlew, writing in 1981, stated that Bob's administration was noted for its stability, its laws to "preserve the purity of the ballot box, promote honest elections, and raise revenue for Schools. . . . Another law confirmed the payment of a poll tax as a prerequisite for voting, as required by the constitution of 1870." One of the issues in the Tennessee Constitution of 1870 was should the poll tax be a prerequisite for voting. The answer was yes and the tax collected would be used to support public education. Bob earned the title of "pardoning governor" because of the clemency he showed to prisoners in the state penal system. He was also known as the "centennial governor." The Tennessee Centennial Exposition, opened one year late, was during his administration a major event for Tennessee with the worldwide attention it gained.

On January 1, 1886, Nathaniel wrote to his son Alf from Happy Valley, congratulating him on the birth of a son, Nathaniel Greene Taylor, Nathaniel's namesake, who was born on December 18, 1885. On the domestic front, Nathaniel related that they were "butchering some good big hogs." He told Alf that one of the family members who had immigrated to Oregon seventeen years previously was returning for a visit to induce others to settle in Oregon. Nathaniel expressed a desire to go for his health and other reasons. He wondered if Alf would be willing to go and suggested that they could pay for the trip if they did some lectures. This is the first mention of the Taylors considering lectures, which were a popular form of entertainment. He added that they should not let the opportunity pass. It is doubtful, however, that this trip took place.

Alf was a delegate to the Republican Convention in Chicago on June 19-25, 1888, where Benjamin Harrison of Indiana was nominated. Harrison won the presidency (1889-1893). In November 1888 Alf defeated Walter P. Brownlow, editor of the Jonesborough *Herald and Tribune*, for the First District Congressional seat. Alf was the second member of the Taylor family to serve as First District Congressman, following in the footsteps of his father Nathaniel Greene Taylor. Alf left for Washington with his family and served in the Fifty-first U.S. Congress, from March 4, 1889, to March 3, 1891. Just after Alf left congress on April 14, 1891, President Benjamin Harrison, traveling by train, stopped in Johnson City to speak. Alf was part of the reception committee and introduced the president to the assembled crowd.

While Alf was running for Congress, brother Bob was working to be reelected governor. Bob had a tough time being nominated in the May 1888 Democratic Convention and did not win the party's nomination until the fortieth ballot. He was vindicated in the election, as he won the most votes for a candidate since the Civil War. Bob was reelected for a second term ending on January 19, 1891.

On July 4, 1890, from the nation's capital, the *Chattanooga Times* wrote a sketch about the wives of the members of the Tennessee congressional delegation. The special correspondent of the *Times* wrote that "these beautiful women of charming and pleasing manners did the social honors for Tennessee. The youngest lady of the Tennessee congressional circle was Mrs. Alfred A. Taylor" who was not quite twenty-four years. The correspondent stated: "Mrs. Taylor was Miss Jennie Anderson, a well-to-do citizen of Carter County, Tennessee. She was educated at Buffalo Institute in her native county. Mrs. Taylor is a lady slightly above medium size, of magnificent figure and charming personal appearance. A perfect type of Tennessee womanhood, she is popular with all. She is fond of domestic life and is devoted to her Tennessee home, which is located on her splendid Chucky [Nolichucky] River plantation—a bridal present from her father. Mrs. Taylor is fond of life at the national capital where she has spent much of her time since her husband has been in Congress. She has two little boys, one named Nathaniel Taylor, and Benjamin Harrison Taylor, the baby. Mrs. Taylor takes a deep interest in the affairs of her husband and proves [she is] a help mate indeed."

Alf was reelected to the Fifty-second Congress, serving from March 4, 1891 to March 3, 1893. He was reelected for a third term to the Fifty-third Congress, serving from March 4, 1893, to March 3, 1895. In 1894 Alf declined to be a candidate for nomination and instead engaged in the practice of law in Johnson City, Tennessee.

Alf and Bob Leave Political Office and Become Lecturers

Bob was without funds when he left the governor's office and moved to Chattanooga to practice law with a Mr. Thompson. His salary as governor was not that large, he did not own a home, he had been helping other family members and was generous to others, depleting financial resources. While he was trying to establish his law practice he had expenses for rent, his office operation, food, and so forth. To economize Sallie and the children moved in with Alf, Jennie, and their family on the Nolichucky farm. Such was the price Bob had to pay for serving in public office. Sallie wrote to Bob from the farm on June 9, 1891, saying that they had arrived there safely. She said "Brother Alf and Jennie are so kind and good and gave us such a warm welcome. I wish you could come soon-hope you can. This is a beautiful paradise, if anything, prettier than Happy Valley. If you only had such a place-you could smile at the cares that best you now. We will work together from this time to gain such a home, 'far from the busy scenes of strife and man.'"

Governor Robert Love Taylor near the end of his second term as governor. After trying his hand in law practice in Chattanooga, he moved in with Alf at his Nolichucky farm. Here Alf encouraged him to join the Chautauqua lecture tour where he became very successful. Adapted from the *Life and Career of Senator Robert Love Taylor*.

On July 10, 1891, Bob wrote to Sallie at Alf's Nolichucky River farm telling of his despair and his aspirations saying "I am miserable and wretched [and] I am sick of politics . . .. Henceforth my battles shall be fought in other fields. I pray for health and strength to make money enough to buy me a farm on [the Nolichucky] close to my brothers where I may find a safe retreat from . . . these whited sepulchers called cities. My heart is brave, and I am going to work with more energy than ever to be free from debt and to have a home of my own." On July 22 he reported to her that he was trying to find a rental house for them in Cleveland, an hour away from Chattanooga, for fifteen dollars a month until he could get into a better financial condition. He said "we are getting plenty of business but no money yet. . . . Alf's failure to give me the help he promised gave me a world of trouble."

Sallie wrote Bob, "My dear papa," in a letter of support and encouragement saying that "Jennie and brother Alf had left the Nolichucky farm for Johnson City" and she was left in charge of the children. She told him she "wanted to talk over . . . plans for the future. We will have to make many sacrifices and be willing to live cheaply till you can again get on your feet. You are now in a good situation to earn money if you begin to make it. You have no one else to provide for except your own family. You have always had from two to three others to provide for and, of course, that would keep any man on a strain." She said the children were barefoot which was to be expected in summer and asked Bob to bring daughters Emma and Retta shoes when he came for a visit. This letter gives us more insight into Sallie and Bob's marriage as well as their financial plight and how Bob had tried to help friends and the larger family. Bob did not have enough funds to maintain his practice as the small routine fees a lawyer earned were not enough to cover his expenses. For cases, such as trials that were lengthy, he was not paid until their conclusion. Bob could not stretch his funds enough to make ends meet. He sold his household belongings to satisfy his creditors, but eventually gave up and left Chattanooga to be with Sallie and the family at Alf's Nolichucky home.

It was Alf who suggested to Bob that he become a lecturer. The occupation of lecturer was fashionable as a result of the Chautauqua movement, founded at New York's Lake Chautauqua in 1874. The original intent of the movement was simply to edify rural teachers, but it soon became a place where thousands of families would gather together for several days of inspiration, education, and enjoyment. People came from miles around to hear speakers of national renown, enjoy bands and plays, and engage in an open forum on the great issues of the day. From there the idea had spread.

In the beginning the Chautauqua was a summer touring program, of lectures, music, and socializing under a big tent. People would bring camping gear and furniture and would set up great tent cities for a week or more. As they became more professional, lecture halls were rented for the speakers. The Chautauqua movement, at its height in 1924, had twenty-one troupes operating in ninety-three circuits, reaching a phenomenal thirty-five million people a year. The movement lasted until about 1932.

Alf while in Congress, may have attended one of the Chautauqua performances. At the least he was familiar with them for in 1886 his father had mentioned doing lectures. Responding to Alf's suggestion, Bob discovered that the peace and quiet of the farm provided an ideal place to write his first lecture "The Fiddle and Bow." He spent three weeks writing and practicing the lecture which was full of the flowery language of the day, telling of a great master playing on the violin. Relating it to childhood, the message to his audience was to play with and nurture children. Other stories mentioning the fiddle kept the audience entertained while keeping alive the myth of the fiddle which surrounded Bob Taylor. On December 29, 1891, the "ex-governor opened his great southern lecture tour in Jobe's Opera House in

Johnson City." He was introduced by his friend Robert Burrows who later reported about the lecture in the *Comet*, saying it was "a magnificent portrayal of the various human experiences. Both the funny and serious sides of life were pictured, and through the whole the melody of the sweetest music ran. He pictured the many scenes of rural life-the old country singing master, courtship and marriage, the song of the disappointed lover, country school life, the old-field school exhibition, and the old fashioned quilting." The admission fee was fifty cents, and $350 was made that night. J.F. Crumley of Johnson City became Bob's first manager. Dr. W.J. Miller of Johnson City was his second manager and loaned him $2,500 for his first extended tour covering several southern states. Bob promptly repaid the loan with interest.

In 1894 while Bob continued his lecture tour, Alf was in the Fifty-third Congress trying to decide if he would run again. He was in debt for endorsing loans for friends and making various contributions that congressmen are called upon to make. Bob urged him not to run but to come on the lecture circuit with him, saying it was lucrative. Alf agreed, and they decided to travel together, developing the very popular "Yankee Doodle and Dixie" lecture which took in $44,000 with the two splitting $22,000 and the rest going to expenses. Bob was now finding success and "succeeding financially for the first time in his life."

Alf would make the Chautauqua Circuit, a quintessential American phenomenon, his on and off career for the next twenty-six years. On February 2, 1896, he wrote Jennie from the Peabody Hotel in Memphis. Always thinking of his children, Alf proudly wrote Jennie that he had paid $150 to former Confederate general and brother-in-law, Alfred E. Jackson, of Jonesborough, for two ponies for their sons Ben and Dave. He instructed Jennie to let Blaine think one of the ponies was his, and he would buy one for him when he was older. Alf's lecture tour continued for twenty nights through Arkansas, Missouri, Kentucky, Indiana, Illinois, Wisconsin, Minnesota, and then back through Missouri to Texas. Continuing his letter, he happily reported that they were guaranteed $400 for that night and $350 at New Orleans, no matter what amount they took in at the door for admission. DeLong Rice was his manager. Alf said he was going to buy the Andrew Broyles farm for brother Bob but not to mention it as he wanted to surprise him. He added that "we [Alf and Bob who were on the tour together] will see five thousand dollars apiece for us in the next two and a half months." Alf claimed that he was building a reputation as good as Bob's as a lecturer, and it was no trouble to make all the money they wanted.

Although Bob Taylor had been on the Chautauqua tour for five years, in 1896 the siren song of politics began calling for him to return to Tennessee and run for governor. Delegations from Tennessee met him in various cities on the tour, urging him to come and rescue the Democratic Party. In 1896 the Democrats were dissatisfied with their own Governor, Peter Turney, as to whether or not he could be reelected. A likely candidate could not be decided upon, but there was a swell among Democratic newspapers and from the people calling for Bob Taylor to return and run for governor. Everyone knew Bob wanted a U.S. Senate seat and was not excited about running for governor, but at the May 6, 1896, Democratic Convention in Nashville, he accepted the Democratic nomination for governor.

On May 25, 1896, Bob wrote his "Dear Sweet Mama" Sallie from the Franklin House, Clarksville, Tennessee, asking her to write him as she had been ill and he was worried. He "was doing double work . . . lecturing and running for governor." On the "State Democratic Executive Committee" letterhead he wrote on July 26, 1896, from their headquarters in the Maxwell House, Nashville, boasting that he was having "the largest crowds that ever assembled in Tennessee." For the next nine days he had speaking engagements on the Chautauqua circuit and was home after August 5 for three weeks. Bob was able to successfully carry most of West and Middle Tennessee against a well organized Republican Party, but he carried only Sullivan County in East Tennessee. Winning the race for "centennial" governor, he served from January 21, 1897, to January 16, 1899.

Bob's wife Sarah Baird Taylor, forty-two years of age, died unexpectedly on Monday, June 4, 1900, at their elegant Queen Anne style home at 308 Fourth Avenue in Knoxville after complications from child birth. She had lost a daughter the preceding Wednesday. Just three weeks before, Bob had finished one of his best Chautauqua lecture tours, and family had come from Texas to join them at the new home Sarah always wanted and which they had purchased after he retired from political life. Bob and Sallie's children were Emily Haynes, Loretta Baird, Katherine Carter, Robert Love Jr., and David Haynes.

In 1900 the only surviving Chautauqua schedule in its entirety found among the Taylor papers, lists Alf as the "attraction." At that time Bob and Alf were on separate Chautauqua circuits. It was, for some unknown reason, called the Southern Five-Day Circuit, beginning on Friday, May 18 and concluding on Sunday, September 3. Alf gave a lecture for 108 out of 109 scheduled nights, and would have talked on the 109th night except that the performance was cancelled. Traveling by train, the circuitous tour covered the states of Arkansas, Illinois, Kansas, Missouri, Oklahoma, and Texas, often crossing back across state boundaries to pick up towns. Although information is sketchy, a later trip in the year gives us further insight into the grueling lecture tour and also into Alf's domestic life. Jennie was left to run the household, and Alf would tell, or remind, her what to do about plowing, planting crops, butchering livestock, and so forth. Jennie would hire teachers for the children. While they tried to keep track of everything by correspondence the mail was at times lost. We do not know where this circuit started, but fifty-two year old Alf traveled from Clinton, Mississippi, to the Edwards House, at Jackson, Mississippi, arriving on October 23, 1900. "I am now traveling toward home—thank the Lord," but he told Jennie he would only have a "scant week" to spend there.

Alf arrived in Monroe, Louisiana, on November 19 and wrote Jennie that this trip was already a "howling success." Alf always sent Jennie money from the different cities to bank or pay expenses. He suggested that she order a dress they had discussed "and let it be the best. Make your own selection of pattern and material making sure that it fits—that is the main point." His next stop was Pine Bluff, Arkansas, and after that, Pascagoula, Mississippi. Alf told Jennie that he was going to "run up" to Memphis, Tennessee, via Mayfield, Kentucky, to see Bob on Saturday afternoon and Sunday.

Bob arrived in Memphis on Friday night and met Alf on Saturday, November 24, 1900. They stayed together at the Peabody Hotel from Saturday until Sunday. Alf faithfully wrote Jennie from the hotel and sent her a $325 check written on the New York Exchange, instructing her to take the check, sign her name directly on the back, and "to take it yourself" to the bank and tell Mr. Earnest (perhaps cashier Tate L. Earnest, Merchants and Traders Bank in Jonesborough) to give you a certificate of deposit (receipt) for it. Alf added that he had heard from Buford Mathes about wiring the house for electric lights but would wait until he came home before letting the contract. Three years earlier, electricity was turned on in Jonesborough, about seven miles away from Alf's Nolichucky farm, and electrical lines were finally reaching out into the rural areas. Alf closed by adding, "stay well . . . and I will go ahead and make us money to pay for our home and for other purposes." Alf left the next morning, November 25, for Birmingham, Alabama, and Bob left for Arkansas. At Birmingham on November 26, Alf wrote that his health had improved and that he missed her very much. He wanted to fill more dates and pay for that place (the Nolichucky farm). He wrote his son and namesake Alf that he was in Madisonville, Kentucky on November 29, but he did not mention that it was Thanksgiving Day. In an undated letter, written from the Hotel Aragon, Atlanta, Georgia, Alf said he would be home Monday afternoon after traveling through Asheville, North Carolina, where he would expect a letter from Jennie. On December 6, from the Peabody Hotel in Asheville, he sent her $375 saying that made $700 he had earned to date above expenses. He added that in a couple of days he would send enough to make it a thousand dollars. On December 13 he wrote to his son Dave from the New State

House in Waco, Texas, while waiting for his train that he was "having a great time in Texas—elegant crowds and much enthusiasm." Alf left Waco in the wee hours of the morning of December 13 for he reached the Read House, Chattanooga, the same day at 10:40 p.m. In the last letter that we have dated December 14, he wrote Jennie telling her that as she "might be cramped for money in buying [a] dress, etc. I enclose you my check for twenty dollars." He had given lectures in Nashville and Murfreesboro and was leaving for Meridian, Mississippi, at 6:10 that evening. He planned to be home on December 24. This was a brutal schedule, and being away from home was very difficult.

In the 1906 senatorial race, Bob Taylor won the popular vote and achieved his life-long dream of becoming a U.S. Senator. The Sixtieth Congress, to which he was elected, first met on March 4, 1907. In Washington, D.C. Bob lived at Stoneleigh Court. Theodore Roosevelt was president when he arrived, and Republican William Howard Taft replaced Roosevelt as president, on March 4, 1909.

On June 14, 1910, the unveiling of the Daughters of the American Revolution Sycamore Shoals Monument near Elizabethton was a significant event honoring the historic Fort Watauga of 1770, the Sycamore Shoals Cherokee Indian Treaty of 1775, and the 1780 gathering of the Kings Mountain men. About six years earlier, the Tennessee General Assembly had appropriated funds for the building of the monument, and Bob was on the commission to select a site and acquire the land. Samuel Cole Williams was master of ceremonies. He was an attorney, noted historian and author of numerous publications about East Tennessee. Senator Robert L. Taylor gave the principal address to a crowd of 2,000. Returning to his beloved Carter County was perhaps one of his favorite senatorial duties. Senator Taylor must have been swelling with pride, as the monument was located in the shadow of the site where his family had settled in 1778. Less than two years after the Sycamore Shoals unveiling, the entire state mourned when Bob died suddenly on March 31, 1912, following a gallstone attack. He was first buried in Knoxville, but in 1941 he and Sallie were reinterred at Monte Vista Cemetery in Johnson City.

In 1906 Alf decided to run as an independent Republican candidate for the First Congressional District against Walter P. Brownlow, nephew of former governor William G. Brownlow of Tennessee. The popular East Tennessee politician was first elected in 1897 as congressman in the First Congressional District. Brownlow was nominated for reelection to Congress by the Republican Convention in Nashville. Brownlow had an impressive record and why Alf chose to run against him is unknown. Brownlow was instrumental in founding Rural Free Delivery for the nation, for establishing the Mountain Home Branch of the Disabled Volunteer

Soldiers at Johnson City, and in the creation of Andrew Johnson National Cemetery at Greeneville, which was dedicated in 1909. During this campaign, the editor of the Jonesborough *Herald and Tribune*, stated in July that "the prospects of electing the Republican ticket were never brighter, [but] there is grave danger that the nominees may be defeated if Alf Taylor ... persists in remaining in the race." He went on to say that if Mr. Taylor and his followers continued, they would prove they were for their own self interests rather than that of the Party. As the election date drew near, Brownlow's supporters contrasted his 1,003 legislative days in Congress with Alf's 860 days. Unfortunately for Alf, his record showed that he was ineffective and had been absent from more than half of the sessions, along with other duties not performed. In November Brownlow was returned to Congress with an 8,500 vote plurality over Alf. Brownlow remained a congressman until his death in 1910.

On Thursday, November 29, 1906, the correspondent for *The Rural Searchlight* stated that Alf was taking his defeat in the race for Congress philosophically and good naturedly. He told the correspondent that his defeat was the result of vote buying, and he hoped that a severe law for this practice would be put in place. Alf was interviewed at his home and the correspondent waxed eloquently and proudly, describing the "home in the picturesque valley, coursed by the sparkling waters of the Nolichucky." Alf's bid for the First District seat is not mentioned in his congressional biography or in other biographies. It may not have been referenced because Alf, a loyal Republican, went against the party and later regretted his action. Further, he not only suffered a humiliating defeat, but his congressional record was open to scrutiny, and he may have preferred that this not be revisited.

In 1908 Alf and Jennie purchased a house facing Buffalo Creek adjacent to the campus of Milligan College where, as Alf believed, his children could get a better education. Alf continued to work the Chautauqua circuit for the first two decades of the twentieth century. On August 18, 1916, from the circuit, he wrote to his son Blaine who was working at the Summers/Parrott Hardware store in Johnson City that he had driven to Seymour, Iowa, so he could catch the Rock Island train for Mercer. He was "in first class trim" he reported, even though he had traveled all night and changed trains four times. Attendance was good, and the Tennesseans in the west, after learning Alf was speaking, "swarmed" to his engagements. It was hot, and Alf confessed that if he did not perspire in streams when speaking, he would collapse. There may have been some discussion about Jennie accompanying him on the circuit, but as he explained to his son, the trip would kill his mama with all its night rides. Alf said he would be home soon, and after he rested, they would take a trip to New York and Washington. Alf was closing the tour in LaGrange and told Blaine that he and his mother should meet him at the Union Depot, St. Louis, on the morning of the 30th, and they would spend a day or so in St. Louis. After the visit the family took the train home to Tennessee via Cincinnati and Louisville.

The Governor's Mansion

In the 1920 election for governor, Alf's Democrat opponent was incumbent Albert H. Roberts. The Democrats were bitterly divided over a sweeping tax reform introduced by Governor Roberts, which gave the Republicans an opportunity to win the state house. In the August 5 primary, Governor Roberts won his Party's nomination. The Republicans narrowed their candidates down to two in the primary, one being Alf, the sentimental favorite of the press and the public, who was nominated in the primary. As reported by the Knoxville *Journal and Tribune* Alf carried with him (as a prop) a fiddle that he said was made at his home in Happy Valley. Alf, according to the newspaper was accompanied by the "Taylor Quartette," composed of his sons and R.C. Wardrep who rendered old time southern melodies upon the guitar, banjo, and violin.

Few issues were more divisive in Tennessee than Women's Suffrage, yet Alf wisely chose not to become involved. Alf, in his campaign, took a page out of brother's Bob political playbook and did not touch divisive issues. During the campaign, Alf's detractors, those who did not care for him for one reason or another, along with the opposition party, said he was too old to run for governor. Alf, an avid fox hunter, responded with what became the legend of Old Limber, a fox hound who everyone thought was too old to hunt. Old Limber was that great fox hound of Happy Valley who is perhaps one of the few, if not the only fox hound to have a book written about him. The author, DeLong Rice, founder of the Rice Lyceum Bureau, wrote that with Alf and Bob Taylor's "eloquence, [about] their fox hounds, they wrought for themselves a niche of eternal melody in the heart of their country." According to Rice, only a Taylor in 1920 could have "called a phantom fox hound out of the woods of the past and set him successfully upon the heels of the staid old Democratic Party in Tennessee." When campaigning, Alf told his audience that he had found the fountain of youth in the Unaka Mountains of East Tennessee, and in vivid descriptive words, he brought the blue and lofty peaks to life for them. He told how by moonlight they took the fox hounds from their kennels. He called many by name, but the most famous, Old Limber, was the oldest of the pack. Alf described the hunt and the melody of the dogs chasing the fox, and how, when sunrise came, the last one, singing the loudest, was Old Limber. The prelude to this was The Fox

Hunters Quartette singing old African American songs. The audience loved the story, and the issue of age was forgotten.

In 1920 Governor Roberts used the National Guard "to break strikes by the street and railway workers in Knoxville and by shoe-factory employees in Nashville." The governor who stressed law and order denounced the unions as a way to suppress their activities and also to keep wages low. Alf agreed on the need for law enforcement, but did not take this up as an issue.

"Roberts was no match for Taylor's . . . folksy, good-humored approach which had served him so well in the primary campaign." The Knoxville *News Sentinel* warned that "folk lore, banjo picking, minstrelsy, and vaudeville are delightful features no doubt, but the conditions and times demand a serious and responsible man at the head of Tennessee's government, not the proprietor of a side show." People loved Taylor's affable, entertaining style, and he drew tremendous crowds throughout the state. Alf did take a stance against the taxation issue, and it gave him a larger return from farmers in the rural areas.

In the final election returns, a higher than usual margin for Alf in East Tennessee was attributed to women who voted for the first time in the gubernatorial race. Seventy-two year old Alf defeated Roberts by a vote of 229,143 to 185,890. Following the election the Knoxville *Journal and Tribune* wrote that Alf, after a political retirement of twenty-five years, had battled his way to the governorship. In this article, as many writers did, they retold the War of the Roses campaign of 1886, thus keeping the story alive.

Jesse Cottrell of the *Chattanooga Times* remarked how Milligan College had converted both Jennie and Alf to women's suffrage. The college, four miles from Johnson City, was surrounded by a beautiful hamlet and at the time was having problems with free roving cattle and other nuisances. To be able to protect themselves, it was proposed to incorporate the town of Milligan. As the newspaper man wrote when it came time to elect a mayor, Alf was nominated. Jennie had worked for the creation of the municipality, but when they went to vote she could not bring herself to do so. Jennie, hesitant because women did not have the right to vote, thought this would be improper. Alf encouragingly asked her to take his arm, and he escorted her to the polling booth, where they voted together. Alf was elected mayor. The reporter remarked this settled the case of women's suffrage in the Taylor home.

Newly elected Governor Alf Taylor (1921-1923) poses with his family. He was the first Republican governor elected since Reconstruction and the oldest person to date to hold the governor's office. James Blaine Taylor was his father's campaign secretary. First row, left to right. Benjamin Harrison, Governor Alf Taylor, first lady Jennie Taylor, Frank; second row, David Haynes, Katherine, Mary Williams; third row, Nathaniel T., Blaine, Robert Love, Alfred. Archives of Appalachia, East Tennessee State University.

Before Alf departed for Nashville, Cottrell interviewed him while he was recuperating from an illness at his home on the Nolichucky River. Cottrell wrote that Alf and Jennie with their "happy family" would leave for the governor's mansion, with the exception of the older sons, Nat and Blaine, who were in business as hardware merchants in Johnson City. Their son "Benjamin H., a brilliant and successful attorney," was not living at home but in Johnson City with his new bride, Lela. The governor-elect wished for "a peaceful administration with harmony between the executive and legislative branches of Tennessee government during the next two years. The handmaiden of that wish [was] a desire that legislation be enacted conducive to further industrial development and economic stability in the state. Efficiency and economy [was] to be [his] slogan, and his every executive act [would] be with that in view."

The Taylors had a good sense of history, which was evident at Alf's inauguration when red and white boutonnieres were worn, reminiscent of the debate thirty-four years earlier in the "War of the Roses." It was an eloquent way for Alf to remember his brother Bob. On Saturday, January 15, 1921, at 11 a.m., the inaugural ceremonies for the Honorable Alf A. Taylor governor of Tennessee were held at the state capitol. Shortly afterwards, the House of Representatives sent him a resolution requesting that he make recommendations toward reducing the state expenses. His message to the Senate and House of the 62nd General Assembly contained eight suggestions, but the Democrats blocked his efforts. Alf served until January 16, 1923, when he was defeated for reelection by Democrat Austin Peay.

Governor Alf Taylor's family pose at their Milligan home in 1929. In the first row, left to right, are children, Alice Jane Taylor, Landon Taylor, Alfred Summers Taylor, Nat Taylor, Emily Taylor, James Taylor, Alfred W. Taylor, and Mary Williams. Second row: Dr. Carter Williams, Mrs. Mary Emeline (Carter) Williams, Carter Williams Jr., Governor and first lady Jennie Taylor, Katherine Taylor Graf, Frank Graf, and daughter Jane Graf, Florence Taylor. Back row: Frank Taylor, Robert Taylor, Mrs. Lela (Ben) Taylor, Mrs. Margaret (Blaine) Taylor, Blaine Taylor, David Haynes Taylor, Mrs. Nell (David) Taylor, Mrs. Fannie (Alfred) Taylor, Alfred Taylor, Mrs. Lucycle (Nathaniel G.) Taylor, Nathaniel G. Taylor. Clifford Maxwell photo, Archives of Appalachia, East Tennessee State University.

Alf had begun on the Chautauqua circuit in 1894, and for twenty-six years, except during World War I and when in political office, this had been his primary occupation and source of income. Whether or not he continued the tour at age seventy-four after leaving the governor's mansion in 1923, we are not certain. Alf, after he was defeated for reelection in 1923, returned to his Milligan home where he resided until his death.

On April 13, 1928, to honor the grand old Republican Alf Taylor, in his declining years, one of the largest fox hunts in America, and perhaps in the world, was held. The fox hunt was held a year and a half before the beginning of the Great Depression that led into World War II. It is unlikely it could have been held at any other time in our history. The decade before had seen America becoming more urban, the automobile was making people more mobile, immigration policy restricted, the Ku Klux Klan strong in the South, prohibition implemented, and through radio, the nation heard a high school teacher in Dayton, Tennessee, being tried for teaching evolution. This hunt, to honor one of Tennessee's most famous fox hunters, was organized by Alex Shell of the Elizabethton Hunt Club. Held on Bogart Knob, an eminence 1,952' in elevation, near the community of Watauga in Carter County, it was three and a fourth air miles north from Alf's Milligan home. A large tent was pitched on the summit, and the road was improved for the 750 friends and admirers, some traveling from Nashville. Governor Henry Horton attended the hunt as well as Senators Kenneth D. McKeller and Lawrence Tyson and Tennessee assemblymen Hill McAllister and George L. Berry. Old Limber, the fox hound made famous by Alf, led the pack of 500 hounds in the all night chase for the fox. The John Sevier Hotel in Johnson City catered the event, and 100 waiters served the guests.

Later, in 1928 another honor came to Alf when he was selected to introduce presidential contender Herbert Hoover when he gave a campaign speech in Elizabethton. Republican Hoover had decided to invade the solid Democrat south to obtain votes. Among those encouraging him to do so was Congressman B. Carroll Reece of the First District. It was Hoover's only southern speech, and he chose Elizabethton because it was solid Republican in a Democratic stronghold, and only one day journey from Washington. Hoover's message was carried nationwide by radio. Further, Carter County made a nice settling as it was so rich in history with the Watauga settlement and the gathering of the 1780 overmountain men for the trip to Kings Mountain. The October 6 date of his speech coincided closely with the anniversary of the famed Battle of Kings Mountain, which had been fought on October 7, the celebration of which was already being planned. Additionally, it was the home of ex-governor Alf Taylor who was nationally known for his Chautauqua lectures and for his humor.

In 1929 Jonesborough, Tennessee, became 150 years old, but the town delayed its sesquicentennial celebration until July of the next year in order to mark the completion of a modern water system at the same time. Congressman John Q. Tilson of Connecticut delivered the Independence Day address in the morning. Ex-governor Alf Taylor, still active in his later years, spoke that afternoon, honoring the founders of the town at the unveiling of the Memorial Fountain located in front of the courthouse.

On the front page of The Nashville Tennessean *Alf's death was portrayed in a sketch* as he poignantly answered *"The Master's Call." His hand reached heavenward toward his destination with Old Limber to comfort him on as many fox hunts as they desired, as he broke earth's tie to the spiritual home of the Taylor Clan, Happy Valley.* B. Harrison Taylor Collection.

On Wednesday, November 2, 1931, at 5:40 a.m., Alfred Alexander Taylor, age eighty-three, passed away at the Appalachian Hospital in Johnson City, from complications of Uremic Poisoning. An editorial simply said with affection "'Uncle Alf' is dead. The grand old man of the Republican Party . . . that has thrilled and moved thousands of people over two generations has been stilled." Outside Tennessee he was known as a political leader, congressman, and as governor of the state of Tennessee. The colorful War of the Roses endeared the two brothers, Alf and Bob, to the state and "commanded the attention of the nation." The editorial stated that at home, he was friend and neighbor and his memory would be a shining light to those who shared his friendship. President Herbert Hoover sent a telegram of condolence to Alf's wife Jennie at Milligan. He stated that in Alf's "public career as governor and as a member of Congress he served the public welfare with diligence and faithfully; his was a high sense of honor and integrity in personal life." Governor Henry H. Horton ordered the flag at the state capitol to be placed at half-mast and said Alf was "the kindest and most generous of men" adding that he led "a life of good will, kindliness of spirit and firm character." Alf was buried in Monte Vista Cemetery, Johnson City. Florence June "Jennie" Anderson Taylor died on February 13, 1943, at Milligan College and is buried beside her husband Alf.

Afterword

The Taylor name has a long political heritage of elected office in Tennessee, dating back to 1803 when Nathaniel Taylor was a state senator. The next Taylor to serve in the Tennessee legislature was Alf who served in 1875. Their imprint also included three members of the family, Nathaniel G., Alf, and Bob who served as congressman in the First Congressional District of East Tennessee. They served for a total of six terms. Bob was Tennessee governor for three terms and also a U.S. Senator. Alf Taylor served as governor from 1921 to 1923. He was the oldest person to date to hold the governor's office in Tennessee. Alf died in 1931, the last of the political dynasty that might have been perpetuated by his son Benjamin Harrison Taylor had he not died at an early age.

Death would not be the end for Alf or Bob, for they would live on in the hearts of Tennesseans. Their legacy was shared far outside the state. For example, on November 2, 1937, Alf and Bob were featured in the nationally syndicated *Ripley's Believe It Or Not*, carried in over 320 newspapers in seventeen languages and forty-two countries. Ripley's newspaper cartoon stated that Alfred Taylor ran against his own brother Robert Taylor for the governorship of Tennessee in 1886. An image of the two brothers was included, and in an explanatory note, it told that Alf, a Republican, ran against Bob, who won. "The campaign was one of the strangest ever seen" as the two brothers canvassed the state in joint debate know as Tennessee's "War of the Roses." Continuing, the note stated that, in 1921, thirty-five years later, Alf became governor of Tennessee.

Chapter 6

Benjamin Harrison Taylor
1888-1930

Alfred and Jennie Taylor, with their small family, moved to Johnson City in 1887, after purchasing property on Rome Hill, according to granddaughter Jennie Taylor Rogers. A son, Benjamin Harrison was born there on August 4, 1888, shortly after Alf returned home from the Republican convention. Alf, an admirer of Benjamin Harrison, named his son after him. It was almost assured from this beginning that Ben, as he was called from birth by his mother Jennie, would be politically inclined.

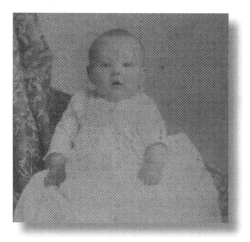

J.A. Cargille, an early Johnson City photographer, took this photograph of Benjamin Harrison Taylor. Alf and Jennie had ten children, and their third oldest was Benjamin Harrison who was born on August 4, 1888, in Johnson City, Tennessee, on Rome Hill. B. Harrison Taylor Collection.

On April 23, 1894, Congressman Taylor wrote to five year old Ben at "Chucky Valley" from Washington, D.C. He told him that he had received his letter and had mailed two books to him and two each to brothers, Nat, Dave, and Blaine. Ben had asked for a fine toothed comb, and Alf promised to get him one. Alf shared that he was miserable being away from his family. One way he furthered their education and comforted himself was to send the children books and other gifts.

In 1896 seven year old Ben was taken seriously ill with pneumonia, one of the leading causes of death in the Unites States at that time. Bob, Alf's brother, shared how distraught Alf was in a letter he wrote on April 28, 1896, to his wife, Sallie, from the Edwards House in Jackson, Mississippi. Both he and Alf were traveling together on the Chautauqua lecture tour when he wrote that "poor Alf had to go home yesterday. Little Ben is very sick. I dread to hear from him. He is so delicate. I fear he can't stand it. I never was as sorry for anybody as I am for Alf. He can't stand that sort of trouble. He dotes on Ben, and if he loses him it will almost kill him. He was the most pitiful looking man I ever saw when he left us, it made my heart bleed."

Fortunately Ben recovered and it is reported that he attended Columbus Powell School in Johnson City. In December 1904 the Taylors sold their Johnson City property and moved back to the Nolichucky River farm. In 1905 at age eighteen Ben graduated from Science Hill High School in Johnson City and entered Milligan College for the fall term of 1905. He was on the Milligan baseball team two years later. In 1908 Alf and Jennie Taylor moved to the campus of Milligan College while still retaining their Nolichucky River home. Benjamin Harrison Taylor graduated from Milligan College with a 94.76 grade average on May 23, 1911.

In 1912 Ben was working in the treasury department of the National Home of Disabled Volunteer Soldiers, Mountain Home Branch, in Johnson City. He entered the National Law School, Washington, D.C., in 1913, one year before World War I began in Europe. On November 8, 1914, Ben wrote his brother Blaine that he was "going to two schools." He was attending law school at night and a stenographer's school during the day. In November 1914 his father Alf Taylor was in Johnson City where he had a long visit with Congressman Sam Riley Sells of the First District. A Spanish-American War veteran and a Republican, Sells had been elected to the Sixty-second Congress, beginning his term on March 4, 1911. Alf had campaigned hard for Sells throughout East Tennessee, and now it was payback time. An a result of this meeting, Alf wrote his son Ben to tell him that Congressman Sells wanted to see him at his Washington office the first Monday in December. Sells was going to offer Ben a job, working two or three hours a day. Alf, always attuned to finances, said this would help Ben pay for his board and other expenses. The experience gained in this job would also benefit Ben in his future political aspirations. Capt. Charles Y. Deaderick, Adjutant and Inspector of the Johnson City veteran home wrote to his friend Ben on December 4, saying that the morning newspaper had announced that Grant Jarvis had been appointed secretary for Congressman Sells and that Ben had been appointed stenographer.

Ben H. Taylor in Washington D.C. He was a student at the National Law School from 1913 to 1915. As a student he worked for Congressman Sam Sells of the Congressional First District and later became a law partner of Thad A. Cox in Johnson City. B. Harrison Taylor Collection.

On June 30, 1915, the Johnson City newspaper reported that Ben H. Taylor had just graduated from law school and returned to his parent's Milligan home for a vacation. The paper reported that he was a very promising young lawyer, an able speaker, and great success was predicted for him. Ben, a member of the Johnson City Bar Association, soon entered a partnership with Thad A. Cox under the firm name of Thad A. Cox and Ben H. Taylor. Earlier, on June 4, 1891, Cox, after his graduation from law school, had opened a law office in Johnson City. At that time he formed a partnership with Walter W. Faw. Cox and Taylor joined together after Faw moved to Franklin, Tennessee, and had their offices in the Thad A. Cox building, 217 ½ Main Street. Thad's residence was at "The Oaks" on South Roan Street. He was a leader of the Democratic Party in East Tennessee, with which Ben Taylor became very involved. This political affiliation made them a natural match. In the courtroom Ben was courteous and considerate, a gifted orator who represented his side of a case with considerable zeal. Samuel Cole Williams told how Ben held the attention of all the associate justices before the Tennessee Supreme Court in a case he pleaded. Williams was from 1913 to 1918 an Associate Justice of the Tennessee Supreme Court. He added Ben had strong legal ethics and a strong love for the law.

In the fall of 1916, Ben tested the political waters by running for Democratic Elector, State at Large, and canvassed the state, making many important political contacts. His travels throughout the state at that time would generate many speaking engagements for him. Ben was recognized as a political figure whose reputation was further enhanced by his father's political career as well as that of his uncle, former governor and senator, Robert Love Taylor. His father was the Republican Elector, State at Large. The *Erwin Magnet*, Erwin, Tennessee, reported that a speech Ben made from the courthouse steps while running as elector lasted one hour and fifteen minutes. Throughout the speech, he was interrupted many times by spontaneous applause, suggesting how successful he was as an orator and candidate. The people loved him, and the newspaper predicted that in a few years he would be governor of Tennessee.

The United States entered World War I on April 6, 1917, and had troops in Europe by June 1917. Ben was called into the army on September 23, 1918, and served as a field clerk, assigned to the Headquarters Southeastern Department, Charleston, South Carolina. On November 11, 1918, the armistice was signed, ending hostilities. On November 20 from Charleston, Ben who was pleased with the news, wrote his "Dear Papa" that he was "waiting anxiously for his discharge from the service," adding "there is no phase of military life that is attractive to me." Ben was trying to get an early discharge from the army, and on the seventeenth of the next month, Thad A. Cox wrote Tennessee Congressman Cordell Hull that "as of December 15 Ben Taylor had not heard anything on his petition [for release from the service] that commanding General Henry G. Sharpe, in view of exceptional circumstances, [has] approved." Democratic Representative Cordell Hull responded to Cox by saying that on "behalf of our mutual friend, Ben Taylor," he was working on the release. The exceptional circumstances mentioned in the letter are unknown, but Ben was discharged shortly thereafter on December 19, 1918. He returned to work at the Thad A. Cox building in Johnson City.

In the fall of 1915, Alf went on the lecture tour with the Midwest Associated Chautauguens. He was not paid $400 owed him for the tour, and after promised payments that did not appear, he engaged his son Ben as his attorney to collect the amount due. On July 6, 1918, Ben, before he entered the military, wrote to Bell and Cross in Chicago on Alf's behalf in reference to the lawsuit filed against S. Boyd White of the Chautauguens. Ben wanted Boyd and Cross to investigate Mr. White and to determine if they could get at least a part payment for the $400 owed. Alf was in a precarious financial situation. He and Ben were very close, and Ben was more than pleased to assist his father. It is not known whether he was successful.

Ben Taylor in the early days of his law career in Johnson City, Tennessee. Ben a member of the First Presbyterian Church, Johnson City, taught a Bible class for several years, and was well thought of among his peers. B. Harrison Taylor Collection.

In 1920 on a Sunday afternoon, a correspondent from the *Chattanooga Times* visited Alf and Jennie Taylor at their Milligan home. The newsman wrote that Ben, their son, was "a brilliant and successful attorney in Johnson City." Jennie was described as a "woman of queenly bearing, comely face, who lived for her children and her husband. Their pleasure and enjoyment is hers. Her devotion to them and their interests is marked, and the children in turn fairly worshiped their mother. Her face lit up with the mention of Milligan College which was dear to her heart and although a non-sectarian school is under the Christian Church." The Taylors were very proud of the new college dormitory building which had recently been completed at a cost of $200,000.

Ben married Lela Amanda Ramsey from Coulterville, Tennessee, on September 28, 1920. She was the daughter of Rev. Samuel Ramsey and Lettie Conner Ramsey and was the oldest of eight children. She was described by a reporter as "a charming girl." As a young lady, she played the piano and sang to her father's accompaniment at his Cumberland Presbyterian Church. After her father's death, she moved to Johnson City and taught school. Lela and Ben moved their wedding date back several weeks so that Alf could attend before entering his campaign for governor. In November 1920 *The Journal and Tribune*, Knoxville, Tennessee, stated that Benjamin Harrison Taylor, a Democrat, was campaigning with his father and was interested in politics. In late November 1920 Ben and Lela were living in the "fashionable Maple Street Section of Johnson City." At the beginning of the New Year, Ben and his bride purchased almost two acres from A.B. Bowman Jr. at the intersection of Commerce Street and Highland Avenue in Johnson City.

On May 31, 1923, Ben and Lela bought an acre of land from S.E. Bottomley for $2,000. This acre joined the property they had purchased in 1921. To illustrate the agricultural nature of the time, when people in town often kept a cow, or a pig, or chickens, Bottomley reserved access to his barn and the right to harvest his clover for hay. Ben loved working in the soil. Thad Cox said Ben would leave the office on a Saturday evening to work on his farm where he could commune with nature and his God better than almost anywhere.

Ben and Lela Taylor pose with their children at the Milligan home of Governor Alf and Jennie Taylor who were celebrating their wedding anniversary in 1929. The children from left to right are Thaddeus Morrison, Jennie Leona, and B. Harrison. Ben died the following year. B. Harrison Taylor Collection.

Ben unexpectedly died of pneumonia on Wednesday, March 26, 1930. He had pneumonia as a child which may have contributed to his death due to a weakened immune system. The place of his death was about eight miles from where Andrew Taylor settled in 1778. Ben's funeral was delayed as his brother, Robert Love Taylor, traveling in the western United States, had to be located. As he made his way back to Tennessee for the funeral, the Southern Railway held train No. 25 at Memphis so that he could make his connection with the Frisco train. Thad A. Cox, Ben's partner for some fifteen years, said Ben was a Christian, as a student, as a lawyer, as a jurist, and as a citizen. He commented that he never saw his equal, and if he had lived, his future would have stabilized the government. From Ben's travels about the state and his speaking engagements, it was evident he was ambitious and had plans to run for political office. Cox said that every time Ben went to Nashville some statesman or friend would urge him to run for governor. Cox thought that he had seemed to be inclined in that direction, and if he had lived, Tennessee would never have had a better man for governor. Congressman Cordell Hull, soon to be Secretary of State, commented that he knew of no person among the younger generation with greater promise and that Ben's passing was an irreparable loss to Tennessee, suggesting the high hopes he had had for him.

Ben's death occurred during the Great Depression, and in 2001 his son, Benjamin Harrison Taylor, wrote that his mother, Lela, "moved to the family farm on the Nolichucky River with her three small children [where she] ran a dairy and taught school." On May 31, 1938, Lela sold the Highland Avenue (now Highland Road) property in Johnson City for $800 to T.F. Thomas. In 1940 "she moved back to Johnson City" where she started construction on a house in the Morningside View Addition at 141 East Highland Road, finishing it in March 1941. While there, her son wrote, she became "a case worker for the Welfare Department. The mayor of Johnson City, Sam H. Sells [son of Congressman Sam R. Sells] requested that she become Judge of the Juvenile Court, a position that she held for several years." Lela, on November 5, 1975, bought from Harry A. Smith lots 13 and 32 in Block 2 of the Morning Side Addition in Johnson City. "Through the hard years of her life, she maintained a life of rectitude, compassion for the poor, fair dealing with all people," and as was later said of her, "she was a true and worthy role model of the independent woman—a woman of faith and trust in God."

Federal Judge Robert Love Taylor and the Clinton Desegregation Case (1889-1987)

Robert Love Taylor was born on December 20, 1899, to parents Jennie and Alf Taylor at their farm on the banks of the Nolichucky River in Washington County, Tennessee. Robert was named for his uncle, a former governor (1887-1891) and senator (1907-1912) from Tennessee. The Taylors were a close knit family, always looking after and assisting each other. For example, attorney James Patton Taylor handled affairs for his mother, Mary, in settling Brig. Gen. Nathaniel Taylor's estate. In 1924 Ben invited his brother, Robert Love Taylor, a fellow Democrat, to practice law with him and Thad Cox in Johnson City upon his graduation from Yale University. In this tradition, when Ben died attorney Robert Love Taylor provided invaluable assistance over the years to Lela and her children.

Robert Love Taylor gained national attention in 1956 during the desegregation of Clinton High School in Clinton, Tennessee. He served in World War I and afterwards graduated from Milligan College in 1921. Taylor studied law at Vanderbilt University and received his law degree from Yale University in 1924. A semi-professional baseball player, he played during the summers to pay for his education. He practiced law with his brother, Benjamin Harrison Taylor, in Johnson City. Active in the Democratic Party, in 1948 he managed the primary campaign of Gordon Browning for governor, and later as chairman of the Democratic State Executive Committee, he managed the successful campaigns of Browning and Senator Estes Kefauver. On November 25, 1949, President Harry S. Truman appointed him as United States District Judge for the Eastern District of Tennessee. Afterwards, Taylor moved with his family to Knoxville, where the court usually met.

Robert Love Taylor in 1957, son of former governor Alf Taylor and brother to Benjamin Harrison Taylor (1888-1930), was brought into the law firm of Taylor and Cox in Johnson City after his graduation from law school. He was practicing law in Johnson City when in 1949 he was appointed as a federal judge and moved to Knoxville. Knoxville News Sentinel.

In 1950 African American families in Clinton, Tennessee, approached Clinton High School principal D. J. Brittain and County School Superintendent Frank Irwin Anderson requesting the enrollment of their children in Clinton High School. Their request was refused, and on December 5, 1950, they filed a federal suit against school officials of Anderson County, Tennessee, citing exclusion from Clinton High School. At the time, Tennessee law prohibited integration as long as there was no inequality in education. The plaintiffs in the Clinton desegregation case, students Joheather McSwain, James Dickey, William Dickey, Lillian Willis, and Shirley Willis, attended the all-black Austin High in Knox County. Their suit was styled *Joheather McSwain, et al. v County Board of Education of Anderson County, Tennessee, et al.* They were represented by Thurgood Marshall, along with other attorneys. Marshall later became associate justice of the United States Supreme Court.

Anderson County did not have a high school solely for African Americans because there were not enough students. When the lawsuit was filed, the Anderson County school board moved their African American students who were attending a high school in Campbell County with a "C" class rating to Austin High in Knoxville which had an "A-1" rating. This rating was higher than the "A" rating of Clinton High School. Thus, according to the officials, the African Americans were now receiving, according to the ratings, an education more than equal to the Clinton High School students.

Patricia Brake, in *Justice in the Valley*, stated that the plaintiffs' counsel argued that laws that only seemed fair on the surface in educational opportunities were prohibited by the Fourteenth Amendment and therefore unconstitutional. Judge Taylor ruled that although the Fourteenth Amendment was a safeguard to opportunity, the schooling of its citizens was a state function. The plaintiffs were seeking an education equal to whites at Clinton High School. Judge Taylor's opinion was that since there was no African American high school in Anderson County, he did not have the authority to "declare segregation in schools unconstitutional," and therefore could not legally admit them to Clinton High School, which the plaintiffs were trying to get him to do indirectly. On May 19, 1952, Judge Taylor dismissed the lawsuit.

Brake wrote that on June 13, 1952, the plaintiffs appealed to the Sixth Circuit Court of Appeals, Cincinnati, Ohio. In October 1953 the McSwain case versus Anderson County was heard. On May 17, 1954, the United States Supreme Court declared that "separate but equal" facilities in public education were unconstitutional. When this decision was made, seventeen states had laws that prohibited integration. On June 3, 1954, the court of appeals reversed Judge Taylor's decision. The court ordered that the final decree must wait for the Supreme Court's decision in *Brown, et al. v The Board of Education, Topeka, Kansas, et* al. On May 31, 1955, Judge Taylor reversed his former decision, awaiting the final decision of the Supreme Court. The final decree was issued in September 1955, and Taylor's District Court decreed that the defendants must integrate. Following the mandate of the Supreme Court to expedite desegregation, Judge Taylor required Anderson County school officials to adopt a "prompt and reasonable start" toward integration. On January 4, 1956, Judge Taylor ordered that racial segregation be ended at Clinton High School, and followed this order by fixing the date for desegregation as the fall term of 1956.

Clinton High School began to prepare for integration. Horace V. Wells, editor of the *Clinton Courier News*, through editorials and regular reporting, made the community aware of the events which were transpiring. The court's action placed Clinton in the forefront of desegregation on a national level. Clinton High School, with a student body of 806, was the first public school in the South to desegregate, when on August 27, 1956, twelve African American students enrolled. These students, from Green-McAdoo Elementary School in Clinton and Vine Junior High

School in Knoxville, had registered peacefully on August 20, but opposition in Clinton and neighboring communities grew to such a level as to interfere with the operation of the school.

Much of the dissension has been attributed to Frederick John Kasper, a twenty-six year old native of Camden, New Jersey, who had headed a white citizens group in Washington, D.C. He arrived in Clinton the weekend before school started. When school opened, Kasper gathered crowds numbering around fifty on Monday and Tuesday morning. The number increased significantly at night, rising to an estimated 800 to 2,000 people. On Wednesday, August 29, Judge Taylor issued a temporary restraining order for potential anti-segregationists. On August 29 and 30, Kasper, the executive secretary of the Seaboard White Citizens Council, with chapters throughout the south, addressed crowds opposing integration. Quick to react to a deteriorating situation, the Clinton school officials, according to Brake, asked Judge Taylor to jail Kasper on contempt charges, which Taylor complied with as Kasper had violated his restraining order. Judge Taylor was closely monitoring the situation, and Brake added that on September 1, a Saturday, Taylor found Kasper guilty of contempt and sentenced him to one year in prison. Kasper was released on bond pending appeal.

Also on that Saturday, Mayor W.E. Lewallen and the board of alderman declared Clinton to be in a state of emergency and requested Governor Frank G. Clement to restore law and order. Governor Clement called out the National Guard and some 600 guardsmen with tanks arrived on September 2 to establish roadblocks and prevent congregating on the square or elsewhere. On September 3 United States Marshal Frank Quarles read Judge Taylor's order in front of the high school, placing all citizens in Clinton under his injunction. Judge Taylor's temporary restraining order was made permanent on September 6, aimed at Kasper and the others who were interfering with the order of the court. The injunction prevented picketing, threatening, or intimidating the African American students along the route they took to Clinton High School.

Through November and December, the harassment continued. For example, on December 4, Reverend Paul Turner, Clinton First Baptist Church, one of three white men who escorted the students to school, was attacked and badly beaten by segregationists. By early December, ten of the original twelve African American students were attending school, although both they and their parents were afraid for their safety as well as the safety of their homes. As author June N. Adamson wrote in 1994, the media hardly interviewed the students, parents, or the African American community to learn their perspective. Adamson said that by not being named in the press, or mistakenly identified, they were dehumanized and thus we lost much of our civil rights history. The media's approach, according to Adamson, was a story of desegregation, not of people. The major networks and print reporters from throughout the United States and internationally swarmed to Clinton.

In December 1957 Bobby Cain became the first black graduate from any integrated public high school in the South, and Gail Ann Epps was the first female African American to graduate from Clinton High School. The other eight attendees included Jo Ann Allen, Minnie Ann Dickey, Ronnie Hayden, Alva J. McSwain (whose parents were among the group who filed the 1950 lawsuit on behalf of an older sister), Edward Lee Soles, Maurice Soles, Regina Turner, and Alfred Williams. Charles Williams apparently did not attend. Theresa Caswell, a freshman, had polio and would have had to be bused in from the Claxton Community about seven miles away. Apparently her parents kept her home because they were afraid she might be injured by the unruly crowds.

The beating of Rev. Turner was a turning point for those who asked U.S. Attorney John C. Crawford Jr. for action. Crawford sought an injunction and Taylor granted it. United States Marshals were ordered to arrest the troublemakers. The Federal Bureau of Investigation assisted, and on December 4, 1956, sixteen people were arrested and charged with violating the judge's order. Clinton was restored to order during the fall and early winter. On February 25, 1957, Kasper and others who were charged with contempt were tried. The defendants did not take the stand, but the jury convicted Kasper and six others. Witnesses told of the threats, insults, and beatings that occurred. Judge Taylor sentenced Kasper to prison, where he served fifteen months of his sentence.

Over the years, Judge Taylor continued to look after his brother Ben's family. Lela Amanda Ramsey Taylor died in Johnson City on July 9, 1985, and was buried in Monte Vista Cemetery. When Ben died he left Lela with three small children. They were Jennie Leona, age eight, who became a housewife, Thaddeus Morrison, age six, was a Naval Academy graduate and became a Naval aviator, and B. Harrison Taylor, age five, earned his doctorate and became a Presbyterian minister. He commissioned this narrative in 2009.

Endnotes

[1] Duane H. King, ed. *The Cherokee Indian Nation, A Troubled History* (1976; reprint, Knoxville, Tenn.: The University of Tennessee Press, 1989), x-xi.

[2] James Mooney, *History, Myths, and Sacred Formulas of the Cherokee* (1900; reprint, Asheville, North Carolina: Historical Images, 1992), 14.

[3] W. Calvin Dickenson, "Watauga Association," in *Tennessee Encyclopedia of History and Culture*, ed. Carroll Van West (Nashville: Rutledge Hill Press, 1998), 1040. Sycamore Shoals State Historic Area, Elizabethton, Tennessee, is part of the cooperative program that honors the historic route of the 1780 Kings Mountain men who marched from there to that famous battle. The National Park Service supports cooperative agreements through the establishment of the 330 mile long Overmountain Victory National Historic Trail established in 1980.

[4] Ben Allen and Dennis T. Lawson, "The Wataugans and the 'Dangerous Example,'" in *Tennessee Historical Quarterly*, vol. 26, no. 2 (Summer 1967): 139.

[5] Hawkins County Register of Deeds, Rogersville, Tennessee, Deed Book 1, pages 147-150, November 1, 1794.

[6] Max Dixon, *The Wataugans* (1976; reprint, Johnson, City, Tenn.: The Overmountain Press, 1989), 36. See also Richard Henderson (1735-1785) in Archibald Henderson, "Richard Henderson and the Occupation of Kentucky, 1775," in *Mississippi Valley Historical Review*, vol. 1, No. 3 (December 1914): 341-363.

[7] Cumberland Gap National Historical Park, National Park Service, now commemorates the famous Wilderness Road. By 1792 the population of Kentucky largely arriving through Cumberland Gap had reached 100,000 and was admitted as a state.

[8] H.T. Spoden & Associates, *Sycamore Shoals State Park and Colonel John Carter House*, (Kingsport, Tenn.: Tennessee Historical Commission, 1974), 154. Hereafter Spoden, *Sycamore* Shoals. The correct name of the site is Sycamore Shoals State Historic Area. Nathaniel Taylor purchase, Carter County Register of Deeds, Elizabethton, Tennessee, Deed Book B, pages 316-317, filed March 13, 1812. A copy of deeds of the "Wataugah Land Purchases" is housed in the Washington County records at Jonesborough, and the original is in the Tennessee State Library and Archives, Nashville.

[9] William L. Saunders, ed. *The Colonial Records of North Carolina, 1775-1776*, vol. 10 (Raleigh: Josephus Daniels, Printer, 1890), 782. Hereafter Saunders, *Colonial Records*, vol. 10. Spoden, *Sycamore Shoals*, 358. A 1973 archeological investigation located the irregular shaped fort at the Daughters of the American Revolution Sycamore Shoals Monument west of Elizabethton on G Street. The reconstructed fort located at Sycamore Shoals State Historic Area is based on the known measurements of the original fort and was part of the park dedication in 1976.

[10] Saunders, *Colonial Records*, vol. 10, 702, 708-711.

[11] Ibid., 702, 708-711.

[12] Ibid., 925-926 951, 978, 998.

[13] http://www.globalsecurity.org/military/agency/army/arng-tn.htm.

[14] W. Eugene Cox and Joyce Cox, *Jonesborough: The Town and Its People* (Jonesborough, Tenn.: Heritage Alliance of Northeast Tennessee and Southwest Virginia, 2008), 14, photocopy. Hereafter Cox, *Jonesborough: The Town and Its People*.

[15] The Taylor and other genealogy throughout the text have been verified by B. Harrison Taylor III, Johnson City, Tennessee.

[16] Elizabeth Taylor McNabb. Widow's pension from Captain David McNabb, Revolutionary War service, North Carolina w. 7438. National Archives Washington, D.C. Andrew Taylor Jr. supporting the pension of Captain McNabb who had married his sister said they (Andrew Taylor Sr. and family) arrived on the Watauga in 1778.

[17] Washington County, North Carolina (Tennessee). Court of Pleas and Quarter Sessions, Book 1, August 1778-October 1799, roll WA-129, 55.

[18] Andrew Taylor, Washington County, North Carolina, October 23, 1782. Grant No. 164, Entry No. 44, entered April 4, 1779, Book 47, page 79, 450 acres on both sides of Buffalo Creek. Original in files Jennie Taylor Rogers Collection, Tucson, Arizona. Goldene Fillers Burgner, *North Carolina Land Grants in Tennessee 1778-1791* (Greenville, S.C.: Southern Historical Press, 1981), 8.

[19] In a letter written May 21, 1963, Frank A. Taylor, North Watauga Avenue, Elizabethton, Tennessee, makes the point Andrew Taylor moved into what they called a lean to. Another viewpoint for the two story log house being Andrew Taylors was described by William and Major George Taylor, grandsons of General Nathaniel Taylor to Franklin D. Love as follows: "The house was constructed of logs, with an open passage way between the north and south ends. It was two stories, and had six rooms, rear and front, and a porch in front and in the rear. It had a shed kitchen." Spoden, *Sycamore Shoals*, 635. Watauga Historical Association Collection 1796-1891, Box 1, Folder 1.19, Archives of Appalachia, East Tennessee State University, Johnson City, Tennessee.

[20] Washington County, North Carolina (Tennessee). Court of Pleas and Quarter Sessions, Book 1, August 1778-October 1799, roll WA-129, 77. Washington County, North Carolina, October 23, 1782. Grant No. 134, Warrant No. 1499, Entry No. 149, entered August 5, 1779, Book 47, Page 65, for thirty-one acres.

[21] Spoden, *Sycamore Shoals*, 649. From Captain David McNabb pension claim by his widow. Andrews Taylor Jr., Claim for a pension for his Service as a Militiaman in 1780 and 1781 During the Revolutionary War, August 25, 1832, Carter County, Tennessee. This pension is probably from Allen Papers, McClung Collection Lawson McGhee Library Knoxville, Tennessee.

[22] Elizabeth Taylor McNabb. Widow's pension from Captain David McNabb, Revolutionary War service, North Carolina w. 7438. National Archives Washington, D.C. Spoden, *Sycamore Shoals*, 649. Lyman C. Draper, *Kings Mountain and Its Heroes* (1881; reprint, Nashville: Blue and Gray Press, 1971), 435, 471. Hereafter Draper, *Kings Mountain*. Allen Papers, McClung Collection Lawson McGhee Library Knoxville, Tennessee.

[23] Draper, *Kings Mountain*, 169.

[24] Ibid., 170-171.

[25] William Gunn Calhoun, comp. *Samuel Doak 1749-1830* (Washington College, Tenn.: Pioneer Printers, 1966), 3-4.

[26] Robert K. Johns. *A History First Presbyterian Church, Elizabethton, Tennessee* (Rogersville, Tenn.: East Tennessee Printing Company, 1989), 3-8. Hereafter Johns, *First Presbyterian Church, Elizabethton*. Andrew's great, great, great, great grandson, B. Harrison Taylor, served as a part time preacher for a few years at the First Presbyterian Church of Elizabethton, concluding in the year 2000.

[27] Draper, *Kings Mountain*, 176. Kings Mountain National Military Park, Blacksburg, South Carolina, a part of the National Park Service, was established to commemorate this historic battle.

[28] Washington County, North Carolina (Tennessee). Court of Pleas and Quarter Sessions, Book 1, August 1778-October 1799, roll WA-129, 140.

[29] J.G.M. Ramsey, *The Annals of Tennessee* (1853; reprint, Johnson City, Tenn.: The Overmountain Press, 1999), 287-288. Hereafter Ramsey, *Annals of Tennessee*.

[30] Cox, *Jonesborough: The Town and Its People*, 17. Michael Toomey, "Our Present Confused Situation": The State of Franklin, 1784-1789" in *History of Washington County Tennessee,* comps. and eds. Joyce Cox and W. Eugene Cox (Johnson City, Tenn.: The Overmountain Press, 2001), 71-96.

[31] Andrew Taylor Sr., Washington County, Jonesborough, Tennessee May 22, 1787, Will Book 1, 10-11. Will is also transcribed in Spoden, *Sycamore Shoals*, 654-656.

[32] Spoden, *Sycamore Shoals*, 635, 654-662.

[33] From Franklin Deaderick Love, *An Outline of the Taylor, Love, and Alexander Families of Eastern Tennessee and Western North Carolina and their Allied Families of Virginia* (Georgetown, Texas, 1929). Hereafter Love, *An outline of the Taylor Family*. Knox County Public Library, McClung Collection, Knoxville, Tennessee, in Spoden, *Sycamore Shoals*, 646.

Notes on Chapter 2

[1] Love, *An Outline of the Taylor Family* cited in Spoden, *Sycamore Shoals,* 640

[2] Washington County Court of Pleas and Quarter Sessions, Book 1, August 1778-October 1799, roll WA-129, February 1787, 273-275, and the May 1787 Term, 279.

[3] Washington County Court of Pleas and Quarter Sessions, Book 1, August 1778-October 1799, roll WA-129, May 1788 Term, 323.

[4] Pauline Massengill DeFriece and Frank B. Williams Jr., "Rocky Mount: The Cobb-Massengill Home First Capitol of the Territory South of the River Ohio." *Tennessee Historical Quarterly,* vol. 25, no. 2 (Summer 1966): 119-134.

[5] The story of Nathaniel going to Rockbridge County for schooling and so forth was told in a July 29, 1941, letter from N.G. Taylor, Limestone, Tennessee, to Nell Taylor (Mrs. David H.), Milligan College, Tennessee. N.G. said that his grandfather Nathaniel Greene Taylor had told this story over and over many times to him. Under the Bounty Act of September 20, 1850, widows and other surviving family of veterans of the War of 1812 or an Indian was since 1790 could apply for 160 acres of land. A.W. Taylor, and attorney, from Happy Valley Post Office, Carter County, Tennessee, on April 12, 1851, applied on behalf of his mother Mary Patton Taylor, Nathaniel's widow. She told of his excursions after the Cherokee Indians when a family by the name of Lewis had been killed. He was ordered out other times in 1793, she believed. She told of their marriage on November 15, 1791. She also mentioned his service as a brigadier general in the War of 1812. Included in a letter from G.P. Taylor, Klamath Falls, Oregon, to N.G. Taylor, Limestone, Tennessee, dated April 4, 1936, and stating the documents came from the National Archives. B. Harrison Taylor Collection, Johnson City, Tennessee.

[6] Nathaniel Taylor and Mary Patton were married by Presbyterian minister Brown in Rockbridge County, Va. Information comes from Mary Taylor applying for a Land Warrant, April 12, 1851, National Archives. B. Harrison Taylor Collection, Johnson City, Tennessee.
Robert McBride, ed. *Biographical Directory of the Tennessee General Assembly, vol. 1, 1797-1861* (Nashville: Tennessee State Library and Archives and Tennessee Historical Commission, 1975), 710. Hereafter McBride, *Biographical Directory of the Tennessee*

General Assembly. Note: The biographical directory was developed by sending family members a questionnaire and although a good source may not be entirely correct.

[7] Love, *An Outline of the Taylor Family* cited in Spoden, *Sycamore Shoals,* 640.

[8] Ernest W. Goodpasture, "General Nathaniel Taylor and Some Papers Relating to His Service in the War of 1812," *The American Historical Magazine,* vol. 9, no.1 (April 1904): 193-200.
Hereafter Goodpasture, *General Nathaniel Taylor and Some Papers.*

[9] Robert M. McBride, editor, *Tennessee Historical Quarterly* in Mrs. John Trotwood Moore, *Record of Commissions of Officers in the Tennessee Militia, 1796-1811* (Nashville: Tennessee Historical Commission, 1947), vii. Frank Merritt, *Early History of Carter County 1760-1861* (1950; reprint, Kingsport, Tenn. : Kingsport Press, 1978), 149. Hereafter Meritt, *Early History of Carter County.*

[10] John H. Dewitt, ed., "Journal of John Sevier," *The Tennessee Historical Society,* no. 3 (October 1919): 162.

[11] Samuel C. Williams, "Brigadier General Nathaniel Taylor," *The East Tennessee Historical Society's Publications,* no. 12 (1940): 29-30.

[12] Ramsey, *Annals of Tennessee,* 584-586.

[13] Edwin Carter, *The Territorial Papers of the United States, Volume 4, Southwest Territory* (Washington, D.C. : U.S. Government Printing Office, 1936), 458.

[14] George Roulstone, *Acts passed at the First General Assembly of the State of Tennessee, March 28,1976,* Chapter 31 (Knoxville, Tenn.: George Roulstone, 1796), 71-74.
Hereafter Roulstone, *First General Assembly of Tennessee.*

[15] *Goodspeed's History of Tennessee* (1972; reprint, Nashville: Goodspeed Publishing Company, 1887), 908. Hereafter *Goodspeed's History of Tennessee.* Merritt, *Early History of Carter County, 34-35, 182.* The other justices of the peace were Andrew Greer, Landon Carter, David McNabb, Zachariach Campbell, Guttredge Garland, John Vaught, Joseph Lands, and Reuben Thornton. Merritt states that Goodspeed Publishing in their 1887 book *History of Tennessee* must have had access to the early record to document the justieces of the peace. Merritt wrote he was able to document in early court records that he had seen Nathaniel Taylor and others listed in their official capacity which he includes in his book. Mrs. John Trotwood Moore, *Record of Commissions of Officers in the Tennessee Militia, 1796-1811* (Nashville: Tennessee Historical Commission, 1947), 6.

[16] Roulstone, *First General Assembly of Tennessee,* 100-102.

[17] Edward Scott, comp., *Laws of the State of Tennessee,* Chapter 5 (Knoxville: Heiskell and Brown, 1821), 637. Early deeds show the name Elizabethton was being used in 1796.

[18] Anne-Leslie Owens, "Carter Mansion," in *The Tennessee Encyclopedia of History and Culture,* ed. Carroll Van West (Nashville, Tenn.: Rutledge Hill Press, 1998), 133. *Goodspeed's History of Tennessee,* 908. March 5, 1795, survey document, B. Harrison Taylor Collection, Johnson City Tennessee.

[19] Merritt, *Early History of Carter County,* 150-151.

[20] Watauga Historical Association Collection 1796-1891, Box 2, Folder 21, Archives of Appalachia, East Tennessee State University, Johnson City, Tennessee.

[21] Robert Tipton Nave, "A History of the Iron Industry in Carter County to 1860" (master's thesis, East Tennessee State College, 1953), 1-5. Hereafter Nave, "History of Iron Industry." Register of Deeds, Washington County, Jonesborough, Tennessee, Deed Book 32, January 16, 1850, 45-46. In an agreement between Samuel Lyle and Robert L. Blair and Brothers with Elijah Embree they were to receive iron and nails manufactured by him from his "lately dissolved" Washington Manufactory Company in exchange for commodities from their store. In 1828 there was not much money in circulation in Carter County and iron served as the principal medium of exchange. A.M. Carter to Nathan Nelson, January 4, 1828, in Thomas B. Alexander, *Thomas A.R. Nelson of East Tennessee* (Nashville: Tennessee Historical Commission, 1956), 6. Hereafter Thomas B. Alexander, *Thomas A. R. Nelson of East Tennessee.*

[22] Nave, "History of the Iron Industry," 15, 92. Godfrey Carriger Jr. from a prominent Carter County family was born on May 13, 1769, and died on May 6, 1827. He was a major in the militia in 1800 and would have served under Nathaniel.

[23] McBride, *Biographical Directory of the Tennessee General Assembly,* 710. Samuel Cole Williams, *Brigadier General Nathaniel Taylor* (Johnson City, Tenn. The Watauga Press, 1940), 9,11.

[24] Elizabeth Roulstone, *Acts Passed by the Sixth General Assembly of Tennessee, July 28, 1806,* Chapter 8 (Knoxville, Tenn.: J.B. Hood, 1806), 76.

[25] Watauga Historical Association Collection 1796-1891, Box 1, Folder 1.19, Archives of Appalachia, East Tennessee State University, Johnson City, Tennessee.

[26] Watauga Historical Association Collection 1796-1891, Box 2, Folder 2.29, Archives of Appalachia, East Tennessee State University, Johnson City, Tennessee.

[27] Watauga Historical Association Collection 1796-1891, Box 2 Folder 2.59, Archives of Appalachia, East Tennessee State University, Johnson City Tennessee.

[28] McBride, *Biographical Directoryof the Tennessee General Assembly,* 710. German born Godfrey Carriger (March 7, 1732-October 8, 1811) came to Carter County in 1779 and was very prosperous.

[29] T.G. Bradford, *The Military Instructor* (Nashville, Tenn.: Thomas G. Bradford, 1812) extract in *Tennessee Historical Magazine,* vol. 8, no. 8 (October 1924): 215-219.

Minuteman National Historical Park, Boston Massachusetts, a part of the National Park Service, commemorates "the shot heard around the world."

[30] Ibid. The book was first published in August 1810 and in 1812 a 142 page copy of *The Military Instuctor* sold for twenty-five cents.

[31] Donald R. Hickey, *The War of 1812 A Forgotten Conflict* (Urbana, Ill.: University of Illinois Press, 1989), 24, 26. Hereafter Hickey, *A Forgotten Conflict.*

[32] Robin Reilly, *The British at the Gates* (New York: G.P. Putnam's Sons, 1974), 15,64,72.

[33] Henry L. Coles, *The War of 1812* (Chicago: The University of Chicago Press, 1965), 151.

[34] Frank Lawrence Owsley Jr., *Struggle for the Gulf Borderlands* Gainesville, Fl.: University Presses of Florida, 1981), 2-4. Hereafter Owsley, *Struggle for the Gulf.* Hickey, *A Forgotten Conflict,* 204-209.

[35] Ibid., 147.

[36] John Buchanan, *Jackson's Way* (New York: John Wiley & Sons, Inc., 2001), 253. Hereafter Buchanan, *Jackson's Way.* Harold D. Moser, ed. *The Papers of Andrew Jackson,* vol. 3, 1814-1815 (Knoxville, Tenn.: The University of Tennessee Press, 1991) 23. Hereafter Moser, *The Papers of Andrew Jackson,* vol.3.

[37] Horseshoe Bend National Military Park, Daviston, Alabama, is part of the National Park Service. www.nps.gov/hobe.

[38] Owsley, *Struggle for the Gulf,* 90-91. Moser, *The Papers of Andrew Jackson,* 280.

[39] Moser, *The Papers of Andrew Jackson,* vol. 3, 407, 411, 424, 425.

[40] James W. Holland, *Andrew Jackson and the Creek War: Victory at the Horseshoe* (Philadelphia: Eastern National Park and Horseshoe Bend National Military Park, 1969), 29. This narrative originally appeared in the *Alabama Review,* October 1968, published by the University of Alabama Press.

[41] Goodpasture, "General Nathaniel Taylor and Some Papers," 193-200. *The Military Instuctor* published in 1812 mentioned militia acts for the state militia as previously cited. The rest of the command staff, which may not be complete, included: Allan Johnson, who was called Brigade Quartermaster, and resigned on November 28,1814; Brigade Quartermaster Thomas P. Winn; Assistant Topographical Engineer James H. Peck; Hospital Surgeon Spencer E. Gibson; Forage Master William B. Carter; Forage Master Joseph Trotter; Assistant Forage Master Johns S. Fulton; Assistant Forage Master John Durgan, Wagon Master David G. Vance; Assistant Wagon Master Joseph McCorkle; Assistant Wagon Master David W. Hailey; and Assistant Topographical Engineer Samuel Bruff who was engaged November 9, 1814, but was absent at Fort Jackson, Bryon and Samuel Sistler, eds. *Tennesseans in the War of 1812* (Nashville,

Tenn.: Bryon Sistler & Associates, Inc., 1992). Hereafter Bryon and Sistler, *Tennesseans in the War of 1812.*

[42] Tom Kanon, "1814 Sept-May 1815 Regimental Histories of Tennessee Units During the War of 1812." Tennessee State Library and Archives, Nashvillle, Tennessee.

[43] Tom Kanon, "Regimental Histories of Tennessee Units During the War of 1812" (Nashville, Tenn.: Tennessee State Library and Archives).

[44] Bryon and Sistler, *Tennesseans in the War of 1812.*

[45] Owsley, *Struggle for the Gulf*, 87. Buchanan, *Jackson's Way*, 296-297.

[46] Owsley, *Struggle for the Gulf*, 90-91. The Trail of Tears National Historic Trail, Santa Fe, New Mexico, is administered by the National Park Service. Moser, *Papers of Andrew Jackson*, vol. 3, 280.

[47] Owsley, *Struggle for the Gulf*, 120-124.

[48] Statute II, April 18.1814, in *Public Statutes at Large of the United States of America* (Boston, Mass.: Charles C. Little and James Brown, 1850), 134-136. Leota Driver Maiden, "Colonel John Williams, *"The East Tennessee Historical Society's Publications*, no.30 (1958), 7-46. Williams was commissioned a colonel on June 18, 1813. Moser, *The Papers of Andrew Jackson*, vol. 3, 473. Mary U. Rothrock, ed. *The French Broad-Holston Country* (Knoxville, Tenn.: East Tennessee Historical Society, 1946), 446,506. Hereafter Rothrock, *The French Broad-Holston Country.*

[49] Moser, *The Papers of Andrew Jackson*, vol. 3, 463-464, 466.

[50] Buchanan, *Jackson's Way*, 310,312.

[51] Walter T. Durham, *James Winchester Tennessee Pioneer* (Gallatin, Tenn.: Sumner County Library Board, 1979), 157. Hereafter Durham, *James Winchester.* Durham shows that General Taylor had 2,000 men while Taylor reported to Jackson on September 28,1814, that he only 1,000 men. River Raisin National Battlefield Park, Monroe, Michigan, is the newest and 393rd park in the National Park Service.

[52] James D. Craig Scrapbook, 2nd Regiment West Tennessee Militia, Department of Archives and History, Montgomery, Alabama. Hereafter, Craig's Scrapbook, 2nd Regiment West Tennessee Militia.

[53] Raymond A. Sears, "East Tennesseeans in the War of 1812 Muster Rolls and Payrolls," *Tennessee Ancestors*, vol. 25, no. 3 (December 2009): 157-161. Another company in this article had eighty-two privates.

[54] Craig Scrapbook, 2nd Regiment West Tennessee Militia. Hart's letter is from Moser, *The Papers of Andrew Jackson*, 467.

[55] Goodpasture, "General Nathaniel Taylor and Some Papers," 193-200. Those signing the letter were Maj. C.F. Spoor, Judge Advocate, Aide-de-Camp George Duffield, Maj.

John Russell, Lt. Col. John Anderson, Maj. Samuel C. Magee, and the Regimental Surgeon Thomas I. Van Dyke.

[56] Goodpasture, "General Nathaniel Taylor and Some Papers," 193-200. Moser, *The Papers of Andrew Jackson*, vol. 3, 176.

[57] Craig Scrapbook, 2nd Regiment West Tennessee Militia.

[58] Moser, *The Papers of Andrew Jackson*, vol. 3, 174-175.

[59] Durham, *James Winchester*, 156. Moser, *The Papers of Andrew Jackson*, vol. 3, 191-193.

[60] Durham, *James Winchester*, 156-159.

[61] Ibid., 156-159

[62] Ibid., 164-166

[63] Alfred Alexander Taylor Family Papers 1815-1962, Archives of Appalachia, East Tennessee State University, Johnson City, Tennessee.

[64] Buchanan, Jackson's Way, 361. Arsène Lacarrière Latour, *Historical Memoir of the War in West Florida and Louisiana in 1814-1815 (*1816; reprint, Gainesville, Fl.: The Historic New
Orleans Collection, 2008), xiii. Hereafter Latour, *The War in West Florida and Louisiana.* Jean Lafitte National Historical Park and Preserve, New Orleans, National Park Service, includes Chalmette Battlefield and National Cemetery which commemorates the Battle of New Orleans, January 8, 1815. On February 12, 1814, Fort Bowyer protecting Mobile Bay fell to the British. It was the last engagement of the War of 1812.

[65] Durham, *James Winchester*, 167. Alfred Alexander Taylor Family Papers 1815-1962, Archives of Appalachia, East Tennessee State University, Johnson City, Tennessee.

[66] Durham, *James Winchester*, 173-174.

[67] Latour, *The War in West Florida and Louisiana*, 140, 263-264, 270-271. Durham, James Winchester, 171-172, 174-175, John Spencer Bassett, *The Life of Andrew Jackson* (New York: The Macmillan Company, 1916), 210. In Latour's book General Winchester wrote the secretary of war on February 17, 1815, stating Lt. Col. Lawrence's garrison was about 360. Durham uses the figure 374 and Bassett lists the garrison as 366. Craig's Scrapbook, 2nd Regiment West Tennessee Militia. Fort Bowyer is part of Gulf Islands National Seashore, a unit of the National Park Service.

[68] Latour, *The War in West Florida and Louisiana*, 277-279.

[69] Goodpasture, General Nathaniel Taylor and Some Papers," 193-200. Jackson's order for the soldier's discharge was issued on March 14.

[70] Ibid., 193-200 Durham, *James Winchester*, 176. Taylor's court martial was referenced in Winchester's letter to Jackson, March 18,1815, Jackson Papers, Library of Congress, in Durhams's *James Winchester*.

[71] Carter County Register of Deeds, Elizabethton, Tennessee, Deed Book C, May 15, 1821, pages 516-517. Registered August Session 1822. B. Harrison Taylor Collection, Johnson City, Tennessee.

[72] Carter County Registrar of Deeds, Elizabethton, Tennessee, Deed Book B, page 219-222. May 1809.

[73] James Patrick, *Architecture in Tennessee* 1768-1897 (Knoxville, Tenn. : University of Tennessee Press, 1981), 45.

[74] An abstractor's report was made of how the land was devised. The first abstracts were made by Messrs. Allen & Allen, Elizabethton, Tennessee, reputable lawyers of Carter County. Date unknown. Then a second abstract was made and is cited here. Author and date unknown. One abstractor reported that a deed was found in the Carter County courthouse showing Nathaniel J. K. Taylor had transferred title of Sabine Hill to A.W. Taylor, his brother. B. Harrison Taylor Collection, Johnson City, Tennessee.

[75] George Wilson, *Acts of a Local or Private Nature of the Thirteenth General Assembly of the State of Tennessee September 20, 1819*, Chapter 78 (Murfreesborough, Tenn.: George Wilson, 1819), 92. Hereafter Wilson, *Thirteenth General Assembly 1819*.

[76] Ibid., 66-67

[77] Spoden, *Sycamore Shoals*, 154. Carter County Register of Deeds, Elizabethton, Tennessee, Deed Book C, pages 119-120, February 15, 1815.

[78] According to her cemetery gravestone Mary Patton Taylor was born on November 5, 1773, and died on August 2, 1853.

[79] Spoden *Sycamore Shoals*, 635, 639-640.

[80] James A. Goforth, "Railroads," in Joyce Cox and W. Eugene Cox, comps. and eds. *History of Washington County Tennessee*, (Johnson City, Tenn.: The Overmountain Press, 2001), 244-245.

Notes on Chapter 3

[1] Pollyanna Creekmore, *Tennessee Newspaper Abstracts 1816-1830* (Knoxville, Tenn.: Clinchdale Press, 1955).

[2] Johns, *First Presbyterian Church, Elizabethton*, 4.

[3] John Haywood, *The Civil and Political History of the State of Tennessee* (1891; reprint, Johnson City, Tenn.: The Overmountain Press, 1999), 464.

[4] Spoden, *Sycamore Shoals*, 641. This house was located near the social center where the Franklin Club now stands.

[5] *Knoxville Republican,* Knoxville, Tennessee, January 30, 1833. Obituary of James P. Taylor.

[6] Nave, "History of the Iron Industry," 15-17, 20-21, 80-81. The initial division of the shares went to James Patton Taylor's sister, Anna, who married Thomas D. Love, and in 1824 James Patton purchased their interest in the iron works for $500. Sister Lorina married Jacob Tipton, and in 1826 James Patton bought their share, as well as brother Alfred W. Taylor's share. His sister, Mary, married William R. Dulaney, and in 1826 all five one-eighth shares were sold to David Waggoner. Sarafina Taylor married Alfred E. Jackson, and they along with Nathaniel J.K. Taylor also sold their one-eighth shares to Waggoner.

[7] James P. Taylor, Alf A. Taylor, and Hugh L. Taylor, *Life and Times of Senator Robert Love Taylor* (Nashville: The Bob Taylor Publishing Co., 1913), 27. Hereafter Taylor, *Life and Times of Senator Robert Love Taylor.* This book must be used with caution.

[8] Wilson, *Thirteenth General Assembly* 1819, 97-98. They were appointed on November 16, 1819.

[9] Frank Merritt, *Early History of Carter County*, 150,153.

[10] Wilson, *Acts of Local or Private Nature of the Thirteenth General Assembly of the State of Tennessee June 26, 1820*, Chapter 4 (Murfreesborough, Tenn.: George Wilson, 1820), 9.

[11] G. Wilson, Heiskell and Brown, *Acts of the Fourteenth General Assembly of the State of Tennessee,* Chapter 161 (Knoxville, Tenn.: Heiskelll & Brown, 1822, 129.

[12] Paul Deresco Augsburg, *Bob and Alf Taylor Their Lives and Lectures* (Morristown, Tenn.: Morristown Book Company, Inc., 1925), 21-22. Hereafter Augsburg, *Bob and Alf Taylor*.

[13] Heiskell and Brown, *Acts of the Fourteenth General Assembly of the State of Tennessee*, Chapter 182 (Knoxville, Tenn.: Heiskell & Brown, 1821) 176-178. The other commissioners were William B. Carter, Charles N. George, William Lindsey, and Johnston Hampton. Wilkesborough is now spelled Wilkesboro and is east 120 miles from Elizabethton on present U.S. Highway 421.

[14] J. Norvell, G.A. and A.C. Sublett, *Acts of the Fifteenth General Assembly of the State of Tennessee*, Chapter 220 (Murfreesborough, Tenn.: J. Norvell, G.A. and A.C. Sublett, 1823), 192-193. Hereafter Norvell and Sublett, *Fifteenth General Assembly*. The others serving with Taylor were John Kennedy, Christian Carriger, William Lindsey, Leonard Shown, and Johnston Hampton.

[15] Norvell and Sublett, *Fifteenth General Assembly*, 77-78. The others were Nathaniel Kelsey, John Kennedy, Samuel Crawford, James Roberts, John G. Eason, Abial C. Parks, and Christian Carriger.

[16] *The Farmers Journal*, Jonesborough, Tennessee, Saturday, September 27, 1828, vol. 3, no. 137.

[17] Spoden, Sycamore Shoals, 641.

[18] Copy of the original letter in files Jennie Taylor Rogers Collection, Tucson, AZ. Original is in Calvin M. McClung Collection, Knoxville, Tennessee. *Goodspeed's History of Tennessee*, 908.
Note that Goodspeed states he was elected in 1819 and not in 1814 which would seem more logical.

[19] *Tennessee Sentinel*, Jonesborough, Tennessee, May 15, 1841, vol. 5, no. 44.

[20] Merritt, *Early History of Carter County*, 43-45.

[21] *Washington Republican and Farmers Journal*, Jonesborough, Tennessee, Saturday, August 27, 1836, vol. 4, no. 195.

[22] Jewell Hamm, "Johnson County" in *Tennessee Encyclopedia of History and Culture*, ed. Carroll Van West (Nashville: Rutledge Hill Press, 1998), 488.

[23] Jonesborough Whig and Independent Journal, Jonesborough, Tennessee, August 7, 1844. Obituary of Mary C. Taylor.

[24] Their other three children were Alfred Moore Carter, Eveline, and Mary Taylor.

Notes on Chapter 4

[1] Noel C. Fisher, *War at Every Door Partisan Politics & Guerrilla Violence in East Tennessee 1860-1869* (Chapel Hill: The University of North Carolina Press, 1997), 11,16,18. Hereafter Fisher, *Partisan Politics & Guerrilla Violence in East Tennessee.*

[2] Rothrock, *The French Broad-Holston Country,* 386.

[3] Michael F. Holt, *The Rise and Fall of the American Whig Party* (New York: Oxford University Press, 1999), 2, 19. Hereafter Holt, *American Whig Party.*

[4] Andrew R. Dodge and Betty K. Koed, eds. *Biographical Directory of the United States Congress 1774-2005* (Washington, D.C.: U.S. Government Printing Office, 2005), 2022-2023. Hereafter Dodge and Koed, *Biographical Directory of Congress.*

[5] *The Jonesborough Whig and Independent Journal,* Jonesborough, Tennessee, May 25, 1842. Abstract by Ed Speer.

[6] *The Jonesborough Whig and Independent Journal,* Jonesborough, Tennessee, August 10, 1842. Abstract by Ed Speer.

[7] Joyce Cox and W. Eugene Cox, comps. and eds. *History of Washington County Tennessee,* (Johnson City, Tenn.: The Overmountain Press, 2001), 1057. Nelson's Chapel was founded before 1790. For an excellent history of early camp meeting see *The Christian Advocate*, Thursday, April 7, 1898, "Brush Creek Campground" by Col. I.C. Reeves. Camp meetings were religious revivals which had been around since 1800. In those early days of sparse settlements, the camp meeting was a great place to renew acquaintances and relax from the year round hard work. The four acre site at Brush Creek was deeded to the Methodist Episcopal Church.

[8] George Fort Milton, *The Age of Hate Andrew Johnson and the Radicals* (New York: Coward-McCann, Inc., 1930), 74-76. Hereafter Milton, *Andrew Johnson.*

[9] *The Jonesborough Whig and Independent Journal*, Jonesborough, Tennessee, February 22, 1843. B. Harrison Taylor Collection, Johnson City, Tennessee. Paul H. Bergeron, "Andrew Johnson (1808-1875)," in *Tennessee Encyclopedia of History and Culture*, ed. Carroll Van West (Nashville: Rutledge Hill Press, 1988), 481.

[10] *The Jonesborough Whig and Independent Journal*, Jonesborough, Tennessee, January 31, 1844, vol. 5, no. 38.

[11] *The Jonesborough Whig and Independent Journal*, Jonesborough, Tennessee, January 31, 1844, vol. 5, no. 38. Emeline is spelled various ways and we are using this spelling throughout the text since the editor and owner of the newspaper, William G. Brownlow, knew both Nathaniel Greene and she. We assume he would have spelled the name correctly. The three sons of Nathaniel and Emeline who wrote about their brother in *Life and Career of Robert Love Taylor* spelled their mother's name Emily.

[12] *Holston Methodism Conferences of 1886,1887, and 1888,* 1912 (?), 381-382, in Jennie Taylor Rogers Collection, Tucson, AZ. Dodge and Koed, Biographical Directory of Congress, 2022-2023. George Roulstone, *Acts of the General Assembly of the Territory of the United States of America, South of the River Ohio*, Chapter 8 (Knoxville, Tenn.: George Roulstone, 1795), 24-27.

[13] Spoden, *Sycamore Shoals*, 155

[14] Original in B. Harrison Taylor Collection, Johnson City, Tennessee. Nathaniel's sister died on August 6, 1842, his mother died two years later, and shortly thereafter he joined the Methodist Church. A story told in many publications relates how after Nathaniel's sister died Nathaniel was so racked with grief that he joined the Methodist Church and became a minister. We have not been able to document that her death encouraged him to join the Methodist Church and if so it was not immediately after her death. Would this also have encouraged him to switch from the Presbyterian Church to the Methodist?

[15] *The Jonesborough Whig and Independent Journal*, Jonesborough, Tennessee, January 10, 1844, vol. 5, no. 35. The editor/owner was William G. Brownlow.

[16] Ibid.

[17] *The Jonesborough Whig and Independent Journal*, Jonesborough, Tennessee, February 28, 1844, vol. 5, no. 42.

[18] Merritt, *Early History of Carter County*, 66-67. *The Jonesborough Whig and Independent Journal*, Jonesborough, Tennessee, February 28, 1844, vol. 5, no. 52.

[19] *The Jonesborough Whig and Independent Journal*, Jonesborough, Tennessee, August 27, 1845. Abstract by Ed Speer. Augsburg in his book Bob and Alf Taylor states on page eighteen and nineteen that the tragic death of Nathaniel's sister Mary changed his life forever and caused him to join the ministry. A few days later he delivered a passionate religious address. Mary died in 1842 and Nathaniel was ordained in 1845. Her death could have influenced his decision but Augsburg does not give a source for his statements. Frank Merritt repeats this claim in his *Early History of Carter County*, 107-108.

[20] *Jonesborough Whig and Independent Journal*, Jonesborough, Tennessee, July 12, 1848, vol. 10, no. 6.

21 *Brownlow's Knoxville Whig and Independent Journal*, Knoxville, Tennessee, June 9, 1849. Abstract by Ed Speer. Milton, *Andrew Johnson*, 83.

22 Holt, American Whig Party, 27, 32, 251, 368, 390. Robert L. Taylor Jr., "An Inquiry into the Background and Personalities of Governors Alf and Bob Taylor 1848-1886," master's thesis, University of Tennessee, 1964, 9. Hereafter Robert L. Taylor Jr., "Governors Alf and Bob Taylor."

23 M'Kennie & Watterson, *Acts of the State of Tennessee Passed of the Twenty-eighth General Assembly 1849-1850*, Chapter 127 (Nashville: M'Kennie & Watterson, 1850), 321-324.

24 Merritt, *Early History of Carter County,* 134-135.

25 *Brownlow's Knoxville Whig and Independent Journal*, Knoxville, Tennessee. January 11, 1851. Abstract by Ed Speer.

26 Postmaster Appointments for the Happy Valley Post Office in Carter County, Tennessee. M841, Microfilm Roll 118, V14F216, V44F218, V44F271, V70F224. The Elizabethton Post Office was not established until February 14, 1857, National Archives, Washington, D.C.

27 Philip A. Hamer, *Tennessee A History 1673-1932* (New York: The American Historical Society, Inc., 1933), 450-451.

28 *Railroad Journal and Family Visitor*, Jonesborough, Tennessee, Saturday, October 18, 1851, vol. 2, no.18.

29 Holt, American Whig Party, 521-522.

30 Ibid., 675, 706-707, 711-712, 727, 754.

31 Saunders H. Henry, "Mill Brook," and Ed Speer, Brookins Campbell (1808-1853)," in *History of Washington County Tennessee*, comps. and eds. Joyce Cox and W. Eugene Cox (Johnson City, Tenn.: The Overmountain Press, 2001), 859, 1187.

32 *Railroad Journal and Family Visitor*, Jonesborough, Tennessee, Saturday, February 11, 1854, vol. 4, no. 2. *Railroad Journal and Family Visitor*, Jonesborough, Tennessee, Saturday, February 18, 1854, vol. 4, no.3.

33 Dodge and Koed, *Biographical Directory of Congress*, 2022-2023. Hans L. Trefousse, *Andrew Johnson A Biography* (W.W. Norton & Co.: New York, 1989), 94. Hereafter Trefousse, *Andrew Johnson*.

34 *Webster's New Explorer Desk Encyclopedia* (Springfield, Mass.: Merriam-Webster, 2003), 147, 970. Hereafter, *Webster's Encyclopedia*.

35 Speech of Hon. N. G. Taylor, of Tennessee on the Nebraska and Kansas Bill Delivered in the House of Representatives, May 18, 1854. (Washington, D.C.: Congressional Globe Office, 1854).

36 Holt, *American Whig Party*, 821-822.

[37] Ibid., 937.

[38] http://www.nps.gov/liho/historyculture/debates.htm.

[39] Merritt, *Early History of Carter County*, 162-169. Merritt's source was the Nelson[Thomas A.R.] Papers, 1828-1861, Lawson-McGhee Library, Knoxville.

[40] Thomas B. Alexander, Thomas A.R. Nelson of East Tennessee, 59. W. Todd Groce, "Thomas A.R. Nelson" in *Tennessee Encyclopedia of History and Culture*, ed. Carroll Van West (Nashville: Rutledge Hill Press, 1998), 685-686. Dodge and Koed, *Biographical Directory of Congress*, 158-159.

[41] Dodge and Koed, *Biographical Directory of Congress*, 2022-2023. [Constitutional Union Party electoral ticket] Bailie Peyton of Sumner County and N.G. Taylor of Carter County electors for the state at large. *Republican Banner and Nashville Whig*, Nashville, Tennessee, July 4, 1860 Abstract by Ed Speer. Thomas William Humes, the *Loyal Mountaineers of Tennessee* (Knoxville, Tenn.: Ogden Brothers & Co., 1888), 306-309. Hereafter Humes, *The Loyal Mountaineers*.

[42] http://www.mrlincolnandnewyork.org/print.

[43] Fisher, *Partisan Politics & Guerrilla Violence in East Tennessee*, 24, 29. Verton M. Queener, "East Tennessee Sentiment and the Secession Movement, November 1860-June, 1861" *The East Tennessee Historical Society's Publications*, no. 20 (1948): 78-79.

[44] Fisher, *Partisan Politics & Guerrilla Violence in East Tennessee*, 181-183.

[45] W. Todd Groce, "Thomas A.R. Nelson" in *Tennessee Encyclopedia of History and Culture* ed. Carroll Van West (Nashville: Rutledge Hill Press, 1998), 685-686. Dodge and Koed, *Biographical Directory of Congress* 1774-2005, 158-159.

[46] Samuel W. Scott and Samuel P. Angel, *History of the Thirteenth Regiment Tennessee Volunteer Cavalry*, U.S.A. (1903; reprint, Johnson City, Tenn.: The Overmountain Press, 1987), 81-82. Hereafter Scott and Angel, *Thirteenth Regiment Tennessee Volunteer Cavalry*. Johnny Graybeal, *The Railroads of Johnson City* (Hickory, North Carolina: Tarheel Press, 2007) 54-55.

[47] Scott and Angel, *Thirteenth Regiment Tennessee Volunteer Cavalry*, 81-82. This was the barn Mary Taylor, widow of Brigadier General Nathaniel Taylor, built prior to 1821.

[48] David S. Hsiung, *A Mountaineer in Motion The Memoir of Dr. Abraham Jobe 1817-1906* (Knoxville, Tenn.: The University of Tennessee Press, 2009), 75-80, 84. Hereafter Hsiung, *The Memoir of Dr. Abraham Jobe*.

[49] Rothrock, *The French Broad-Holston Country*, 129-130. Fisher, *Partisan Politics & Guerrilla Violence in East Tennessee*, 102, 173.

50 B. Harrison Taylor Collection, Johnson City, Tennessee. In all Nathaniel and Emma had ten living children and as we understand an infant, Rhoda Haynes, died early. Sannie McClung, the tenth, was born in 1862.

51 Carter County Register of Deeds, Elizabethton, Tennessee, Deed Book D, page 184.

52 *The Nashville Daily Union*, Nashville, Tennessee, Sunday, April 9, 1865, vol. 4, no. 17, 1.

53 Scott and Angel, *Thirteenth Regiment Tennessee Volunteer Cavalry*, 95. Roan Mountain is 6,394 feet in elevation.

54 John T. Moore. *Tennessee, The Volunteer State*, Vol.II, 1923, in Spoden, *Sycamore Shoals,* 642.

55 Humes, *The Loyal Mountaineers*, 306-309.

56 *The Nashville Daily Union*, Nashville, Tennessee, Sunday, April 9, 1865, vol. 4, no. 17, 1.

57 William C. Harris, "The East Tennessee Relief Movement of 1863-1865," *Tennessee Historical Quarterly* 48 (1989): 86-96. Hereafter Harris, "East Tennessee Relief Movement." *The Nashville Daily Union*, Nashville, Tennessee, Sunday, April 9, 1865, vol. 4, no. 17, 1. Nathaniel's March 1865 letter in this newspaper states that William Brownlow was one of those who wrote a glowing introduction for him.

58 James B Campbell, " East Tennessee During the Federal Occupation, 1863-1865" *The East Tennessee Historical Society's Publications*, no. 19 (1947): 64-80. Rothrock, *The French Broad-Holston Country*, 143-144. Humes, *The Loyal Mountaineers*, 310, 323. Humes gave the date of the association's formation. See Harri, "East Tennessee Relief Movement," 86-96. He states other first members of the relief association were Joseph T. Thomas, secretary, Caleb Cope, treasurer, J.B. Lippincott, chairman on the committee on collections, and Lloyd P. Smith, chairman of the executive committee. There would be changes to the officers. Aid was sought from the federal government in the form of payments for lost property and also for transportation for relief supplies.

59 "List of Applications made through Thos. A.R. Nelson to the East Tennessee Relief Association in 1864, "*The East Tennessee Historical Society* 26 (April 2010): 3. Thomas A.R. Nelson, Nathaniel's friend, was on the executive committee of the East Tennessee Relief Association.

60 Rothrock, *The French Broad-Holston Country*, 409-410, 417, 431-432. Humes, The Loyal Mountaineers, 309.

61 *The Philadelphia Inquirer*, Philadelphia, Pennsylvania, Friday, January 29, 1864, 4.

62 Harris, "East Tennessee Relief Movement of 1864-1865," 86-96.

63 Ibid. Faneuil Hall is a unit of Boston Historical Park, National Park Service.

64 Ibid. Humes, *The Loyal Mountaineers*, 313, 317.

65 "Relief for East Tennessee, Address of Honorable N.G. Taylor at the Cooper Institute (New York: Wm. C. Bryant & Co., 1864).

[66] Ibid.

[67] Harris, "East Tennessee Relief Movement of 1864-1865," 86-96.

[68] B. Harrison Taylor Collection, Johnson City, Tennessee. When Alfred A. Taylor was preparing a press release for his talk "If Columbus Should Wake" for the Chautauqua circuit, he suggests he was aided and influenced by the oratory of Edward Everett.

[69] *The War of the Rebellion*, Series 2, vol. 8 (Washington, D.C.: U. S. Government Printing Office, 1890), 321-322. Mark M. Boatner III, *The Civil War Dictionary* (New York: David McKay Company, Inc. 1959), 866.

[70] Dodge and Koed, *Biographical Directory of Congress*, 2022-2023. Eric Foner, *A Short History of Reconstruction 1863-1877* (New York: Harper & Row, 1990), 104, 109-111. Cox, *Jonesborough: The Town and Its People*, 74.

[71] http://www.whitehouse.gov/about/presidents/andrewjohnson/.

[72] *Letter of N. G. Taylor of Tennessee, on the Political Situation* (Washington, D.C.: Intelligence Printing House, 1866). Ford's Theatre National Historic Site is a unit of the National Park Service. *The Bristol News*, Bristol, Tennessee-Virginia, March 7, 1867, vol. 2, no. 83.

[73] Carla Homstad, Janene Caywood, and Peggy Nelson, *Cultural Landscape Report: Golden Spike National Historic Site, Box Elder County, Utah* (Denver, Co,: National Park Service, Site, Brigham City, Utah, a unit of the National Park Service.

[74] *Journal of the House of Representatives* 1853-1854 (Washington, D.C.: Robert Armstrong, National Monument of America in Nebraska is a unit of the National Park Service. The Pony Express National Historic Trail is under the administration of the National Park Service, Salt Lake City, Utah. The Pony Express operated from April 3, 1860, to October 24, 1861.

[75] Thomas H. Johnson, *The Oxford Companion to American History* (New York: Oxford University Press, 1966), 602. Robert Utley, The Indian Frontier of the American West 1846-1890 (Albuquerque: University of New Mexico Press, 1984), 40. Hereafter Utley, *The Indian Frontier of the American West*. The Oregon National Historic Trail, Salt Lake City, Utah, is administered by the National Park Service in partnership with other agencies.

[76] LeRoy R. Hafen and Francis Marion Young, *Fort Laramie and the Pageant of the West, 1834-1890*(1938, reprint: Fort Laramie, Wyoming: Fort Laramie Historical Association, 1984), 27, 177-178, 193-194. Fort Laramie National Historic Site, Wyoming, is a unit of the National Park Service.

[77] *Proceedings of the Great Peace Commission of 1867-1868* (Washington, D.C.: Institute for the Development of Indian Law, 1975), 3. Hereafter *Proceedings of the Great Peace*

Commission of 1867-1868. We used liberally from this document which gave the daily meetings of the commission.

[78] Henry G. Waltmann, "The Interior Department, War Department and Indian Policy, 1865-1887," dissertation, University of Nebraska, 1962, 35. Hereafter Waltmann, "The Interior Department, War Department and Indian Policy, 1865-1887."

[79] Ibid., 93-94, 96-100, 132.

[80] Sherman to Hunt at Fort Smith, March 12, 1866 in Athearn, *William Tecumseh Sherman and the Settlement of the West* (1956; reprint, Norman, Okla.: University of Oklahoma, 43. Hereafter Athearn, *William Tecumseh Sherman*. Jefferson National Expansion Memorial, St. Louis, Missouri, is a unit of the National Park Service.

[81] Ibid., 43-44.

[82] Waltmann, The Interior Department, War Department and Indian Policy, 1865-1887," 101-102. Athearn, *William Tecumseh Sherman*, 33, 46.

[83] Waltmann, "The Interior Department, War Department and Indian Policy, 1865-1887," 49.

[84] Bogy to Browning in Waltmann, "The Interior Department, War Department and Indian Policy, 1865-1887," 110-112. Bogy was Commissioner of Indian Affairs from November 1, 1866 to March 26, 1867. For more on the Fetterman Fight see Utley, *The Indian Frontier of the American West* and John H. Monnett, *Where a Hundred Soldiers were Killed* (Albuquerque: University of New Mexico Press, 2008).

[85] Paul H. Bergeron, ed., *The Papers of Andrew Johnson*, vol.11 (Knoxville, Tenn.: The University of Tennessee Press, 1994), 607-608.

[86] Utley, *The Indian Frontier of the American West*, 107.

[87] Waltmann, "The Interior Department, War Department and Indian Policy, 1865-1887," 112-113.

[88] Robert M. Kvasnicka and Herman J. Viola, eds. *The Commissioners of Indian Affairs, 1824-1977* (Lincoln, NE.: University of Nebraska Press), 116.

[89] Ibid., 116-117. Typescript copy of letter in B. Harrison Taylor Collection, Johnson City, Tennessee.

[90] *Senate Executive Journal*, 40the Congress, 1st sess., March 27, 1867, 565-566.

[91] Roderick Nash, *Wilderness and the American Mind* (New Haven, Conn.: Yale University Press, 1967), 24, Utley, *The Indian Frontier of the American West*, 33-35.

[92] Waltmann, "The Interior Department, War Department and Indian Policy, 1865-1887," 25-26.

[93] *Proceedings of the Great Peace Commission of 1867-1868*, 2.

[94] Utley, *The Indian Frontier of the American West*, 36,40.

[95] Ibid., 42-43.

[96] Waltmann, "The Interior Department, War Department and Indian Policy, 1865-1887," 25-26.

[97] Utley, *The Indian Frontier of the American West*, 46.

[98] Ibid., 44-46.

[99] Athearn, William Tecumseh Sherman, 15, 29.

[100] Susan Badger Doyle, ed. *Bound for Montana Diaries From the Bozeman Trail* (Helena, Montana: Montana Historical Society Press, 2004), 1,3,7-9. Bighorn Canyon National Recreation Area, Fort Smith, Montana, is a unit of the National Park Service and has sites related to the Bozeman Trail.

[101] *Annual Report of the Commissioner of Indian Affairs for the Year 1868* (Washington, D.C.: U.S. Government Printing Office, 1868) 378-382, in No. 131, Statement showing the population, wealth, and education of the different tribes of Indians within the United States for 1867. Hereafter *Annual Report of the Commissioner of Indian Affairs 1868*.

[102] Waltmann, "The Interior Department, War Department and Indian Policy, 1865-1887," 4-7, 13, 18, 24. Rothrock, *The French Broad-Holston Country*, 31.

[103] *Annual Report of the Commissioner of Indian Affairs 1868*, 37-38, containing the "Report to the President by the Indian Peace Commission, January 7, 1868, signed by all eight commissioners with Nathaniel Taylor as president.

[104] Waltmann, "The Interior Department, War Department and Indian Policy, 1865-1887," 128-131. 1868 *Annual Report of the Commissioner of Indian Affairs 1868*, 38 containing the "Report to the President by the Indian Peace Commission January 7, 1868, signed by all eight commissioners with Nathaniel Taylor as president.

[105] Utley, *The Indian Frontier of the American West*, 108.

[106] *Senate Journal*, 40th Congress, 1st sess., July 8, 1867, 136-137.

[107] Ibid.

[108] Ibid.

[109] Waltmann, "The Interior Department, War Department and Indian Policy, 1865-1887," 133.

[110] *Senate Journal*, 40th Congress, 1st sess., July 8, 1867, 136-137.

[111] *U.S. Statutes at Large*, 15: 17-18 in Francis Paul Prucha, *Documents of United States Indian Policy* (Lincoln, Nebraska: University of Nebraska Press, 1975), 105-106. Douglas C. Jones. *The Treaty of Medicine Lodge* (Norman, Okla.: University of Oklahoma Press, 1966), 17-18. Hereafter Jones, *The Treaty of Medicine Lodge*, Francis Paul Prucha, *American Indian Policy in Crisis: Christian Reformers and the Indian, 1865* (Norman, Okla.: University of Oklahoma Press, 1976), 18-19. Hereafter Prucha, *American Indian Policy in Crisis.* Waltmann, "The Interior Department, War Department and Indian Policy, 1865-1887," 138-141.

[112] Robert M. Utley, *Frontier Regulars The United States Army and the Indian 1866-1891* (1973; reprint, Lincoln, Nebr.: University of Nebraska Press, 1984), 130. Hereafter Utley, Frontier Regulars.

[113] Jones, *The Treaty of Medicine Lodge*, 17.

[114] Ibid., 18.

[115] Ibid., 20.

[116] http://home.nps.gov/bica/historyculture/hayfield-fight.htm. http://www.philkearny.vcn.com/wagonboxfight.htm.

[117] *Proceedings of the Great Peace Commission of 1867-1868*, 10-11.

[118] Ibid., 30.

[119] Ibid., 31.

[120] Ibid., 32, 41.

[121] Ibid. 47, 49.

[122] Ibid. 51-53.

[123] Ibid. 55-56.

[124] Utley, *The Indian Frontier of the American West*, 207.

[125] *Proceedings of the Great Peace Commission of 1867-1868*, 54-55.

[126] Ibid., 56.

[127] Ibid., 57-58.

[128] Ibid., 58.

[129] Ibid., 60-61.

[130] Ibid., 61-63.

[131] Ibid., 65

[132] Jones, *The Treaty of Medicine Lodge,* 28-29, 30, 37-39.

[133] *Proceedings of the Great Peace Commission of 1867-1868*, 8-10, 29-33, 41-43, 48-49, 51-65.

[134] Jones, *The Treaty of Medicine Lodge*, 48, 55, 62. Henry M. Stanley, "A British Journalist Reports the Medicine Lodge Peace Council in 1867," *Kansas Historical Quarterly* 33 (Autumn 1967): 257. Hereafter Stanley, "A British Journalist Reports the Medicine Lodge Peace Council in 1867,"

[135] Jones, *The Treaty of Medicine Lodge*, 66, 69.

[136] Ibid., 70, 72.

[137] Ibid., 70-71.

[138] Ibid., 72-73.

[139] Ibid. 74, 79-81.

[140] Stanley, "A British Journalist Reports the Medicine Lodge Peace Council in 1867," 265, 277, 279.

[141] Waltmann, "The Interior Department, War Department and Indian Policy, 1865-1887," 144-145. Utley, *Frontier Regulars*, 133.

[169] Leon Wier Jr., *Remington Society of America Journal* (Second quarter 2002), 36-39. George M. Chinn, *The Machine Gun* (Washington D.C.: Department of the Navy, 1951), 117-118. The Taylor Battery Gun is housed at the Smithsonian National Museum of American History. Sandy Hook is part of Gateway National Recreation Area, New York/New Jersey, a unit of the National Park Service.

[170] Carter County Register of Deeds, Elizabethton, Tennessee, Deed Book D, page 529. Dave Shackelford, "Taylor vs. Turley: Fortunes and Misfortunes of War in Post-Civil War America" in *The Archivist's Bulldog, The Maryland State Archives*, Annapolis, Maryland, vol. 14, no. 22 (November 2000). Turley vs. Taylor, Tennessee Court of Appeals, September Term, 1873.

[171] Paul Bergeron, Patricia Anthony, Glenna R. Schroeder-Lein, Marion O. Smith, and Richard M. Zuczek, eds. *The Papers of Andrew Johnson*, vol. 16, May 1869-July 1875 (Knoxville, Tenn.: University of Tennessee. Andrew Johnson National Historic Site, Greenville, Tennessee, is administered by the National Park Service.

[172] These letters were in possession of Mrs. Lela Taylor, widow of Benjamin Harrison Taylor, Alf's son, and father of B. Harrison Taylor, Johnson City, Tennessee. Hereafter Bob and Sarah Taylor Correspondence. B. Harrison Taylor Collection, Johnson City, Tennessee.

[173] *Knoxville Tribune*, April 2, 1879, *The French Broad-Holston Country*, 242-248.

[174] William Perry Bailey Jr., M.D., *History of First United Methodist Church of Johnson City, Tennessee 1865-1990* (Johnson City, Tenn.: The Overmountain Press, 1990), 21-22. 175 Dodge and Koed, *Biographical Directory of Congress*, 2022-2023. *Knoxville Journal*, Knoxville, Tennessee, April, 1887.

Notes on Chapter 5

[1] The children of Nathaniel Greene Taylor and Emeline Haynes Taylor were James Patton (1844-1924), Rhoda Anne (1846-1851), Alfred Alexander Taylor (1848-1931), Robert Love Taylor (1850-1912), Nathaniel Winfield Scott (1852-1904), Rhoda Emma (1855-1943), Mary Eva (1855-1916), David Haynes (1857-1890), and Hugh Lawson McClung (1859/1860-?), and Sanna R. (1862-?).

[2] Ned L. Irwin, "Education," in *History Washington County Tennessee*, comps. and eds. Joyce Cox and W. Eugene Cox (Johnson City, Tenn.: Overmountain Press, 2001), 518-519.

[3] *The Philadelphia Inquirer*, Philadelphia, Pennsylvania, Thursday, September 1, 1864, 8. Correspondence with A. Melissa Kiser, Director of Public Relations, The Pennington School, Pennington, New Jersey, April 12, 2010. Mary Alice Quigley, School Archivist, "What's in a Name," October, 2006. A letter written on September 12, 1864, to Andrew Johnson in Nashville by Nathaniel supports where they were living. Dodge and Koed, *Biographical Directory of Congress,* 2018. Alfred A. Taylor is listed in his biographical sketch as attending "the schools of Edge Hill and Pennington Seminary, New Jersey." Dodge and Koed, *Biographical Directory of Congress*, 2023. Robert Love Taylor in his biographical sketch states he "attended Pennington Seminary in New Jersey." Nathaniel Greene Taylor, Haddonfield, New Jersey, to Andrew Johnson, Nashville, Tennessee, September 12, 1864. B. Harrison Taylor Collection, Johnson City, Tennessee. The school is still in existence and is known today as "The Pennington School." In a letter to the *Nashville Daily Union* dated March 31, 1865, Nathaniel gives his return address as Longacoming, New Jersey.

[4] Jones, *Treaty of Medicine Lodge*, 68.

[5] Stanley, "A British Journalist's Account of the Medicine Lodge Peace Council of 1867," 249, 308. Jones, The Treaty of Medicine Lodge, 160-163.

[6] Stanley, " A British Journalist's Account of the Medicine Lodge Peace Council of 1867," 308-309. Alfred A. Taylor, "Medicine Lodge Peace Council of 1867," *Chronicles of Oklahoma*, vol. II (June 1924): 98-118. Alf stated the Sun Dance Lodge was five miles from camp giving us a third mileage from the distance.

[7] Jones, *The Treaty of Medicine Lodge*, 162, 164.

[8] Dodge and Koed, *Biographical Directory of Congress*, 2018.

[9] Taylor, *Life and Career of Senator Robert Love Taylor*, 88.

[10] Taylor, *Life and Career of Senator Robert Love Taylor*, 88-90, 98. *Herald and Tribune,* Jonesborough, Tennessee, Thursday, December 14, 1871, vol. 3, no. 15. The performance was on Monday, December 11. W. Eugene Cox and Joyce Cox, *Jonesborough's Historic Main Street* (Jonesborough, Tenn.: Heritage Alliance of Northeast Tennessee and Southwest Virginia, 2008), 31, photocopy.

[11] B. Harrison Taylor Collection, Johnson City, Tennessee.

[12] Taylor, *Life and Career of Senator Robert Love Taylor*, 99. Robert L. Taylor Jr., "Governors Alf and Bob Taylor," 40.

[13] Bob Taylor letters to Sallie Baird, B. Harrison Taylor Collection, Johnson City, Tennessee. Typed copies of the originals. W. Eugene Cox and Joyce Cox, *Jonesborough's Historic Main Street* (Jonesborough, Tenn.: Heritage Alliance of Northeast Tennessee and Southwest Virginia, 2008), 150, photocopy.

[14] Bob Taylor letters to Sallie Baird, B. Harrison Taylor Collection, Johnson City, Tennessee. Typed copies of the originals. *The Jonesborough Journal*, Jonesborough, Tennessee, Wednesday, January 27, 1875, vol.1, no.1.

[15] Bob Taylor letters to Sallie Baird, B. Harrison Taylor Collection, Johnson City, Tennessee. Typed copies of the originals.

[16] Dodge and Koed, *Biographical Directory of Congress*, 2018. Trefousse, Andrew Johnson, 371-372.

[17] DeLong Rice, *"Old Limber"* or *The Tale of the Taylors* (Nashville, Tenn.: McQuiddy Printing Company, 1921), 52-56. Hereafter Rice, *"Old Limber"* of *The Tale of the Taylors.*

[18] Frank Merritt, *Later History of Carter County 1865-1980* (Kingsport, Tenn.: Arcata Graphics, 1986), 227-228. Hereafter Merritt, *Later History of Carter County.*

[19] Taylor, *Life and Career of Senator Robert Love Taylor*, 118.

[20] Bob Taylor letters to Sallie Baird, B. Harrison Taylor Collection, Johnson City, Tennessee. Typed copies of the originals.

[21] For how the brothers joined their respective parties see Taylor, *Life and Career of Senator Robert Love Taylor,* 111-112, 119-120. Bob Taylor letters to Sallie Baird, B. Harrison Taylor Collection, Johnson City, Tennessee. Typed copies of the originals.

[22] Bob Taylor letters to Sallie Baird, B. Harrison Taylor Collection, Johnson City, Tennsessice. Typed copies of originals.

[23] Paul M. Fink, *Jonesborough The First Century of Tennessee's First Town 1776-1876* (Johnson City, Tenn.: The Overmountain Press, 1989), 151.

[24] *Herald and Tribune*, Jonesborough, Tennessee, August 19, 1980, vol. 2, no. 44.

[25] Genealogy from B. Harrison Taylor Collection, Johnson City, Tennessee.

[26] Register of Deeds, Washington County, Jonesborough, Tennessee, Deed Book 58, pages 491-492, April 3, 1890.

[27] Jennie Taylor Rogers Collection, Tucson, Arizona. Register of Deeds, Washington County, Jonesborough, Tennessee, Deed Book 58, page 147, March 8, 1890.

[28] Johnny Graybeal, *The Railroads of Johnson City* (Hickory, North Carolina: Tarheel Press, 2007), 137-138, 141, 145.

[29] Walter T. Pulliam, "Newspapers," in *History of Washington County Tennessee*, comps. and eds. Joyce Cox and W. Eugene Cox (Johnson City, Tenn.: The Overmountain Press, 2001), 312. Lane L. Boutwell, "The Oratory of Robert Love Taylor."

[30] Robert L. Taylor Jr. "Apprenticeship in the First District: Bob and Alf Taylor's Early Congressional Races, "*Tennessee Historical Quarterly* 28 (1969): 38. Robert E. Corlew, *Tennessee A Short History* (Knoxville, Tenn.: The University of Tennessee Press, 1989), 377. Hereafter Corlew, *Tennessee A Short History.*

[31] Daniel Merritt Robison, *Bob Taylor and the Agrarian Revolt in Tennessee* (Chapel Hill, North Carolina: The University of North Carolina Press, 1935), 58 Hereafter Robison, Bob Taylor and *The Agrarian Revolt.*

[32] Ibid., 22-23. Boutwell, " The Oratory of Robert Love Taylor," 16.

[33] Robison, *Bob Taylor and the Agrarian Revolt in Tennessee*, 58-65.

[34] Ibid., 64-68.

[35] Robert L Taylor, *Echoes, Centennial and other Notable Speeches and Lectures and Stories* (Nashville, S.B. Williamson & Co., 1989), 172-173. Taylor, Life and Times of Senator Robert Love Taylor, 164.

[36] Taylor, *Life and Times of Senator Robert Love Taylor*, 164-165. The legend is carried on in Augsburg's, Bob and Alf Taylor, 51.

[37] Robert L. Taylor Jr., "Tennessee's War of the Roses as Symbol and Myth," Tennessee Historical Quarterly 61 (1982): 337. Margaret I. Phillips, *The Governors of Tennessee* (Gretna, Lousiana: Pelican Publishing Company, 1978), 105-0106. Corlew, *Tennessee A Short History,* 311, 348, 380.

[38] Original which is typed is in Jennie Taylor Rogers Collection, Tucson, Arizona.

[39] Ray Stahl, *Greater Johnson City A Pictorial History* (1983; reprint, Norfolk, Va.: Donning Company, 1986), 81.

[40] Robison, *Bob Taylor and The Agrarian Revolt*, 94-96.

[41] Alfred Alexander Taylor Family Papers 1815-1962. News clipping 1890, Accession 404, Series IV. Archives of Appalachia, East Tennessee State University, Johnson City, Tennessee.

[42] Dodge and Koed, *Biographical Directory of Congress*, 2018.

[43] Bob and Sarah Taylor Correspondence. B. Harrison Taylor Collection, Johnson City, Tennessee.

[44] Ibid.

[45] Ibid.

[46] Augsburg, *Bob and Alf Taylor*, 61.

[47] http://www.nancho.net.

[48] http://www.nohumanitiesprg/programs/chatuque. In 1878, the New York Chautauqua initiated the first book club in our country. By the turn of the twentieth century they sponsored more than 10,000 local reading circles in towns all across the land.

[49] Robert L. Taylor, *Echoes, Centennial and other Notable Speeches Lectures and Stories* (Nashville, Tennessee: S.B. Williamson & Co., 1899), 111.

[50] Taylor, *Life and Career of Senator Robert Love Taylor*, 184-189. Augsburg, Bob and Alf Taylor, 62-66.

[51] Augsburg, *Bob and Alf Taylor*, 66-68. Boutwell, "The Oratory of Robert Love Taylor,"18.

[52] Bob and Sarah Taylor Correspondence. B. Harrison Taylor Collection, Johnson City, Tennessee.

[53] Augsburg, *Bob and Alf Taylor*, 66-68. Boutwell, "The Oratory of Robert Love Taylor," 18.

[54] Robison, Bob Taylor and *The Agrarian Revolt*, 179, 191-193, 197, 203.

[55] Bob and Sarah Taylor Correspondence. B. Harrison Taylor Collection, Johnson City, Tennessee. Robison, *Bob Taylor and The Agrarian Revolt*, 179, 191-193, 197, 203.

[56] Obituary, *Knoxville News Sentinel*, Knoxville, Tennessee, Tuesday, February 19, 1900. Copy in B.Harrison Taylor Collection, Johnson City Tennessee. The Knoxville home the Taylors lived in burned down on February 18, 1985. *Knoxville News Sentinel*, Knoxville, Tennessee, Tuesday, February, 19, 1985.

[57] The original "Southern Five-Day Circuit" and the letters cited are in the B. Harrison Taylor Collection, Johnson City, Tennessee.

[58] The letters cited here are from the Blaine Taylor Papers 1896-1935, Box 1, Series I, Archives of Appalachia, East Tennessee State University, Johnson City, Tennessee. On Saturday, August 14, 1897, Jonesborough turned on its first electric lights in Cox, *Jonesborough: The Town and Its People*, 39-40.

[59] Robert L. Taylor Jr., "Demagoguery, Personality, and the Gospel of Democracy: Family Influence on Centennial Governor Taylor," *Tennessee Historical Quarterly*, 60 (1996): 171-172. On the Sycamore Shoals Monument it is engraved that it was dedicated September 26, 1909.

Bob was there one year later. *Johnson City Press Chronicle*, Johnson City, Tennessee, Sunday, November 23, 1941.

[60] W. Eugene Cox and Joyce Cox, *Jonesborough's Historic Main Street* (Jonesborough, Tenn.: Heritage Alliance of Northeast Tennessee and Southwest Virginia, 2008), 173-175, photocopy. Brownlow and his family lived at 421 West Main Street in Jonesborough. *Herald and Tribune*, Jonesborough, Tennessee, Wednesday, July 25, 1906, vol. 38, no. 17. *Herald and Tribune*, Jonesborough, Tennessee, Wednesday, October 24, 1906, vol. 38, no. 30. *Herald and Tribune*, Jonesborough, Tennessee, Wednesday, November 7, 1906, vol. 38, no. 32.

[61] *The Rural Searchlight*, Limestone, Tennessee, Thursday, November 29, 1906, vol. 2, no. 34.

[62] Jennie Taylor Rogers Collection, Tucson, Arizona. An earlier owner was Joshua Williams from 1838 to 1880 that provided land for the college. The house was restored by Milligan College as a hospitality facility in 2002 and is now known as the Taylor/Phillips House. Clarinda Jeanes, wife of college president Don Jeanes, was responsible for the renovation. All receipts derived from the use of the hospitality center are used for scholarships.

[63] Blaine Taylor Papers 1896-1935, Box 1, Series I, Archives of Appalachia, East Tennessee State University, Johnson City, Tennessee.

[64] Gary Reichard, "The Defeat of Governor Roberts," *Tennessee Historical Quarterly* 30 (1971): 94, 96, 104. Hereafter Reichard, "The Defeat of Governor Roberts." *Journal and Tribune,* Knoxville, Tennessee, November 4, 1920, in the B. Harrison Taylor Collection, Johnson City, Tennessee.

[65] DeLong Rice, *"Old Limber" or The Tale of the Taylors*, 15, 17, 65, 70. *Chattanooga Times*, 1920, in Blaine Taylor Papers 1896-1935, Archives of Appalachia, East Tennessee State, Johnson City, Tennessee.

[66] Gary Reichard, "The Defeat of Governor Roberts," 96, 107-109. *The Journal and Tribune*, Knoxville, Tennessee, Thursday, November 4, 1920, in Jennie Taylor Rogers Collection, Tucson, Arizona. Alf did campaign in 1906 for Congress. *The Nashville Tennessean* on Sunday, November 14, 1920, reported the vote as 229,519 for Alf and 182,841 for Roberts. Other records were established with Alf's election. At that time he was the oldest elected candidate for governor, and he and Bob were the second set of full brothers to be governors of the state. Neill S. Brown and John C. Brown were the other set of full brothers. William Blount, governor of the Southwest Territory (1790-1796) and Willie Blount governor of Tennessee (1809-1815) were half-brothers.

[67] Jesse S. Cottrell, *Chattanooga Times*, November 1920 in Blaine Taylor Papers 1896-1935, Archives of Appalachia, East Tennessee State University, Johnson City, Tennessee.

[68] Ibid.

[69] Program "Inaugural Ceremonies of Honorable Alf A. Taylor as Governor of Tennessee, Saturday, January 15, 1921." McClung Collection, Lawson McGhee Library, Knoxville, Tennessee. *Message of Governor A.A. Taylor to the 62nd General Assembly of Tennessee* (Nashville: Printing Department, Tennessee Industrial School, 1921).

[70] Merritt, *Later History of Carter County*, 70. Bob Cox, February 1, 2010, "'South's Greatest Foxhunt' in 1928 Honored Ex-Gov. Alf Taylor" in a review copy for newspaper release.

[71] Merritt, *Later History of Carter County*, 253-260. Herbert Hoover National Historic Site, West Branch, Iowa, is a unit of the National Park Service.

[72] *Johnson City Chronicle*, Johnson City, Tennessee, Sunday, June 29, 1930, in Alfred Alexander Taylor Family Papers, Archives of Appalachia, East Tennessee State University, Johnson City, Tennessee.

[73] Jennie Taylor Rogers Collection, Tucson, Arizona.

[74] Ibid.

Notes on Chapter 6

[1] The children of Alf and Jennie Taylor with date of birth are John Anderson, March 3, 1883, Nathaniel Greene, December 18, 1885, Benjamin Harrison, August 4, 1888, David Haynes, February 19, 1891, James Blaine, September 15, 1893, Alfred Alexander Jr., August 10, 1895, Robert Love, December 20, 1899, Mary Emmaline, August 8, 1902, Ann Catherine, July 16, 1905, and Frank Jones, May 8, 1908.

[2] Alfred A. Taylor letter, typescript, April 23, 1894 B. Harrison Taylor Collection, Johnson City, Tennessee.

[3] B. Harrison Taylor Collection, Johnson City, Tennessee, Letters of Robert L. Taylor.

[4] *Johnson City Press Chronicle*, Friday, October 20, 1930, Milligan baseball team. *Eulogy of Ben H. Taylor* (Johnson City, Tenn.: The Union Printing Co., 1930), 1. Benjamin Harrison Taylor Family Papers 1833-1977, Archives of Appalachia, East Tennessee State University, Johnson City, Tennessee. Hereafter *Eulogy of Ben H. Taylor.*

[5] B. Harrison Taylor Collection, Johnson City, Tennessee.

[6] Dodge and Koed, *Biographical Directory of Congress*, 2005, 1887. Benjamin Harrison Taylor Family Papers 1833-1977, Archives of Appalachia, East Tennessee State University, Johnson City, Tennessee.

[7] *Johnson City Chronicle*, Johnson City, Tennessee, June 30,1915, John L. Kiener, "Court System and Legal Profession" in *History of Washington County Tennessee*, comps. and eds. Joyce Cox and W. Eugene Cox (Johnson City, Tenn.: The Overmountain Press, 2001), 575. *Eulogy of Ben H. Taylor*, 15, 17-18.

[8] *Erwin Magnet*, Erwin, Tennessee, November 8, 1916.

[9] *Webster's Encyclopedia*, 1323. Benjamin Harrison Taylor Family Papers 1833-1977, Archives of Appalachia, East Tennessee State University, Johnson City, Tennessee. Information about service time is from a January 1, 1919 letter Ben wrote the Treasurer of the Bureau of War Risk Insurance, Washington D. C., about a policy he had.

[10] Benjamin Harrison Taylor Family Papers 1833-1977, Archives of Appalachia, East Tennessee State University, Johnson City, Tennessee.

[11] *Chattanooga Times*, 1920, in Blaine Taylor Papers 1896-1935, Archives of Appalachia, East Tennessee State University, Johnson City, Tennessee.

[12] *Chattanooga Times*, Chattanooga, Tennessee, November 21, 1920, in Blaine Taylor Papers 1896-1935, Box 1 Series I, Archives of Appalachia, East Tennessee State University, Johnson City Tennessee. B. Harrison Taylor, "Lela Amanda Ramsey Taylor (1892-1985)" in *History of Washington County Tennessee*, comps. and eds. Joyce Cox and W. Eugene Cox (Johnson City, Tenn.: The Overmountain Press, 2001), 1216. Hereafter Taylor, "Lela Amanda Ramsey Taylor (1892-1985)." *The Journal and Tribune*, Knoxville, Tennessee, Thursday, November 4, 1920. Jennie Taylor Rogers Collection, Tucson, Arizona. Register of Deeds, Washington County, Jonesborough, Tennessee, Deed Book 146, page 94, January 12, 1921.

[13] Register of Deeds, Washington County, Jonesborough, Tennessee, Deed Book 158, page 384, May 31, 1923, *Eulogy of Ben H. Taylor*, 25.

[14] *Eulogy of Ben H. Taylor*, 25.

[15] Taylor, "Lela Amanda Ramsey Taylor (1892-1985)," 1216. Washington County Register of Deeds, Jonesborough, Tennessee, Deed Book 203, page 242, June 29, 1938. Washington County Register of Deeds, Jonesborough, Tennessee, Deed Book 495, page 169, November 17, 1975.

[16] History of the Sixth Circuit. Robert Love Taylor (1899-1987) at http://www.ca6.uscourts.gov/lib_hist/Courts/district.

[17] Patricia E. Brake, *Justice in the Valley A Bicentennial Perspective of the United States District Court for the Eastern District of Tennessee* (Franklin, Tenn.: Hillsboro Press, c1998), 102-103, 105-117.

[18] Patricia E. Brake, *Justice in the Valley A Bicentennial Perspective of the United States District Court for the Eastern District of Tennessee* (Franklin, Tenn.: Hillsboro Press, c1998), 102-103, 105-117. Bill Hawkins, "Integration Riots Sadden Judge who Ordered Mix, Taylor Family Helped Shape State History" *Chattanooga News-Free Press,* September 5, 1956, in Benjamin Harrison Taylor Papers, Box 2, Folder 2.1, Archives of Appalachia, East Tennessee State University, Johnson City, Tennessee. "Judge Taylor's Charge to the Jury provides clear Background of Events Leading to Arrest, Trial, Convictions in Clinton Case," *The Knoxville News Sentinel*, Knoxville, Tennessee, Sunday, July 28, 1957. Clinton Beauchamp and Amanda Turner, "The Desegregation of Clinton Senior High School: Trial and Triumph," http://www.docstoc.com/docs/18251700/The-Desegregration-of-Clinton-Senior High-School. Nearby Oak Ridge schools, also in Anderson County, were integrated in 1955 as they were in a federal installation not governed by state or local government. June N. Adamson, "Few Black Voices Heard: The Black Community and the Desegregation Crisis in Clinton, Tennessee, 1956," *Tennessee Historical Quarterly* 53 (1994): 30-41. Time, August 5, 1957. *The Knoxville Journal*, Friday, August 9, 1957. "Robert Love Taylor (1899-1987),"

History of the Sixth Circuit. http://www.ca6.uscourts.gov/lib-hist/Courts/district. Janice M. McClelland, "Clinton Desegregation Crisis," in Tennessee Encyclopedia of History and Culture, ed. Carroll Van West (Nashville: Rutledge Hill Press, 1998), 182. Readers researching the Clinton desegregation case will find the citations we used conflicting in their details and interpretation of events. We have placed more credence in Brake's *Justice in the Valley* and the court records she used and not so much on interpretation. This is an excellent book for the Clinton case. We did not note anyone citing the *Clinton Courier News*, Thurgood Marshall's papers, or Anderson Couty School board minutes or correspondence (if still available). The history of the civil rights movement has not been adequately told. Judge Robert Love Taylor served the United States District Court for the Eastern District of Tennessee from 1949 to 1985 and died in 1987.

Index